KARL KAUTSKY

KARL KAUTSKY

Marxism, Revolution & Democracy

John H. Kautsky

Transaction Publishers
New Brunswick (U.S.A.) and London (U.K.)

Library of Congress Catalog Number: 93–228
ISBN: 1–56000–109–7
Printed in the United States of America

Library of Congress Cataloging-in-Publication Data

Kautsky, John H., 1922
    Karl Kautsky : Marxism, revolution, and democracy / John H.
Kautsky.
       p.   cm.
    Includes bibliographical references (p.   ) and index.
    ISBN 1–56000–109–7
    1. Kautsky, Karl, 1854–1938.   2. Communists — Germany — Biography.
3. Communism — Soviet Union — History.   I. Kautsky, Karl, 1854–1938.
II. Title.
HX274.7.K38K38   1993
335.4'092 — dc20   93–228
[B]   CIP

Contents

Preface

For many years after Karl Kautsky's death in 1938, his work received almost no scholarly attention. References in the literature tended to treat it superficially or misunderstood it, often, as I stress in my Introduction below, because, consciously or not, they saw it through Lenin's eyes. In the past two decades, however, a striking change has occurred. Nearly a dozen full-length books devoted to Kautsky have appeared in German, English, Italian, and Polish. They analyze — rather than praise or denounce — his thought and usually seek to explain it with reference to his position in his political environment. I refer to the most outstanding of these works below and may here merely mention one very recent one, *Marxismus und Demokratie* (edited by Jürgen Rojahn, Till Schelz, and Hans-Josef Steinberg), which is based on an international conference held in Bremen in 1988 that I had the privilege of attending and found extremely stimulating.

The remarkable growth in recent years of scholarly interest in Kautsky encouraged me to bring together in one volume two papers I have written in the past two or three years and three essays I had published some years ago. At the same time, the thoughtful and insightful literature now available on Kautsky, produced by sophisticated experts on the subject who were not yet active when I turned to it, makes me keenly aware of the shortcomings of my own expertise and work.

As his grandson, I have had an interest in Karl Kautsky all my life, though when I knew him personally it was more as a kindly old man with a white beard than as a political thinker. Later, however, in 1949–51, I wrote my doctoral dissertation at Harvard on Kautsky's political thought and so, in a sense, in publishing the present volume, I have come full circle, although my perspective on Kautsky has undergone some change in the past four decades. My dissertation was of some use as the first and for quite some time the only scholarly study of Kautsky's thought to systematically present many of his ideas. Like all too much work in the field of political thought, especially in those days, however, it made no effort to explain these ideas by relating them to the situations and the conflicts that gave rise to them. This seems particularly inexcusable in an analysis of Marxist thought, which puts such emphasis on the sociological explanation of ideologies.

I soon came to recognize this defect of my dissertation and, feeling unqualified at the time to place Kautsky's work in the context of the political and intellectual history of his period, gave up my efforts to revise it for publication. The only result of these efforts that was eventually published was my 1961 article reprinted below, comparing Kautsky's and Schumpeter's theories of imperialism. It still neither explains Kautsky's ideas nor treats them critically, but I hope that it is nevertheless worth reproducing now for the light it throws on Kautsky's relatively little-known thought on imperialism and on its intriguing relation to Schumpeter's.

As my academic career evolved in the 1950s, 1960s, and 1970s, I turned to work on Kautsky only rarely, as when the University of Michigan Press asked me to write an introduction, also reprinted below, to its new 1964 edition of his *Dictatorship of the Proletariat,* and when I was asked to contribute the article on Kautsky to the *International Encyclopedia of the Social Sciences* in 1968. While I always maintained my interest in Kautsky and, more generally, in Marxism and European socialism, most of my writing and teaching in these three decades was devoted to the politics of modernization in underdeveloped countries. Although no doubt still influenced by my earlier concern with Kautsky's thought, I now gradually came to evolve my own conception of politics, which eventually enabled me to view Kautsky's approach more critically.

In the 1980s my interests turned back to European politics and also back to Karl Kautsky, whom I could now see in the context of the history of European labor movements. I did so first in my article on Kautsky and Eurocommunism, written in 1980, that appears below. What I said there about the French and Italian Communist parties is, of course, no longer up-to-date (although, on rereading the piece, I was not too embarrassed by my tentative predictions about them).

What matters in the present context, though, is the view of Kautsky's thought as a chronologically transitional and ideologically "centrist" phenomenon in the history of the Continental labor movement. In emphasizing both revolution and democracy, Kautsky's thought retained the focus on the former of the preceding phase of that history and paved the way for labor's participation in the parliamentary politics of the next phase.

Later, in the 1980s, I undertook the time-consuming task of producing an abridged edition of Kautsky's magnum opus *The Materialist Conception of History,* published in German and in English translation in 1988, and I also edited a special issue of the *International Journal of Comparative Sociology* on "Karl Kautsky and the Social Science of Classical Marxism" (1989).

There followed the two until now unpublished papers included in this volume, on "Lenin and Kautsky on the Role of Intellectuals in the Labor Movement" and on Kautsky's book *The Road to Power.* The latter was written as an introduction to a new translation of that book, which will be published by Humanities Press. I have also recently completed my forthcoming book, *Marxism and Leninism, not Marxism-Leninism,* which argues that these are quite different ideologies employing a single terminology and views each from a perspective not available to Kautsky.

Finally, I have now written an Introduction to the present book, in which I try incidentally to introduce some biographical data on Kautsky, but above all to link the five articles that make up the body of this book, different as they are. I do so through some remarks focusing on two questions: whether Kautsky's thought remained consistent, a question raised by the reputation as a renegade that Lenin attached to him, and how relevant that thought is in the present, a question that is now being raised.

Given the richness of Kautsky's writings and also of much of the more recent secondary literature on him, I was often tempted to go off in various directions in more detail than may be appropriate in an introduction. Since, according to my present plans, it may well be the last thing I write on Kautsky, I did not always resist that temptation and maintain proper self-discipline. The result is an essay that is not only much longer but also much more discursive and in some places more reflective and even opinionated than I had intended when I began writing it.

I should add that if this Introduction and my more recent writings on Kautsky see him more critically than my earlier ones, this should not be taken to mean that my respect for my grandfather as a thinker and as a man has diminished. I should like to devote the rest of this Preface to a personal explanation of why I respect him for his scholarship and for his values.

The range of Kautsky's knowledge is truly impressive. In addition to his writings on politics, which I emphasize in this volume, Kautsky wrote a number of still quite respectable studies in the field of history, including ancient and medieval history, and worked extensively on problems of economics and demography, race and nationality. Obviously, Kautsky was a very learned man with broad interests in history and the social sciences and in their relation to natural science. He read widely all his life, and he was always eager to learn.

On Kautsky's tombstone in a cemetery near Amsterdam are the words with which he concluded an autobiographical sketch in 1923: "So I shall die as I have lived, an incorrigible Marxist." His statement does not do justice to Kautsky, for he was in some ways a quite "corrigible" Marxist. He was certainly convinced that Marxist theory was valid and sought to interpret data to fit the theory. But, the theory as left by Marx and Engels being by no means clear or rigid, it could also be interpreted and modified to fit the data. It was Kautsky's contribution to Marxism that he adapted it to an environment different from the one Marx and even Engels had been familiar with, but not yet so different as to render Marxism quite irrelevant. Kautsky meant it when he stated time and again that what mattered in Marxism was the method or approach, not the results reached by Marx and Engels, which were subject to change. Particularly in his late *Materialist Conception of History,* he was outspokenly critical in some respects of Marx and even more of Engels.

Kautsky was always searching for explanations of social phenomena and for patterns and regularities in their interrelationships; that is, he was a social scientist. His goal was to encompass the study of development in nature and in society in a single consistent system of thought, to reconcile them in what he liked to call a *widerpruchsloser Gesamtzusammenhang,* a total context free of contradictions. He may not have succeeded, but the goal and the quest seem to me not only ambitious but admirable.

In all his writings, even the polemical ones, Kautsky appealed to reason, not to emotion. His style was simple and, as is often charged, dry and even pedantic. He always saw his role as that of a teacher, not a propagandist; he sought to instruct and to persuade, not to excite. As Hans-Josef Steinberg points out in his sensitive introductory essay to *Marixmus und Demokratie,* this may be one reason why, for the past fifty years, no significant branch of socialism has invoked Kautsky's name or claimed his inheritance.

In our time, a person with Kautsky's talents, interests and inclinations would be a professor and scholar. In his time, and especially in the growing world of socialism, he could play the role of a party intellectual; he could put his scholarship at the service of his party and his cause. In this sense, he was a politician as well as a scholar, for he sought to and did influence the political world around him. But if a politician seeks power to carry out his goals, while a scholar seeks clarity and truth, he was above all a scholar. Kautsky was influential as long as his truths, as he saw them, served the needs of socialist parties. He lost much of his influence when that was no longer the case, but he never considered changing his "truths" to regain his influence.

If I respect Kautsky for the depth and breadth of his scholarship, for his appreciation of learning and culture, and for his integrity as a scholar, I also share the values that guided his work. His faith in democracy, which, like most people, he never clearly defined, was unshakable, and he strongly rejected all political authoritarianism — German imperial and fascist as well as Leninist, Trotskyite, and Stalinist. That he stood and hoped for a society with equality and opportunity for all and without poverty, discrimination, or oppression goes without saying. Today these values are, of course, more widely held, or at least professed, than in his time. But I also sympathize with Kautsky's attitudes with respect to the means by which he wanted his goals to be achieved. Here he was, in his lifetime and thereafter, attacked from two sides, finding himself in what he characterized as the "Marxist Center."

From the right, he was denounced as rigid, doctrinaire, and unrealistic for his insistence on the need for a political revolution to achieve democracy in the German Empire. Eduard Bernstein is often described as a realist for urging the German Social Democrats to give up their commitment to revolution and to work for a gradual and imperceptible "growth into socialism." Given the character of the imperial regime, the forces supporting it, and their unrelenting antagonism to Social Democracy and its objectives, it seems to me that the argument is more persuasive that Kautsky was the realist in his conviction that gradual political change toward democracy, let alone socialism, was impossible in the Empire and that an eventual confrontation with the regime was inevitable.

The fact is that until its end and even during World War I, when the majority of the Social Democratic party supported its war policies, the imperial regime made no concession in the direction of democratization. Electoral district lines were never redrawn; the extraordinarily unequal Prussian three-class suffrage remained intact throughout the entire history of the Empire; the constitutional position of the Reichstag remained weak until a few weeks before the collapse of the imperial regime in November 1918. That the later Nazi regime, which in good part rested on institutional and ideological elements that had grown strong in the Empire, was so much more arbitrarily, violently, and cruelly oppressive must not cause one to forget the quite undemocratic character of that Empire, and one must see Kautsky's political attitude until 1918 in that context.

If Kautsky was too revolutionary for some, he was not sufficiently revolutionary for others; indeed, it is often said that he was revolutionary only in words and not in deeds. That accusation rests on a misunderstanding of what the word "revolution" meant to Kautsky, a matter I hope to clear up in some of my articles below. It is quite true, however, that Kautsky was a cautious man. He did not shy away from engaging those he disagreed with in polemics, but when it came to "revolutionary" confrontations of the labor movement with the regime, as in the mass strikes advocated by Rosa Luxemburg, he hoped to postpone them until the chances for victory were improved.

As I stress at the end of my Introduction below, Kautsky also wanted to avoid violence whenever possible, and he saw no glory in bloodshed, whether it served the cause of reaction or of revolution. This peaceable, cautious, and responsible attitude has been described with much irony in some of the literature as that, not of a revolutionary, but of a mere *Stubengelehrter*. I can only admire it myself, perhaps because I, too, have been a mere ivory-tower theorist, though, I hasten to add, not in the same league with my grandfather.

I have added three appendices to my articles. In Appendix A I combine biographical and bibliographical data on Kautsky, for his life was inseparable from his work. To list, year by year, along with major events in his personal and public life, his more important writings, as I do here, is the best way to summarize his interests and commitments, his contributions and achievements, the conflicts he was engaged in. In Appendix B I list a number of edited volumes consisting entirely or in part of writings by Karl Kautsky, along with three volumes containing, respectively, his correspondence with Friedrich Engels, August Bebel, and Victor Adler and an article with another correspondence. In Appendix C I provide a bibliography of selected works on Karl Kautsky, with some emphasis on the rapidly growing scholarly literature of the past two or three decades.

The arrangement of the five articles appearing below in any sequence is inevitably arbitrary. Rather than arranging them in the chronological order in which they were written, I have tried to put them in an order corresponding very roughly to phases in Kautsky's life and in his evolving concerns, though this cannot be done at all consistently.

Of course, I would not today say everything I said in my articles published in 1961, 1964, or even in 1981; nor would I say it in quite the same way. I would not, for instance, use the concept of totalitarianism, as I did in 1964. Also, I would no longer say, as I did at that time, that communism and democratic socialism parted ways only in 1918 or, as I wrote in 1980, that they are the two major ideological branches that grew out of Marxist roots. As I indicate in my piece on Lenin and Kautsky, I now see Leninism — though not so clearly Western European Communism — as ideologically distinct from Marxism from its beginnings.

I hope that any reader who goes through this book from beginning to end will forgive me for occasionally being repetitive. Writing over a period of three decades, I sometimes developed similar or identical thoughts. Because some of these repeated thoughts are tied to different contexts, I found it impossible now to eliminate them completely.

I have decided, then, that if I did not want to rewrite my three earlier and previously published pieces — and I certainly do not — I would have to live with a few formulations I would now no longer employ and with a few repetitions, which is probably harder on me than on any reader. I have confined my revisions of the three earlier articles almost entirely to very minor stylistic ones and to modification of tenses of verbs and of chronological references (such as "in the past decade" or "last year") that would now, years later, be confusing. In one or two cases, I did abbreviate and clarify a passage or eliminate brief digressions, including the introductory paragraph of the article on Schumpeter and Kautsky. I have also, in some articles, added note references to other articles in this book.

When I quote Kautsky from his original writings in German, the translation is my own. Even when I cite an English-language edition as my source, I have modified the translation whenever it seems less than accurate or precise, which is all too often the case.

I acknowledge my debts for the individual articles where appropriate. Here I wish to thank the following publishers of the three previously published articles for their permission to reprint them: *The Midwest Journal of Political Science, Studies in Comparative Communism,* and the University of Michigan Press.

1

Introduction:
Karl Kautsky — Consistency and Relevance

Lenin revered Karl Kautsky as an oracle of Marxist wisdom until 1914 and thereafter denounced him as a renegade. His image of Kautsky, particularly the post-1914 image, has, at least until recently, powerfully influenced the view of Kautsky in the literature, thus making the question of Kautsky's consistency a central one. On the other hand, with the breakdown of the regimes Lenin founded or inspired, Kautsky's democratic Marxism in general and especially his condemnation of the Bolsheviks from 1918 till his death in 1938 appear to be highly relevant once again.

In this introductory essay, I try to answer the questions: How consistent was Kautsky's thought? How relevant is it today? I do so especially with reference to themes taken up in the five articles that follow, and I also introduce some biographical data on Kautsky. I first deal with Lenin's view of Kautsky and how it came to focus much of the literature on the question of his renegadism. In section II, I mention some examples of changes in Kautsky's thought and then point out that his theory of imperialism has often been distorted as a result of being seen through Lenin's eyes. I then turn, in section III, to Kautsky's very consistently held convictions on revolution and democracy during the period 1880–1925, and, in section IV, to his work in his Vienna years (1924–38), when he had to confront fascism.

Even earlier, as I show in section V, Kautsky could not come to terms with the bureaucratization of the labor movement and divisions in the working class. I then find his thought largely irrelevant to recent developments in democratic industrialized countries (section VI) and

1

in what was the Soviet Union (section VII). I conclude in section VIII with a look at what remains relevant in Kautsky's thought, his approach to the study of politics and his political values.

I

Karl Kautsky was the outstanding Marxist party intellectual of German Social Democracy in the three decades before World War I. In 1883, at the age of twenty-nine, he founded *Die Neue Zeit,* which was the leading Marxist journal as long as he edited it — for the next thirty-five years — and became the central international organ of Marxism as a school of thought. In 1891 Kautsky wrote the section on the principles of the Erfurt Program, the first Marxist program of the German Social Democratic Party (SPD), which became a model for other socialist parties.

After Friedrich Engels' death in 1895 and until World War I, Kautsky was generally recognized as the most authoritative Marxist thinker in Germany and in the Second (Socialist) International. Between 1883 and 1918 he wrote nearly forty books, some big and some small, about five hundred journal articles, and well over three hundred pieces in newspapers in at least sixteen countries, not to mention innumerable brief notes, book reviews, speeches, and resolutions and not counting translations of his writings into at least twenty-six languages.[1]

During the thirty-five-year period when Kautsky was most prominent and influential as a Marxist theorist and publicist and as the champion of "orthodox" Marxism in controversies with other tendencies among socialists, most notably Eduard Bernstein's Revisionism and Rosa Luxemburg's radicalism, Lenin did not figure significantly in Kautsky's thought. In 1883 Lenin was thirteen years old; he became a controversial figure in the tiny and divided grouping of Russian Social Democrats around the turn of the century and especially after he published *What Is to Be Done?* in 1902, but he was known much more as a brilliant sectarian politician and polemicist than as a major theorist.

Lenin's name hardly appears in Kautsky's published writings before 1918. (I touch very briefly on Kautsky's lack of interest in Lenin, on his position in the conflict between Bolsheviks and Mensheviks, and on his interest in Russian affairs in my article on Lenin and Kautsky on the role of intellectuals; see pp. 58-59, below.) In November 1917, however, Lenin was catapulted from being the leader of one faction of a minor political movement in backward Russia to becoming world famous and widely seen as the leader of the first socialist revolution, a revolution that millions had been hoping for and millions dreaded. As a result, even though his relationship with Lenin was anything but central in Kautsky's life and thought before World War I, the literature on Kautsky, both by Communist and non-Communist authors, was for long heavily influenced by Lenin's view of him.

Only in the past twenty-five years — and mostly much more recently — have a number of major scholarly works on Kautsky appeared that are not so influenced, most notably those by Steinberg (1967), Steenson (1978), Salvadori (1979), Gilcher-Holtey (1986), and most of the contributions to the collective work edited by Rojahn, Schelz and Steinberg (1992).[2] Perhaps, now that Lenin has been widely discredited and Communist regimes have virtually disappeared in Europe, Kautsky will be less likely to be seen through Lenin's eyes in the future,[3] though well-established major themes in the literature have a way of remaining unexamined and of being repeated for a long time.

In the literature on Kautsky, the major theme that is due to Leninist influence and that has unfortunately distorted the image of Kautsky's role in history is an emphasis, often even a focus, on what is in fact a nonproblem. Much of the general literature on socialism takes it for granted that Kautsky, who for the decade from 1899 to 1909 was the principal opponent of Revisionism, somehow during or after this decade himself underwent a drastic change in the direction of Revisionism. The Leninist-influenced literature specifically concerned with Kautsky often focuses on a search for the nature and timing of this drastic change from Marxism to "opportunism." As some of the books I have just referred to, perhaps most notably those by Gilcher-Holtey and Salvadori, show, no such drastic change ever occurred. What is the origin of this influential myth? It was a drastic change, not in Kautsky, but in Lenin's view of Kautsky. I refer to that change in my article on Lenin and Kautsky on pp. 73-76, below, but would here add more generally the following.

It seemed to the adherents of Marx and Engels, like Kautsky, that the thought of these two was vastly superior to that of others, not only because it demanded and promised the better world they were hoping for, but because it was, they felt, based on science and hence empirically valid. This may account for the tradition among them to regard their masters with the utmost respect and to cite their writings as ultimate authority. Russian Marxists were, if anything, even more inclined to do so than German Marxists.

Both because Marxism seemed to Lenin to hold out the scientific promise of a successful revolution and because one's prestige and authority in the circles in which he moved were heavily dependent on one's adherence to Marxism, it was of the utmost importance to Lenin to appear, both in his own eyes and in the eyes of his followers and his rivals, as an orthodox Marxist. By the time Lenin joined the ranks of Russian Marxists Kautsky was the outstanding living orthodox Marxist, and so Lenin treated him with almost as much awe as he did Marx and Engels. He frequently invoked Kautsky's name and writings in support of his own views—my article below deals with a particularly striking and misleading instance of this—and thought of himself and wanted to be thought of as a follower and disciple of Kautsky. (See the long quotation from Max Shachtman in my introduction to *The Dictatorship of the Proletariat* on pp. 208-209, below.)

In fact, Lenin never understood Kautsky; indeed, Lenin was not a Marxist. This is not the place to justify this seemingly daring or extremist statement. I have recently done so in my forthcoming book *Marxism and Leninism, not Marxism-Leninism,* in which I argue, on sociology-of-knowledge grounds, that Marxism and Leninism are best analyzed as quite distinct ideologies, as responses of people with different interests to different environments. They have generally, even by their own adherents, been thought to be one and the same, because they have employed the same terminology. I make the same point briefly in section IX of my article on Lenin and Kautsky on the role of intellectuals, below.

Lenin's failure to understand Kautsky, then, was due not to some intellectual or moral deficiency on his part, but to the very different roles the two thinkers played in two very different contexts. Kautsky was a theorist of a mass labor movement in an industrialized country; Lenin was a modernizing revolutionary in an underdeveloped country. At their time, unlike now, the latter type of political actor was not yet well known. Especially in Russia, where intellectuals had long identified themselves with Western counterparts, this type of political actor could easily be confused with the first type of politician in industrialized countries, who also described himself or herself as revolutionary.

Kautsky and Lenin both favored "revolution," and they mistakenly thought that they favored the same thing because they employed the same word. Thus, in 1909, Lenin referred with approval to the "pronouncedly revolutionary wing of Kautsky" within German Social Democracy.[4] In that year, Kautsky had published *The Road to Power,* usually considered his most revolutionary work for reasons I discuss in my article on that book below. As I make clear there and as is, indeed, clear from all of Kautsky's Marxist writings through more than half a century, he meant by "political revolution" the conquest of power by the working class through a socialist party. Kautsky assumed that in industrialized countries the working class would constitute the majority of the population (I stress below how wrong he was in this assumption), and that it therefore would capture control of the government by winning a parliamentary election and would then gradually carry through the social revolution by introducing socialism. If this process was going to be other than peaceful, as Kautsky feared would be the case in the German Empire, it would be because of the resistance of the old regime and the interests it represented.

Obviously, Lenin, with tsarist Russia rather than industrialized countries in mind, was bound to have a different concept of revolution. Not only was the electoral and parliamentary route not open to him, but, even if it had been, the small working class and the tiny and bitterly divided socialist party could not have hoped to come to power by taking this route. As in all underdeveloped countries under the early impact of industrialization emanating from advanced industrialized countries, it is intellectuals inspired by modern values who hope for and make revolutions against traditional-aristocratic and colonial regimes to bring about rapid modernization. If they can mobilize mass support at all, it is among the long-suffering peasants who constitute the huge majority of the population.[5] Neither the bourgeois revolution against feudalism nor the class struggle of the proletariat against the bourgeoisie culminating in the socialist revolution, all categories Marx derived from past and future Western European history as he envisaged it, are relevant in underdeveloped countries like tsarist Russia at the turn of the century.

Lenin's writings are full of the Marxian words "bourgeoisie" and "proletariat," but their reader soon discovers that Lenin, quite rightly, did not expect what native bourgeoisie there was in Russia to make the bourgeois revolution; rather, he looked to the peasants to make a revolution, which he nevertheless called bourgeois. Nor did he expect what proletariat there was in Russia to acquire "proletarian," that is, socialist, class consciousness or to make the socialist revolution unless it was led by his party. That party would be largely composed of and certainly led by intellectuals, but Lenin associated it verbally with the proletariat. A survey of Lenin's *Collected Works* reveals strikingly the persistence of two major themes from his beginnings to his death: the program and the organization of the party, and the revolutionary potential of the peasantry. He was, that is, concerned with the leadership and the major potential support group of the modernizing revolution in underdeveloped countries.

Lenin and Kautsky both spoke the language of Marx, who had attempted to analyze and predict the economic, social, and political consequences of capitalist industrialization. But while Kautsky applied Marxian terminology to a capitalist environment more industrialized than Marx's, Lenin applied it in an industrially underdeveloped environment, where Marx's analysis was largely irrelevant. Although Lenin was strongly motivated to identify his thought with Kautsky's, and although their common language long concealed their substantive differences from both of them, these differences were bound to emerge into the open sooner or later. They did so at the outbreak of World War I in August 1914, when Lenin was furiously disappointed with the position taken by Kautsky (see p. 73, below), and even more clearly when Kautsky attacked Lenin's seizure of power in November 1917 on the grounds that it was undemocratic and that the prerequisites for a socialist revolution were then lacking in Russia (see my introduction to Kautsky's *The Dictatorship of the Proletariat,* pp. 213–14, below).

It is quite understandable that neither Lenin nor his followers ever since could admit that he had been wrong in his understanding of Kautsky for at least a decade and a half before 1914. Therefore they had to believe that Lenin had been quite right in admiring Kautsky all those years and that, when he denounced him beginning in 1914, it was due to a sudden change on Kautsky's part. This is how the myth of the drastic change began, and how a man who for over sixty years wrote a huge number of books and articles on a very wide range of subjects and who for at least a quarter of a century played a key role in the complex politics of German and international socialism came to be known widely mostly by the one designation of "renegade."[6]

It was Lenin himself who initiated the search for the beginnings of Kautsky's renegadism that has preoccupied the Communist literature on Kautsky. As I note in my article on Lenin and Kautsky, p. 75, below, Lenin, notably in his *The State and Revolution,* retrospectively discovered symptoms of "opportunism" in Kautsky's earlier thought, even in his attacks on Bernstein of 1899 and in his *Road to Power* of 1909 — works which Lenin had admired without reservation when they were written — and in Kautsky's position in the "Marxist Center" in 1910.

Even though Lenin had sided with Kautsky not only in his controversy with the Revisionists but also in his conflict with Rosa Luxemburg over the mass strike in 1910 (see pp. 72–73, below), more recent Communist scholarship has focused on Kautsky's move to the Marxist Center in 1910, or even earlier in 1906, as the point when he became a renegade (see my note 66 on German literature on "Centrism" in chapter 3, below, and my denial that there was a drastic change between 1909 and 1910 on pp. 115–16, below).[7]

The East German Communists in particular were preoccupied with this problem, for they traced the descent of their Socialist Unity Party (SED) back, via the German Communist Party (KPD), to the radical wing of the SPD, of which Kautsky was a principal representative. He was thus both an honored ancestor and a hated renegade to them, and the question is when he turned from one into the other. Not only is there disagreement on just when that happened — possibly as early as 1899, perhaps in 1906 or more probably in 1910, clearly by 1914 and absolutely definitively by 1917 — but there has never been a persuasive explanation as to why an outstanding Marxist (and Communists must see him as such, because Lenin's pre-1914 writings are full of praise for Kautsky) betrayed his commitment and took the side of those he had fought for years.

Certainly Kautsky's failure to understand the Marxian dialectic, his insufficient appreciation of the subjective factor in history, his more scholarly than activist personality, or his cowardice (all of which have been ascribed to him), being presumably permanent characteristics, cannot account for a more or less sudden change on his part. His supposed failure to understand politics in the new age of monopoly capitalism and imperialism is not so much an explanation of his alleged renegadism as a mere assertion of it. In any case, Lenin had not noted such a failure when, even in December 1914, he discussed Kautsky's *Road to Power* at some length as "containing a most complete exposition of the tasks of our times."[8]

In the same article, Lenin himself raised the question "how *could* it have come to pass . . . that the leading authority in the Second International . . . has sunk to something that is worse than being a renegade?" But the only answer he can come up with is

that Kautsky is "dead." The political bankruptcy of individuals is not a rarity at turning points in history. Despite the tremendous services he has rendered, Kautsky has never been among those who, at great crises, immediately take a militant Marxist stand (recall his vacillations on the issue of Millerandism).[9]

Seventy-four years later, an East German scholar was still at a loss to explain Kautsky's supposed shift:

One will have to continue to ponder and argue about the causes of this behavior in 1910 that introduced a change in Karl Kautsky's development. A reasonably good explanation of its causes and reasons, in the context of his biography and of the history of the Party, will probably be most likely to be found if one considers many circumstances and factors of an objective and subjective nature.[10]

II

I hold that neither the date of Kautsky's shift from Marxism to "opportunism" nor the reasons for it can be established, simply because there was no such shift. I do not argue, however, that Kautsky consistently and persistently maintained the same views throughout his life, though he himself tended to emphasize his consistency and to see himself as, at least basically, unchanging. It is, indeed, unimaginable that a person could remain politically aware and relevant in an environment undergoing great changes without changing himself or herself.

Kautsky's environment did, indeed, change drastically in his lifetime. He became politically active in the German Empire (which had been founded when he was sixteen years old) in the period of Bismarck's Anti-Socialist Law (1878–90), under which all socialist organizations were prohibited, hundreds of party members were expelled from their homes and sentenced to prison, and the only socialist agitation permitted was in election campaigns because candidates running for elections were legally seen as individuals rather than as representatives of political parties.

Kautsky became the principal theorist of a party that after 1890, could function more freely, but that was still rigidly opposed and constantly harassed by the imperial regime. It grew from a minor party polling 6.1 percent of the vote in the Reichstag election of 1881 (it had obtained only 3.2 percent in the first election in 1871) to a mass movement and the biggest party in the country, polling 34.8 percent of the vote in 1912.[11]

Kautsky witnessed World War I; the Russian Revolution and the subsequent split of European labor movements by the rise of Communist parties; the replacement of the German Empire by the parliamentary Weimar Republic, with which the SPD was closely identified; and its replacement in turn by the Nazi regime during the last five years of his life. Austria, where Kautsky lived as a child and young man until 1880 and as an old man after 1924 and to whose socialist party (SPOe) he was always close, passed, somewhat like Germany, through the phases of monarchy, republic, and fascism in his lifetime.

In the articles appearing below, mention is made of several changes in Kautsky's political position. In my article on Kautsky and Eurocommunism, I draw a parallel between the Western European Communist parties' shift in the 1960s and 1970s from separatism to Eurocommunism and Kautsky's shift from his opposition to socialist coalitions with "bourgeois" parties in the German Empire to his advocacy of such coalitions in the Weimar Republic (see pp. 176, 184–85, below). In my article on Kautsky's *Road to Power,* I stress that his rejection of coalition politics was linked to the specific conditions in imperial Germany. Obviously, it was the change from Empire to Republic that accounted for his change in this respect (see my note 70 in chapter 3, below).

However, not only in the Weimar Republic but also in the Empire, Kautsky did attack the concept that vis-à-vis the working class all other classes were only "one reactionary mass," because this popular Lassallean phrase wrongly suggested that all nonsocialist parties were equally hostile to the SPD and thus ruled out any limited cooperation with some of them, especially agreements in runoff elections. Yet in his *Road to Power,* as I note in my article on that book (see p. 106, and note 31 in chapter 3, below), he argued that the "one reactionary mass" had become reality when in the Reichstag election of 1907 the left liberals, with whom the Social Democrats had earlier sometimes cooperated, supported the imperial government.

On the other hand, the change in Kautsky's attitude from that in *The Road to Power* in 1909 to that in his response to Rosa Luxemburg on the mass strike in 1910 (which I discuss on pp. 115–16, below) was, in my view, at most a change in emphasis. Its importance and extent is greatly exaggerated by those who find in it the beginning or a major symptom of Kautsky's supposed renegadism.

The conditions in the first decade of the twentieth century, to which Kautsky responded in *The Road to Power* and which I note in my article on that book below, notably the failure of the labor movement to continue to score striking successes and the imperial government's emphasis on colonialism and armaments, may also account to some degree for the shift in Kautsky's explanation of imperialism, with which I deal in section IV of my article below, comparing his and Schumpeter's theories on the subject. While he had associated imperialism with preindustrial forces and considered industrial capitalism anti-imperialist in his writings at the end of the nineteenth century, he explained it in terms of the needs of industrial capitalism after the turn of the century. He did so because he saw industrial capital as having merged by then with preindustrial banking capital into what Hilferding, in his major work of 1910 by that title, called finance capital.[12]

I need not repeat here what I say in my article about this change in Kautsky's theory of imperialism, but would like to digress to call attention at greater length to something I mention only in passing there. Kautsky's thought on imperialism is another aspect of his work that has been distorted in much of the literature because it has been seen through Lenin's eyes. Lenin's pamphlet *Imperialism,* written in 1916 and first published in 1917,[13] is one of his best-known works, possibly his single best known one. In it he repeatedly and at great length attacks Kautsky on the subject of imperialism, but he confines his attention entirely to two articles written by Kautsky, one in 1914 and one in 1915.[14] In these articles, Kautsky made the point that capitalism could function without imperialism and war, which flies in the face of Lenin's principal argument that imperialism was a necessary final phase of capitalism and that capitalism must therefore be overthrown if international wars were to be ended.

In his pamphlet, Lenin deals only with the articles of 1914 and 1915 because it was at the outbreak of World War I — the first of these articles was drafted a few weeks before and published a few weeks after that date — that Lenin turned against Kautsky. He completely ignored Kautsky's writings on colonialism and imperialism in the quarter-century preceding World War I, evidently because in that period he had admired and respected Kautsky, even though in some of them Kautsky had also stressed that imperialism was a policy industrial capitalism could well do without. What is more (as I point out in note 35 of my article on Schumpeter and Kautsky, below), the writings Lenin attacked are closer to Lenin's own thought (like Lenin's thought they are influenced by Hilferding, and they link imperialism to finance capitalism), than are the writings he ignored, among which the earlier ones linked imperalism to preindustrial forces.

As a result of Lenin's emphasis, Kautsky's ideas on imperialism have in much of the literature come to be identified with those expressed in the two articles Lenin attacked, especially the first one, "Der Imperialismus." While important, it is by no means representative of Kautsky's thought on the subject, which he developed in well over a dozen articles, pamphlets, and books both before and after 1914. The few sentences Lenin quotes from Kautsky have been read by millions, while his many pages on imperialism — virtually none of them translated into English — have remained widely unknown. It was generally Kautsky's bad luck to be known for several decades after his death principally through Lenin's attacks on him, and this is particularly true of his thought on imperialism.

Indeed, not only has this body of complex, sophisticated and changing ideas been widely ignored in favor of a single brief article, but most of this article has been ignored in favor of a single sentence in it, which I quote on p. 147, below, on the possibility of a future phase of "ultra-imperialism." Nine months after writing it, Kautsky explained why he had done so:

> The retreat of the movement for protective tariffs in England, the reduction of tariffs in America, the efforts at disarmament, the quick reduction of capital exports from France and Germany in the last few years before the War, and finally the growing international interpenetration [*Verfilzung*] of the various cliques of finance capital caused me to consider whether it might not be possible for the present imperialist policy to be pushed aside by a new ultra-imperialist one, which replaces the struggle of national finance capitals against each other by the joint exploitation of the world through internationally allied finance capital. Such a new phase of capitalism is, in any case, imaginable. The necessary preconditions are still lacking to decide whether it is also realizable. . . . The present war . . . can totally

stamp out the weak sprouts of ultra-imperialism by greatly increasing the national hatred also of the finance capitalists, by spurring on the armaments race, by making a second world war inevitable. . . . But the war can also . . . strengthen the weak sprouts of ultra-imperialism. . . . Temporarily, . . . ultra-imperialism could bring an era of new hope and expectations within capitalism."[15]

Lenin quotes from this passage as well as the sentence from "Der Imperialismus" and violently pours out his contempt and hatred for what he calls Kautsky's "theory of ultra-imperialism." He denounces it as "ultra-nonsense," "utterly meaningless talk," a "silly little fable," "the reactionary attempt of a frightened philistine to hide from stern reality," "a reformist 'pious wish,' " a "notorious theory," and "a lifeless abstraction,"[16] and he says that

> the only objective, i.e., real, social significance of Kautsky's "theory" is this: it is a most reactionary method of consoling the masses with hopes of permanent peace being possible under capitalism, by distracting their attention from the sharp antagonisms and acute problems of the present times, and directing it towards illusory prospects of an imaginary "ultra-imperialism" of the future. Deception of the masses — that is all there is in Kautsky's "Marxist" theory.[17]

I do not recall seeing the term "ultra-imperialism" used by Kautsky except in the two passages of 1914 and 1915 cited above and also in a passage of 1927, which I quote on pp. 147–48, below. In these passages and in the one of 1917 just referred to, he merely suggests that a phase of ultra-imperialism is one possible alternative development of capitalism, "only one among many other possibilities," that it is "not inconceivable," that it is "imaginable" and "by no means impossible," and he stresses that it was quite impossible to predict whether such a phase would in fact occur.[18] Surely, a couple of brief statements advanced so hesitatingly and with such deliberate caution can hardly be considered a theory. And yet, simply because Lenin in 1916 needed to attack Kautsky's reference to "ultra-imperialism," that one word has been widely identified as the very essence of Kautsky's thought on imperialism.

III

Kautsky was by no means a rigid, dogmatic theorist, as he has often been described. In the course of his long career, he changed his mind on some issues, such as those I have now mentioned. On the other hand, he did not deserve the label "renegade," which Lenin so successfully attached to his name. Much of the recent scholarly literature on Kautsky confirms both these points.

With respect to the two principal themes of Kautsky's political thought, which can be designated with the two words "democracy" and "revolution," he did remain remarkably consistent from the time he became a Marxist and an intellectual leader of the German Social Democratic Party in the early 1880s. For at least a quarter of a century, his position was regarded as the "orthodox" Marxist one; there was no opposition to it on the issue of democracy, and those who disagreed with it on the issue of revolution were seen as "revisionists." It was only when a different ideology responding to conditions in underdeveloped Russia claimed the mantle of Marxist orthodoxy that Kautsky's unchanged views could be seen as those of a renegade.

I deal with Kautsky's insistence that the proletariat develops its organizational and intellectual strength best under parliamentary democracy and that it must maintain this form of government once it is in power in my introduction, reprinted below, to his *The Dictatorship of the Proletariat*. In that pamphlet of 1918, in which he attacked the new Bolshevik regime for its rejection of democracy and pleaded with German and European socialists to remain faithful to democracy, Kautsky voiced views that now became highly controversial but that had until then been generally accepted among Marxists.

Some quotations from Kautsky's writings and letters of the 1890s in my article on *The Road to Power* (p. 111; note 42; pp. 115–16; and note 72, in that article, below) show that he had held these views all along. Throughout this article and, in more summary fashion, in my article on Kautsky and Eurocommunism, also reprinted below, I analyze Kautsky's concept of revolution and its relation to his view of democracy. In both pieces, I try to explain it with reference to the peculiar character of the German Empire, where the SPD could compete in free elections and yet could not hope to come to power within the existing political order. The article on Eurocommunism and my introduction to *The Dictatorship of the Proletariat* also refer to Kautsky's postwar views.

Kautsky, living in Vienna as a child and young man, had developed his interest in history and in natural science—the two fields were linked in his mind by an evolutionary or Darwinian perspective — in the 1870s. In early 1874, at the age of twenty, he had joined the fledgling Austrian socialist party, in which he functioned as a writer and lecturer. All this laid the basis for his future thought and work, but the political ideas to which he then remained faithful all his life were developed principally in response to conditions in the German Empire, as I noted, at first in the period of the Anti-Socialist Law.

In the early 1880s, Kautsky spent about three years in Zurich, where he moved in German socialist emigré circles and, together with Eduard Bernstein, studied Marxist works, especially Engels' *Anti-Dühring*, to become a convinced Marxist. In 1881 he met Marx and Engels in London, in 1883 he established *Die Neue Zeit* in Stuttgart, and from 1885 to 1888 he worked in the British Museum under Engels's guidance. Incidentally, while in England, he was impressed with British parliamentarism and he remained an Anglophile all his life. In the 1880s, then, Kautsky was launched on his career as the theoretician of the radical or revolutionary wing of the SPD in the Empire and as the champion of "orthodox" Marxism against socialists who opposed or deviated from it.

Even after the lifting of the Anti-Socialist Law in 1890, given the nature of the German imperial regime and its continuing implacable hostility to the Social Democratic Party, Kautsky felt that, being a democrat, he had to be a revolutionary. The remarkable growth of the German working class, of its trade unions, and of the Social Democratic Party seemed to Kautsky to confirm the Marxian promise of socialist success and never left any doubt in his mind that the working class, through the SPD, would have to come to power, that is, to make a political revolution to establish democracy. He hoped that democracy could be introduced through socialist electoral victories and other forms of working-class pressure that could overcome the possibly violent resistance of the old regime. He did not expect democracy to be attained before the working class was ready to defeat the ruling classes, so that in Germany the achievement of democracy and of proletarian power would coincide.

Pro-labor reforms and trade-union advances and electoral victories on the national and local levels seemed to Kautsky highly desirable and electoral victories, at least, also seemed highly probable. Unlike his Revisionist adversaries in the SPD, however, he was convinced that the imperial regime and its supporters would not permit a gradual and imperceptible "growth into socialism" by such methods and would eventually provoke some sort of confrontation with the SPD.

Unable to predict when and in what form such a confrontation would occur, Kautsky could only advocate that the proletariat be prepared for it by improving its organization, advancing its education, and avoiding demoralizing entanglements with the regime. If this were done, time was working on the side of the inevitably growing proletariat, and it was not in its interest or its party's interest to provoke a clash with the regime prematurely.

Such a clash never occurred, but the political revolution Kautsky had desired did occur when the imperial government fell in 1918 as a result of defeat in World War I. With the establishment of the parliamentary democratic Weimar Republic in 1919, there was in his view no longer any need for a political revolution. The way to the peaceful gradual realization of socialism through SPD electoral victories and legislation by an SPD parliamentary majority was now open,[19] though there might be a transitional period of socialist participation in coalition governments with left bourgeois parties.

In the next section, I will say enough on Kautsky's analysis of fascism to show that by 1933 he had to realize that Weimar democracy had not yet opened the road to power to the working class and that yet another struggle, presumably violent, would have to be fought by that class, the goal of which must once again be the achievement of democracy.

Kautsky's position as a revolutionary theorist in the Empire and his concern as such with the need and the prospects for revolution did not prepare him well for the new situation that arose in 1919. He had all along advocated the institution of parliamentary democracy, but he had seen it merely as the desirable alternative to the status quo under the Empire. More concerned with that status quo, he had given little thought to the problems of parliamentary democracy, for example, with respect to voting behavior and representation, policy formation, and the role of the bureaucracy.[20] As I will note in a moment, after parliamentary regimes supplanted imperial regimes in Germany and Austria, Kautsky hardly dealt with the role and the problems of socialist parties under this new form of government. Rather, he concerned himself with developments in the Soviet Union, where he could continue to call for the democratization of a regime rather than analyze the situation under a democratic regime.

Democracy, much like socialism, represented for Kautsky the good future with which to confront the bad present. Under socialism public policy would reflect the interests of society. Who would select, control, and influence those who would decide what was in the interest of society, and how their decisions would differ from those of pre-socialist politicians who, after all, had also been convinced that they represented the interests of society, are the kind of basic questions that Kautsky either did not confront or answered with the simple word "democracy."

Under the Empire, Kautsky, like most Marxists, including Marx and Engels, had not paid much attention in his thought and writings to the details of the future socialist order.[21] He identified socialism with social ownership — but by no means only state ownership — of the means of production, but he felt that its forms could not and should not yet be predicted. They would emerge through trial and error and would vary greatly in different countries, times, and branches of the economy.

From a Marxist perspective, the failure to think systematically about the nature of the future socialist society and of the governmental measures that would be required to convert capitalism into socialism was not irresponsible; Marxists were proud to be "scientific" socialists, whose job it was to analyze the present and the tendencies inherent in it, but not, like the earlier utopian socialists, to paint wishful but necessarily quite unscientific pictures of an unpredictable distant future society. That attitude had not changed at a time when the future society did not seem so distant any more but when Marxists were still preoccupied with their problems in the present.

After the German Revolution, Kautsky did give some thought to the problems of the transition to socialism. He served as chairman of the German revolutionary government's socialization commission for a few weeks immediately after the overthrow of the Empire. In 1922 he published a substantial book on the political and economic problems that would confront a new socialist government,[22] which deals at some length, but in quite general terms, with such topics as democracy and coalitions, bureaucracy and planning, and socialization in industry and agriculture.

In 1925 Kautsky drafted the section on the Party's principles of the Heidelberg Program of the reunited SPD, repeating, sometimes verbatim, what he had written in the Erfurt Program thirty-four years earlier. But he also noted the growing significance of white-collar workers and intellectuals and the newer phenomena of finance capital and the danger of war, and he stressed that the working class now possessed "in the democratic republic the form of government whose preservation and expansion is an indispensable necessity for its struggle for emancipation."[23]

This, however, was Kautsky's last major contribution to German Social Democracy, to which he had been so closely tied for more than four decades. He never regained his prewar influence in the SPD, in part because he had left it to join the antiwar Independent Social Democratic Party (USPD) in 1917 and lost the editorship of *Die Neue Zeit*, which had been his principal voice for thirty-five years. But, above all, he was no longer actively involved in the politics of Social Democracy because his role as a revolutionary thinker had been appropriate to a party rigidly excluded from power and in opposition to the existing political and social order. With the victory of the revolution and of democracy, which Kautsky had advocated all along, the SPD became a pillar of the new Weimar Republic, a situation that Kautsky approved of but for which his experience had not really prepared him.

That Kautsky had not, until 1918, analyzed the transition to socialism in any detail soon proved to be irrelevant, for the Social Democrats failed to gain parliamentary majorities. However, he had also never had any interest in "social policy,"[24] and thus could not make any contributions in an area where the SPD could be active. Finally, his longstanding opposition to any coalition participation by the SPD in the Empire did not help him to understand the complex role of the Party in Weimar politics, where it not only participated in coalitions with other pro-democratic parties, which Kautsky agreed with, but also had to support governments of which it was not a member. In 1932, to keep Hitler out of the presidency, the SPD even had to support the candidacy of Paul von Hindenburg, a Prussian Junker who represented everything the Party and Kautsky had opposed in the Empire.

IV

In Germany after 1918 the revolution for democracy and, through it, for working-class power was no longer an issue. The great battles Kautsky had fought in the last two decades of the Empire were no longer relevant. The conflict with Revisionism had been focused specifically on the question of whether democratization and the continued progress of the socialist movement were possible in the German Empire without a drastic political change or whether they were possible only by way of revolution. Now that this issue had disappeared, Kautsky could renew his old friendship with Bernstein.

Rosa Luxemburg's emphasis on the spontaneity of unorganized workers hardly needed to be fought by Kautsky now that he himself faced the antipathy or indifference of a bureaucratized labor movement, while the German Communist Party, founded by Luxemburg, had been taken over by the followers of Lenin, to whom spontaneity was a dirty word and organization the key to success.

Thus, in the Weimar period, we do not find Kautsky engaging in polemics with fellow Social Democrats, as he had done again and again in the Empire. We look in vain in the pages of the Berlin *Gesellschaft* and the Vienna *Kampf* for the kind of articles by Kautsky that had filled the pages of *Die Neue Zeit*. Of some fifty articles he contributed to these two journals between 1919 and 1933, twenty-nine are devoted to historical topics or more general problems of historical and social analysis and nineteen to attacks on Communism and the Soviet regime and to the defense of democracy.

These were the subjects that preoccupied Kautsky in the last fourteen years of his life, when he had also physically separated himself from German Social Democracy by moving to Vienna in 1924. Although Austro-Marxists, including Otto Bauer, who led the Austrian Social Democratic Party in opposition to the clerical government, regarded him as their teacher,[25] Kautsky did not become publicly and actively involved in Austrian socialist politics.[26] His writings also show no interest at all in the remarkable achievements of the socialist municipal administration of "Red Vienna" in the fields of welfare, health, education, and housing.

In his Vienna period Kautsky published two of four projected books on the politics of war and on socialist attitudes toward war, especially World War I, and he began work on what remained a massive fragment of his autobiography.[27] But before these three big volumes Kautsky produced two others, his magnum opus *The Materialist Conception of History*.[28] In it, Kautsky, as he says in his preface, fulfilled his old wish "to give a systematic and comprehensive account and justification" of the materialist conception of history. He saw this conception as compatible with and linked to natural science and attempted to encompass the study of development in nature and in society, while recognizing their differences, in a single, consistent system of thought. This is not the place to discuss Kautsky's approach,[29] but in our context it must be noted that in integrating the interests of his youth with those he had developed in the subsequent fifty years, Kautsky presents in this work remarkable testimony to the continuity and consistency of his thought.

Although Kautsky had withdrawn from the German Social Democratic Party and had remained out of Austrian Social Democratic Party politics after 1924, he was passionately involved in another area of current politics even while, now in his seventies, he produced the five big volumes I have just mentioned, which were quite detached from current affairs. Ever since he had, in August 1918 — less than a year after the October Revolution in Russia and three months before the fall of the German Empire — attacked the Bolsheviks in his *Dictatorship of the Proletariat,* Kautsky followed with the greatest interest and commented on developments in the Soviet Union and the Third (Communist) International. While his long-standing concern with revolution and democracy may have been outdated in the parliamentary Weimar and First Austrian Republics, it seemed very relevant here.

I shall return to Kautsky's writings on Communism below, when I turn to the present-day relevance of his thought on the Soviet Union. Here I may merely note that in several books, pamphlets, and articles — I cite some below and also in my introduction to *The Dictatorship of the Proletariat* — Kautsky elaborated on the themes I mention in that introduction, notably the absence in Russia of the prerequisites for a socialist revolution, that is, not only advanced industry, but also a mature proletariat, which can develop only under democracy. Because these prerequisites for socialism did not exist and because the regime had therefore become dictatorial, he was certain it was bound to collapse. Kautsky came to regard the Soviet regime as a counterrevolutionary enemy of the proletariat not only in Russia but also internationally, as it had split the labor movement in the West and thus facilitated the rise of fascism.[30]

It might seem that in Germany and Austria concepts of revolution and democracy — and of the achievement of democracy through revolution — became relevant again when fascist regimes came to power there. Kautsky, however, never fully understood fascism. He thought that "the eighteenth century overestimated the influence of thought, of reason, on the behavior of men" and stressed that "the unconscious plays a big role in society and history,"[31] but in most of his writings he clearly assumed that individuals and classes would become aware of their class interests and act accordingly. His optimism regarding the inexorable advance of science, democracy, and socialism rested on his faith that knowledge must triumph over ignorance and reason over irrationality.

More specifically, Kautsky recognized that the workers' "socialist drive or instinct" may lack clarity, which needed to be spread by intellectuals like himself (see my article on Lenin and Kautsky on the role of intellectuals on pp. 61, 65, below), but he took it as self-evident that socialism expressed the interests of workers. While he had less respect for the political insight of the peasantry and the petty bourgeoisie than for that of the proletariat, he assumed that the achievement and maintenance of democracy was in the interest of all three of these classes. An antisocialist and especially an antidemocratic mass movement of the dimensions of Nazism therefore simply did not fit into Kautsky's conception of modern politics.

Kautsky explained the Nazi success in Germany as the result of the weakness of Weimar democracy, which in turn was due to the weakness of the proletariat produced by the World War and its dehumanizing effects, by the Great Depression, and by the splits and confusion introduced by the Communists and the Nazis. He also blamed some aspects of the Versailles treaty, which provided for a professional German army rather than a militia, and of the Weimar constitution, which gave too strong a position to the Reich president.[32]

On the problem of how to remove fascism from power, Kautsky, writing a few months after Hitler's seizure of power in Germany, had this to say:

> What methods the struggle against fascist dictatorship requires is difficult to determine at the moment. Modern dictatorships are something so new, so unheard-of in world history that it is to be expected that the way of overcoming them would assume quite new, hitherto unheard-of forms.

He recognized that "the struggle against fascism absolutely requires illegal, secret organizations" and that, if these were to be effective in preparing insurrections, "dictatorial, undemocratic methods" would be necessary.[33] But in the same year, Kautsky also wrote:

> The momentary victory of Hitlerism does not in the least cause us to

become "hard," as we have recently been urged to become, if becoming hard means becoming ruthless and unscrupulous, resorting to the Nazi methods of lies, deceit, torture, and assassination of political opponents. The brown barbarians may arrest us, may drag us into concentration camps, may shoot us "while escaping," but they shall not succeed in making us prisoners of their depravity. Under all circumstances, we shall remain champions of democracy and of humanism. We reject as senseless and cruel and ruinous for our cause and our people the suggestion that we seek to arrive at humanity through bestiality.[34]

Whatever means of removing fascism from power Kautsky may have had in mind — and he was obviously, and surely could be, only uncertain and vague on the matter — he emphasized and insisted repeatedly that the goal of the struggle by the working class, as distinguished from its methods, had to be the restoration of democracy and not some kind of dictatorship to counterpose to and succeed the fascist one.

Kautsky escaped from Vienna on 12 March 1938, when German troops entered Austria; he died seven months later in exile in Amsterdam as the optimist he had always been.[35] He remained convinced that

the rise of dictatorship in some states signals a local transitory interruption of a process that has been advancing for more than a century in the entire civilized world. It is a consequence of the World War. We need not fear that it may become general and lasting enough to lead to the "Decline of the West" that one of the pioneers of National Socialism prophesied.[36]

Kautsky had no doubt that democracy and socialism were bound to triumph, because the proletariat was bound to grow in strength and insight.

I will turn below to the failure of Kautsky's firm prediction of the unstoppable forward march of the socialist proletariat, but I should, in fairness, add here that his failure to develop a systematic analysis of fascism is quiet understandable. Although when he was in his eighties he was no doubt inclined to repeat ideas that had been relevant in the past, and in his writings on fascism he tended to draw historical parallels, he was, as he indicated in the passage I just quoted, quite aware that fascism was something wholly new and unheard of in world history. It was this novelty that kept him — and so far as I know, all of his contemporaries — from a wholly adequate understanding of fascism.

Indeed, one could even argue that Kautsky's understanding of fascism, limited as it was, was superior to that of many Marxists of his time, who tended to see fascism as a reaction by advanced capitalism. In 1927, Kautsky wrote that "the emergence of Fascism does not demonstrate that it will everywhere be the answer of capital to a victory of the working class under democracy." At that time, he argued that the conditions that had given rise to fascism in Italy were not likely to recur elsewhere, especially not in Germany.[37] When that prediction proved disastrously wrong six years later, Kautsky, ever optimistic but this time also mostly more correct, wrote:

> Fascism will not cross the Rhine, let alone the North Sea. In France, England, and America, it will remain the fashionable folly of a few insignificant political show-offs [*Gecken*].[38]

Deeply rooted parliamentary democracy would be an insuperable barrier to fascism.

Karl Kautsky's thought had been a relevant response to historical developments in Western Europe, and especially in the German Empire, in the few decades before World War I. The growth of industry and, with it, of the working class and of socialist parties in that period seemed to him to confirm his view that there were regularities in history or laws governing it and that these laws guaranteed the eventual victory of socialism.

His confidence both in that victory and in the existence of regularities in history remained unshakable, but he recognized that politics in the two post-World-War-I decades he lived through was different from pre-War politics and hence in his view, abnormal. His inability to understand it by seeing it through the application of the laws derived from prewar history troubled him. In 1937, in his preface to his last completed work, he wrote that the world was moving in "extreme and abnormal ways" since World War I. Current developments were difficult to understand because regularities in them could not yet be discovered. "Insofar as our present-day social and political thought rests on scientific foundations, on the recognition of regularities, these were gained through the observation of social processes before the World War."[39]

V

Although by no means entirely inflexible and rigid, Kautsky was on the whole a remarkably consistent thinker. However, to consistently adhere to unchanging views in a changing world is no virtue. Concepts and theories that helped one to explain and to act appropriately in one situation may become obstacles to an understanding of a new and different situation. Kautsky effectively avoided this problem when he refrained from participating in or commenting on the politics of the last decade of the Weimar and First Austrian Republics and concentrated instead on Soviet and Communist politics. There his concern with the prerequisites of a socialist revolution and the need for democracy seemed, at least at the time, to be more relevant. When forced to confront the phenomenon of fascism, however, his old concepts and theories proved inadequate, and he, like other Marxists in that period, was unable to develop new and more appropriate ones.

Even much earlier, however, in the last decade of the German Empire, Kautsky's old way of viewing his environment kept him from adequately appreciating a gradual change in the German labor movement and in his own Social Democratic Party. He had always stressed that the growing working class must become highly organized and educated. The SPD and the trade unions associated with it approached that goal with remarkable success. One consequence of that success, however, which Kautsky had not clearly foreseen, was the bureaucratization of the Party.[40]

Kautsky must have become aware of this development at the latest by 1909, in a period he saw as one of stagnation and of no progress by the labor movement, especially when early in that year he faced the opposition of his Party's Executive Committee to the publication of his *Road to Power,* which I discuss in my article on that book below. A few months later, he wrote an unusually pessimistic letter to Victor Adler about German Social Democracy "retrogressing" at that time:

It is not Revisionism that is becoming dominant but incompetence and pettiness. Or, rather, even very competent people become incompetent and petty as soon as they occupy leading positions.

What is so depressing in this entire business is exactly that there is no prospect of improving matters by a change in personnel, for instance by changes in the Executive Committee. The causes lie deeper. For one thing,

I believe one of these causes must be sought in the excessive growth of bureaucratism, which kills every initiative from below and thus also any daring, for only the irresponsible mass is daring and takes risks, not the responsible leaders, who have their doubts and hesitate, not out of coward-ice but out of conscientiousness. I, too, would not dare to press for mass action, which the mass itself does not press for, because only when the action is initiated by the mass can one count on the necessary power and passion.

But in Germany the masses are drilled always to await commands from above. The people on top, however, are so absorbed by the administrative tasks of the immense apparatus that they have lost all wider vision, all interest for anything that is beyond their bureaucratic concerns. We saw this first in the case of the trade unions; we see it now, since the political organization has grown so much, in it as well. . . . We suffer from the division of labor, from the idiocy of specialization, which is inevitable.[41]

But though Kautsky sees the trends he insightfully diagnoses here as inevitable, he cannot quite accept them, because they are incompat-ible with his belief in the revolutionary nature of the working class and its party. Even in his pessimistic letter to Adler, he says that he does not despair. "Some event" would soon break up the existing state of balance and stagnation in the society and would unleash a powerful movement.

Similarly, as I note in my introduction to *The Dictatorship of the Proletariat* — see pp. 215–16, below — Kautsky admits in that work that, in the mass movements made possible by the democracy he ad-vocates, workers — not just the leaders he was worried about two de-cades earlier — may be bogged down in petty day-to-day work and concern with passing events and may develop opportunism and con-tempt for theory. But he quickly concludes:

The antagonisms in capitalist society grow; again and again they cause big conflicts and pose great problems for the proletarians that lift their minds above daily routines. . . .

Under democracy, the proletariat does not constantly think and talk only of revolution, as it does under despotism. For years and even entire de-cades, it may be immersed in mere day-to-day work, but eventually situa-tions must everywhere again and again arise that kindle in it revolutionary thought and aspirations.[42]

Kautsky sees a situation that deviates from the model he has in mind and he even admits that this situation may persist for decades, but he can adhere to his model nevertheless by asserting that the situation cannot last forever.

Kautsky was also keenly aware of divisions within the working class. Even in *The Road to Power,* where he stresses that "economic development continuously effects the growth of the revolutionary elements in the population, those who have an interest in removing the property system and the political order of today,"[43] he admits immediately that these elements are only potentially and not in fact revolutionary. "Many proletarians," stemming from the petty bourgeoisie and the small peasantry, feel like would-be property-owners. Others hope to advance by becoming strikebreakers or by joining company unions. Others look for help to bourgeois parties and governments. Even many believers in the class struggle doubt that the proletariat will be victorious. Kautsky concludes this listing of nonsocialist elements in the working class by noting that "the faster economic development and thus the proletarization of the population proceeds, . . . the more numerous the elements in the proletariat who have not yet grasped the significance for them of a social revolution, who do not even understand the class antagonisms in our society."[44]

But here again Kautsky does not accept that the situation he diagnoses might last. Some workers have "not yet" grasped the need for a social revolution; they are "still" caught up in petty-bourgeois ideology. "It is the task of Social Democracy to unite the various ways in which the proletariat reacts to its exploitation into goal-conscious and uniform behavior, which reaches its peak in the great final struggles for the conquest of political power."[45]

There is no doubt in Kautsky's mind that the Social Democratic Party will succeed in overcoming the divisions within the proletariat, particularly when it is guided by the proper theory, that is, Kautsky's Marxist theory. "Only knowledge of the social process, its tendencies and goals, is capable of . . . concentrating the forces of the proletariat, to combine them in great organizations that are united by great goals and that subordinate in planned fashion personal and momentary actions to lasting class interests."[46]

Thus, though he knows very well that the working class was in fact politically divided, Kautsky throughout his works keeps referring to "the" proletariat as if it were a single political actor. In part, this may be due to no more than the tendency of all politicians to ascribe their views to a much larger constituency than they in fact enjoy, as when American politicians routinely attribute their views to "the" American people.

There is more involved here, however. Kautsky's theory of social development convinced him that workers must, of historical necessity, develop common interests and must become aware of them and be united by a common goal. In turn, these interests and that goal must be represented by the socialist party. Kautsky could, then, spend much of his time engaging in controversies dividing the SPD and still regard it as a basically united force. The divisions within the party and within the working class that he saw very clearly were in his view either relatively superficial or bound to disappear; they were never such as to induce him to abandon his optimistic convictions.

That Kautsky, at the beginning of the century, could not fully grasp the nature and consequences of the bureaucratization of the Social Democratic Party is not surprising, for there was no precedent for this process; the SPD was the first mass party in history.[47] And that Kautsky believed in the growth of the working class, not only in numbers but also in its organizational and ideological unity, is not at all surprising either, for there were powerful tendencies in this direction in the period of the German Empire that seemed to confirm Kautsky's theory. In the two decades between the fall of that Empire and Kautsky's death, he did not think very much or very clearly about factors affecting the nature of labor movements in industrialized countries or he could not come to terms with them and regarded the conditions of that period as abnormal.

VI

In the half-century since Kautsky's death and since World War II, as I state more briefly in my introduction to *The Dictatorship of the Proletariat* on p. 215, below, the industrialized world has changed so much that Kautsky's views of its development have become largely irrelevant.[48] The bureaucratization of labor's mass organization was not a temporary phenomenon, as Kautsky had thought. The working class has not only remained divided in ways that Kautsky recognized but thought were only temporary, but it has also become far more heterogeneous as a result of technological changes not foreseen by Kautsky. The bureaucratization of capitalism through the rise of big corporations and the development of the social welfare state are processes whose beginnings, at least, Kautsky was aware of, but which he never analyzed systematically to modify his view of social development.[49] Yet they have drastically changed the nature of capitalism, the position of workers, and the role of government in industrial societies.

Not only have the living standards of workers greatly improved; not only do they no longer feel excluded from society, labor being accepted as a legitimate social partner in most industrialized countries; not only is the working class more heterogeneous than in Kautsky's day; but that class, that is, its blue-collar component, is shrinking in size. Consequently, the socialist parties that Kautsky insisted must be and that in fact very largely were working-class parties can no longer hope to win elections with workers' votes alone, nor can they appeal to a distinct working-class interest shared by class-conscious workers. Socialist parties have therefore sought to expand their constituency by becoming "people's parties" and by appealing especially to the growing professional and white-collar strata, whose interests are not sharply distinct from or opposed to those of workers, especially of workers in the service sector.

It is both obvious and crucially important in a consideration of the continuing relevance of Kautsky's thought, that it cannot accommodate these facts. Kautsky took it for granted that with growing industrialization the working class must grow to become the great majority of the population — though he was also one of the first Marxists to call attention to the growth of a new white-collar middle class.[50] The growing working class must become class-conscious and socialist, and it was therefore just a question of time when it would come to power through democratic elections. Kautsky's faith in the labor movement, his faith in democracy, and his faith in socialism were closely linked.

Now, socialist parties in Western and Central Europe have achieved more strength and power in the years since World War II than they ever enjoyed in Kautsky's lifetime. They have, alone or in coalitions, formed governments and they have used their influence to improve the status of workers in their societies. They have done all this through electoral and parliamentary means, and to that extent Kautsky proved right in his insistence that labor would advance through democracy. But in doing all this, socialist parties have helped change their societies and they have had to change themselves in ways Kautsky could not have imagined.

In Kautsky's day it was obvious, and he certainly took it for granted, that workers were poor and constituted the lower class in society. Since the working class developed in the old European societies dominated by aristocracies, workers were widely regarded as inferior, and many came to regard themselves as separate, different, and disadvantaged and were, in this sense, class-conscious. Today, workers are widely regarded and regard themselves as members of a huge, ill-defined middle class; the working class is not the lower class any longer. This is particularly true in the United States, where, with the possible exception of the very rich, most people have either thought of themselves as belonging to the middle class or have never identified themselves with a class at all. But, with the disappearance of the last remnants of aristocratic ideology and institutions, Europe is becoming more like America in this respect. In America, at least, the middle class appears to be vaguely defined as those who work, presumably to distinguish it from the upper and lower classes.[51]

The lower class, then, consists of those who do not work, that is, those who, having no skills and little education, have no place in the modern economy and are therefore either permanently unemployed or hold more or less temporary menial service jobs. Their poverty, their lack of skills and work experience, their poor housing or homelessness, their poor schools, and their poor medical care all reinforce each other, making it difficult for them to rise out of their lower class and keeping that class quite sharply distinct from the rest of society. That distinction is even sharper in the case of the large part of this lower class that is made up of members of ethnic minorities and particularly of recent immigrants from agrarian areas, whether at home or abroad.

The present-day lower class differs from Kautsky's lower class, that is, the working class of the late nineteenth and early twentieth centuries. It makes up a smaller proportion of the population and, while it may at times grow when immigration or economic depression provides new members for it, it is not steadily growing in size as a result of long-term economic change and is never likely to approach majority status. It may also be more invisible to the rest of the population, because it is less numerous and its members do not work with members of other classes, and hence its plight arouses even less sympathy on the part of members of the middle and upper classes than did the misery of early workers. Indeed, members of the working middle class may resent the fact that members of the lower class do not work and may blame their laziness for their misfortunes.

Above all, workers, because they worked together under similar conditions and became aware of common interests, could be organized. And because they occupied an essential place in the economy, their organizations could become powerful and bargain successfully with employers and governments. The new lower class, the new poor, are unorganizable and they have no bargaining strength. Having no jobs, they cannot strike; having little education and little involvement in the larger society and being unorganized, they do not vote in great numbers; having no hope, they either do not protest or, rarely, they protest by means of riots, arson, and looting that have no positive goals and quickly end. They can make trouble, but they cannot make policy.

Kautsky's conviction and prediction that the working class, as the lower class, would come to power has proved wrong. The working class and the lower class have become distinct. Workers will not come to power as a class, because they do not constitute a class; they differ greatly among themselves and collectively constitute merely a shrinking part of a vast heterogeneous middle class. The new lower class will not come to power because of its numerical and organizational weakness.

To Kautsky it was still obvious that democracy favored the lower classes — the growing industrial working class and the growing lower white-collar strata as well as the shrinking petty bourgeoisie and peasantry — because they would form the overwhelming majority of the population. Today, it is the middle class that forms the majority of the population and the even greater majority of the voters. In modern industrial societies, for the first time in human history, the poor are a minority. Add to that the fact that winning elections and influencing public opinion through the media of communication cost a lot of money, much of which can only come from those who have it, and it becomes clear that democracy does not favor the poor. In order to govern, politicians must appeal to and must in their policies represent those who have votes or money.

Of course, it is not likely that any form of government other than democracy would be more favorable to the poor for any length of time. On the contrary, under democracy, the poor may have some representation and some influence where they are concentrated in urban areas. Clearly, however, Kautsky's assumption that democracy would bring the poor to power is no longer valid, though it may continue to help workers who are no longer poor. As democracy favors numerical and organizational strength, in his time it made sense for Kautsky to equate the rise of labor and the rise of democracy, for he saw, as Marx had seen, that the working class was one lower class — the first and so far the last one in history — that had the potential of becoming both numerous and organized.

It was the function of the labor movement, primarily the trade unions and the socialist parties, to organize workers. It was Kautsky's function and contribution to the labor movement to provide workers with the hope for a better future that would inspire them to cooperate and to organize. He did so by linking, through Marxist theory, the reformist practical day-to-day work of the unions and the party with what he called "the great final goal of socialism." Of course, that goal was never realized and was, in this sense, a mere myth, though a very powerful and effective one (see also my note 48 in chapter 2, below). It can also be argued that, to the extent that the hopes expressed by that myth focused on a better world for industrial workers, they have to a considerable extent been fulfilled.

However that may be, Kautsky has proved to be mistaken in his conviction that an ever bigger and ever more united and class-conscious working class, produced by advancing capitalist industry, would fight the class struggle against the bourgeoisie and would, through electoral and parliamentary victories, make its political revolution and then more gradually its social revolution. These ideas of his are irrelevant for an understanding of present-day politics in industrialized countries.

Of course, this does not mean that there is not much in Kautsky's voluminous writings that still strikes the reader as insightful or that can be interpreted to throw light on present-day conditions. I can quickly refer to two areas that may seem relevant in the context of the present volume. Kautsky's thought on imperialism, which I discuss below, stressed that capitalism could survive without imperialism and as such proved superior to Lenin's insistence that imperialism was the necessary last phase of capitalism. Even Kautsky's hopes for disarmament among the major powers may seem relevant today,[52] but he could not know about the cold war or nuclear weapons, and it would be unreasonable to look to Kautsky for guidance to an understanding of recent or present-day international relations.

I can also allude to the ideas relevant to their needs that Western

Communist parties, most notably the Italian one, could have discovered in Kautsky in their "Eurocommunist" phase, especially in the 1970s, which I discuss in the article on that subject reprinted below. But, as I noted there, some Eurocommunists had already gone beyond Kautsky in their de-emphasis on class conflict. Kautsky always insisted that democracy would not put an end to the class struggle and that a socialist party must therefore remain a workers' party. Eurocommunism, on the other hand, represents the same shift from workers' party to people's party that the SPD made only in 1959 in its Godesberg Program, two eventful decades after Kautsky's death.

VII

It is less with reference to politics in the Western democratic industrial countries than in connection with the collapse of the Communist regime in the Soviet Union that Kautsky's ideas have recently been seen as highly relevant. Here I can quote the editors of a volume on Kautsky who in their preface of 1990 stress his view that

> the working class requires democratic rights and liberties both in order to take power and in order to exercise it. . . . [Kautsky's] merciless critique of the Bolsheviks . . . currently gains new relevance. After the failure of the . . . socialism that bases itself on the teachings of Marxism-Leninism, any serious discussion of a model of a socialist society . . . will not be able to bypass Kautsky. Gorbachev's remark that socialism needs democracy as a man needs air to breathe points directly to him. . . . The key thesis of his critique of the Bolsheviks that a merely moderately industrialized country was not ready for a socialist transformation so that the latter can be carried through only by force, in an undemocratic way, whereby socialism itself is deformed, this thesis will play a central role in future discussions.[53]

Kautsky's prediction, developed in 1918, that the Bolshevik regime would be a minority dictatorship resting on terrorism and a powerful bureaucracy and that the regime was bound eventually to collapse can, indeed, be seen as remarkably accurate and insightful.[54] His predictions were based on his insistence, stated time and again in his works — for one quotation from 1909, see note 66 in chapter 2, below — that socialism could not be introduced unless certain prerequisites were present: a highly developed industry and a highly developed proletariat that was not only numerous and well organized but mature in its knowledge and understanding, its discipline and solidarity. This intellectual and moral maturity can develop only under conditions of democracy. The fulfillment of the prerequisites for socialism, Kautsky thought, was close at hand in Germany and Britain, but certainly not in Russia.[55]

In one of his earliest reactions to the Russian Revolution, written three weeks after the abdication of the tsar and still seven months before Lenin's seizure of power, Kautsky wrote:

> To emancipate themselves, the proletarians must not only encounter certain material conditions and be numerically strong, they must also have become new men, endowed with the capacities that are necessary for a new ordering of state and society. These capacities they acquire only through the class struggle, which requires democratic rights and freedoms if it is to be conducted as a struggle of self-governing proletarian masses not of masses managed by secret committees.

> Whatever the new Russian government may at the moment offer the proletarians with respect to material achievements and positions of power, this question is much less significant than the one of the maintenance of democracy. That is by far the most important aspect of the present-day Russian Revolution.[56]

Given Russian industrial backwardness, it was very clear to Kautsky that the Bolshevik revolution could not be proletarian and socialist as he understood these adjectives. He stressed this in his efforts to draw a clear distinction between Communism and Social Democracy, which he undertook partly in order to oppose various "united front" efforts between the two movements. This involved him in sharp differences with other Marxists, notably Otto Bauer, who was eager to reunite the Western labor movements split into socialists and Communists. Bauer regarded dictatorship and terrorism as a road to socialism, undesirable and inappropriate in the West (except perhaps if the democratic road was closed by fascism), but holding out hope for a democratic future in Russia.[57] For Kautsky there could, by definition, be no nondemocratic road to socialism. As he wrote in *The Dictatorship of the Proletariat* in 1918:

> For us, socialism without democracy is unthinkable. By modern socialism we understand not only social organization of production, but also a democratic organization of society. Socialism is therefore for us indissolubly linked to democracy.[58]

It was important that Kautsky understood well what the Russian Revolution and the Soviet regime were not. He—as well as his adversaries among Social Democratic Marxists—could not, however, understand what they were. They could analyze developments in the East only in terms of categories derived from Marx and from Western European, especially French, history. Thus, they debated at length whether the Bolsheviks were Jacobins or Bonapartists.

In Marx's scheme, there are only bourgeois revolutions and proletarian revolutions, so—as I state in my introduction to *The Dictatorship of the Proletariat* on p. 218, below—to Kautsky the Bolshevik revolution, not being proletarian, had to be bourgeois. It was erecting a form a bureaucratic state-capitalism in which the state bureaucracy and the capitalist bureaucracy merged into a single arbitrarily ruling bureaucracy.[59] Unlike earlier radical bourgeois revolutionaries, who were defeated and replaced by reactionaries, the Bolsheviks carried on the counterrevolution themselves.[60] They became Bonapartists and, as such, were, according to Kautsky, much like fascists. He notes the very different origins of Bolshevism and fascism but stresses that the repressive results of both of them for the proletariat are the same.[61]

In retrospect, we can see that, while valid parallels between French and Russian revolutionary history can no doubt be drawn, Kautsky's and similar conceptions cannot account for the development of the Soviet Union. With the benefit of hindsight and of our acquaintance with the type of revolution that has occurred with great frequency in underdeveloped countries since World War II, but was rare and little understood earlier, we can develop a perspective on the Russian Revolution and the Soviet regime that was not available to Kautsky and his contemporaries.

That perspective—from which I also, at the beginning of this essay, characterized Lenin's position on revolution—sees the process of political change in Russia in the context not of Western European history but of the politics of underdeveloped societies. Here, as a reaction to contacts with industrialized countries and to early industrialization, intellectuals with modern Western values, often trying to mobilize mass support among the huge peasantry and the small working class, overthrow aristocratic or colonial rulers who maintain the traditional political order.

These modernizing intellectuals, thinking and speaking in the language of Western politics and emphasizing such terms as "nationalism" and "socialism," aim at the rapid industrialization of their societies in the belief that it will bring power and wealth to their countries and to the mass of their population. Such a drastic transformation of a largely agrarian into a largely industrial society can only be accomplished at the expense of workers and peasants and by a government playing a dominant role in both industry and agriculture.

This is not the place to elaborate on my view of modernizing revolutions and regimes in underdeveloped countries or on my interpretation of the Bolshevik revolution and regime as modernizing ones. I already hinted at it nearly thirty years ago in my introduction to *The Dictatorship of the Proletariat* on pp. 217–19, below, and I refer to it in my article on Lenin and Kautsky on pp. 76–79, below, and I list some of my writings on the subject in note 76 in chapter 2. My forthcoming book *Marxism and Leninism, not Marxism-Leninism* also sees Leninism in this context. Modernizing revolutions began in China and Mexico even before the Russian Revolution of 1917 and have since then occurred in many countries of Asia, Africa, and Latin America, but few have gone very far toward the attainment of their goal of industrialization. What distinguishes the Soviet regime from most other regimes growing out of such revolutions is its success. At tremendous costs in human suffering and environmental damage, it did turn the Soviet Union from an agrarian into an industrial society.

Kautsky could not understand the Russian Communists' revolution and regime as those of modernizing intellectuals, as I believe they should be understood. He came closest to this conception, not in any of his writings on Soviet developments, but in his *Materialist Conception of History* of 1927, in a brief chapter on underdeveloped countries, which he sees, quite unrealistically, in the context of "the advance and ultimate victory of the non-European proletariat."[62] Two paragraphs there hint at remarkable insights on the revolutionary role of intellectuals, but they also seem to equate or confuse their revolution with a proletarian one. Clearly with Russia in mind, Kautsky writes:

> The intelligentsia of the East, which is familiar with the history of the revolutions of the West, easily sees in its own revolution merely a continuation of the Western revolution, ... which makes it less perceptive of the peculiar nature of its own revolution. ... This intelligentsia is influenced by the theories of Western European socialism.

> If the proletariat comes to power in an Eastern state, the intellectuals of

this kind feel obligated to use that power for the immediate establishment of socialist production, for which the economically advanced West has hardly yet created the rudimentary bases. These intellectuals then believe that they are ahead of the West, serving as an example to it and showing it the way. In making this attempt, which exceeds its strength, the proletariat must necessarily fail and lose its hard-won democratic freedom, to a new despotism, a bureaucratic-militarist despotism under the leadership of a dictatorship of intellectuals, with whom the proletariat feels itself allied. To that extent, the dictatorship is of proletarian origin. But it does not mean rule by the proletariat."[63]

Kautsky did not, as far as I know, pursue this line of thought on the role of intellectuals in the Russian Revolution, but he did come to see the rulers of Russia as a new class and thus went beyond the traditional Marxist categories of bourgeoisie and proletariat. In one of his last articles on the subject, he refers to this new class again as "a new aristocracy that disposes of the new means of production and exploits them for itself." Above the enslaved peasants and the workers who are said to be the ruling class and are preferred to the peasants, there arises a lower nobility of bureaucrats, a higher one of Communist Party members, and the highest one of the political police, all under the top level, the central authority of the state. "After the destruction of the old classes, there thus grows a new class division, a hierarchy with the dictator at the top."[64] Kautsky continued:

The only thing Lenin achieved was that the old exploiting classes disappeared, but he could not prevent classes of new exploiters and rulers from arising. They are entirely unique, corresponding to the peculiar character of the Russian people and its particular historical situation after the collapse of the old system in the World War.[65]

In the same article, Kautsky also states very clearly that the Soviet regime is neither capitalist (or at least private capitalist) nor socialist. "The militarized monopoly economy in the Soviet state is certainly very different from the economy of private capitalism, but no less different from the goal of the emancipation of the working class from any exploitation and servitude."[66]

Still, Kautsky, like the other Eurocentric Marxists of his time, with little knowledge of or sustained interest in underdeveloped countries, could never develop categories, like modernizing revolution or modernizing regime, that would be more relevant to the politics of underdevelopment — and hence of the early Soviet Union — than such Marxian ones as bourgeois and proletarian revolution, capitalism and socialism, a point I also made at a little greater length in my introduction to *The Dictatorship of the Proletariat* reprinted below. Even Lenin, one of the most successful modernizing revolutionaries, and his followers described the revolution he made and the regime he founded in the inappropriate Marxian terminology of Western politics, thus causing unending confusion.[67]

But if Kautsky was wrong or vague in identifying the social actors in the Russian Revolution and in the Soviet regime and their objectives, was he not nevertheless right in prophesying the collapse of the Communist regime in the Soviet Union that has now occurred? Few experts foretold this collapse even a short time before it happened, yet Kautsky had already in March 1918 written that it had been inevitable that the Russian proletariat under the leadership of the Bolsheviks "undertook the attempt . . . to realize socialism. . . . But as inevitable as this undertaking is, as certain is its failure."[68] And in 1919 he predicted that the then new bureaucracy, which had replaced economic anarchy, would also fail. "The economic and thus also the moral failure of the Bolshevik method is inevitable."[69] Two years later, Kautsky wrote:

> We must count on the collapse of the Communist dictatorship in the foreseeable future. A definite date cannot be stated. It can come overnight or may occur later than is apparently to be expected. But one thing is certain: Bolshevism has passed its peak and is in decline, the speed of which naturally accelerates."[70]

In 1930 Kautsky, while always opposing foreign intervention in the Soviet Union, thought that a massive peasant revolt, possibly joined by parts of the Red Army, was a likely response to starvation induced by Stalin's collectivization of agriculture. If workers, to protect their privileges, fought the peasants and won, the Communist Party could remain in control; if the peasants won, reactionaries could benefit; but if the workers joined the peasants and intellectuals, democracy would triumph. All of these possibilities could be realized in different parts of the country, and, in any case, chaos was inevitable.[71]

Three years later, Kautsky spoke again of possible "worker and peasant movements" and of chaos in Russia:

According to the laws of social development researched by Marx, a backward agrarian country cannot point the way to modern socialism. In this it must fail. That was clear from the beginning. The only question is when and in what way this will become evident. . . . The day is not far off when even those most eager to believe will recognize: This road does not lead upward to socialism but only downward to open bankruptcy or quiet decay. . . . But the failure of socialist construction in Russia is not tantamount to the fall of the Bolshevik regime. . . . The rule of the Bolsheviks may last for some time yet, but it will more and more lose the capacity to survive a significant test of strength. Through such a test, it can fall overnight. In Russia, we must always be ready for surprises.[72]

Even though the Soviet regime has now collapsed, we cannot give much credit to Kautsky for the accuracy of his prediction. He never set a date for the collapse, but clearly did not expect the regime to last seven decades. A person who predicts the imminent sunrise for 6, then 7, then 8 o'clock on a winter evening cannot claim to have been right when the sun rises the next morning.

But Kautsky also imagined the process and the nature of the collapse quite differently from what eventually occurred. He did mention the possibility of splits in the army and the bureaucracy and among the rulers, but only in response to revolutionary movements of peasants and workers. In fact, the collapse came from above, as the culmination of gradual changes in the dominant strata of Soviet society, the managerial and governmental bureaucracy. These strata, to a considerable extent, continue to exercise power after the collapse of the Communist Party as an organization because there is no substitute for them. Certainly workers and peasants have not taken their place and do not seem well represented by the post-Communist governments.

What collapsed in the Soviet Union was not, after all, Lenin's regime or Stalin's regime of the first two five-year plans, which Kautsky still knew. The regime collapsed not because of the failure to build heavy industry but because of the consequences of its success. In building up industry, the Stalinist regime had also built up a huge new professional and bureaucratic upper and middle class, which eventually demanded more consumer goods and more freedom of movement, of thought, and of expression. The regime, with its reliance on terror, regimentation, and propaganda, had been capable of building industry, but it could not satisfy these growing demands; under their pressure it was first modified, then it crumbled and collapsed.

Although Kautsky, wrongly, assumed from the beginning that the purpose of Soviet industrialization was the immediate improvement of the standard of living of the mass of the population, he was right in insisting that this kind of industrialization could not succeed under the rule of a centralized bureaucracy. Similarly, if he, wrongly, thought that the collectivization of agriculture was designed to improve the lot of the peasants rather than to advance industrialization, he was right in predicting its failure (see also my note 13 in chapter 6, below).

As future developments in what was the Soviet Union are quite unpredictable now, it is impossible to tell with certainty whether Kautsky's ideas on what might and should happen there after the collapse of the Communist regime will prove to be realistic. Of course, he did not expect as much industrialization by the time the regime collapsed as now exists. On the other hand, he evidently assumed that workers and peasants would be in a much stronger political position than they are now. He expected that, at least after a period of chaos, a parliamentary democratic regime would emerge. So far, there has been some chaos and some democracy, but either or neither might prevail in the future.

Kautsky thought that a new regime would provide far-reaching social insurance and labor-protective legislation and that a mixed economy would develop in industry. In the interest of the undisturbed continuation of production, large-scale socialized properties should be preserved and could maintain themselves if workers and their unions and councils, as well as managers, were freed of bureaucratic control. Private, communal, and cooperative enterprises should compete with state-owned ones. If they

> work more successfully, supply cheaper or better products, pay higher wages, and so on, then the state enterprises should be abandoned, but not before. The transition to a different, perhaps a capitalist enterprise, should occur only when and where it is of advantage for consumers and workers.

Trade should be returned to private ownership, as should the land to the peasant, except where peasants were willing and equipped to work it collectively.[73]

VIII

The developments that Kautsky predicted have not occurred, either in democratic advanced industrialized countries or in the Soviet Union.

In the case of the democratic industrialized countries, of whose history and society he had an excellent understanding, Kautsky paid insufficient attention to certain trends already appearing in his lifetime and did not foresee and could not imagine the profound changes their societies would undergo in the half-century after his death.

In the case of the Soviet Union, Kautsky did not understand the immense processes of change at work there. It is fair to say that there was probably no one in his time who did, because what happened there was — or seemed to be — as yet unique, and unique developments, being incomparable, are incomprehensible. In all of history, there had never been a revolution that clearly brought modernizing intellectuals to power — who, moreover, in the Russian case concealed their character as such by their use of Marxian terminology — nor had any country ever been industrialized through a mechanism other than that of private capitalism.

Kautsky, quite deliberately and explicitly, based his predictions on historical precedents; his predictions therefore failed because there were no precedents. The Western European ones he chose, because they were the only ones he was familiar with and the only ones on which the Marxian conception of history rests, proved to be inappropriate for an understanding of Soviet development, and, indeed, for an understanding of the development of all underdeveloped countries. I might add that the study of the politics of these countries has suffered all along, down to the present, from the employment of concepts derived from Western historical experience.

None of this minimizes Kautsky's importance in history. He was a key figure in the politics and, especially, the ideological development of the European socialist labor movement for more than half a century and as such is worth studying. Those of his writings emphasized in the present volume should be read for an understanding of his time, not of ours. In addition, there is a significant body of historical works by Kautsky that I have almost completely ignored here, which, though no doubt in many respects outdated by the findings of more recent research, is still of interest for his interpretations based on his Marxist conception of history.[74]

It seems to me quite unreasonable to expect thinkers of the past to have had a degree of clairvoyance or a gift of prophecy that no sensible present-day thinker would claim for himself or herself.[75] If any social scientist were asked today what aspect of his work he expected to be relevant fifty or a hundred years from now, he could sensibly refer, not to his substantive findings, but, at most, to his methods and his approach. This much Kautsky could perhaps claim, too.

Some of the key concepts Kautsky used — revolution, class struggle, perhaps even class — either are no longer useful or, like democracy, are not precise enough for an analysis of modern industrialized societies. But Kautsky's more general approach to the study of society and particularly of politics remains relevant and useful today. He always viewed politics as dynamic, focusing on change and inclined to trace phenomena back to their origins. And he viewed politics as conflict and therefore focused on the groupings participating in politics and on their interests.

Both the emphasis on change and development and the emphasis on conflict Kautsky derived from his "materialist" conception of history, but he was always anxious not to oversimplify. Indeed, in response to both adherents and opponents of that conception who did oversimplify it, he sometimes suggested that it was one of its virtues that it was very complicated. In explaining social change, he referred to all kinds of interacting factors and insisted only that economic and specifically technological change was responsible for social change "in the last analysis," a concept that either cannot be objectively defined at all or that refers to the very beginnings of technological change in the beginnings of mankind.[76]

As to conflict, Kautsky certainly stresses the class struggle between proletariat and bourgeoisie, but time and again he emphasizes divisions within these two classes and the role of other classes and groupings. Thus, even his early work of 1889 on class conflicts in the French Revolution that I just cited in note 74 was primarily designed to do just that.

A conception of politics as dynamic rather than static and as involving conflict of interests may be less unorthodox today than it was in Kautsky's time, but it remains as fruitful. More generally, Kautsky's view that explanation requires an understanding of the origins and the development of the phenomenon to be explained, while not the only possible conception of explanation, is to me attractive one.

Finally, as much as our societies have changed since Kautsky's time, the values that motivated his work remain relevant today. Some may even be more widely shared now, though they are certainly not held universally. I would mention first Kautsky's tremendous appreciation of knowledge and understanding. The twenty-seven-year-old Karl Marx, in his famous Eleventh Thesis on Feuerbach, had written: "The philosophers have only *interpreted* the world, in various ways; the point, however, is to *change* it." Considering how he spent most of the remaining thirty-eight years of his life, one could argue that Marx did not comply with his dictum himself. Kautsky, at any rate, was always at least as concerned with interpreting and understanding the world as he was with changing it, though, no doubt like Marx, he believed that his kind of understanding would lead to change.

What attracted Kautsky to Marxism was not only its commitment to the labor movement's struggle for a better world and its promise that that struggle would succeed, but also, above all, its social science, which seemed to him far superior to other then-prevalent approaches in its ability to explain social change. The pure Marxist social science was, in Kautsky's view, in principle value-free, socialism being merely applied science derived from it.[77]

Many of Kautsky's writings — my emphasis in the present volume is on some of these — grew out of debates with other socialists on questions of current policy, but even these writings frequently contain long excursions into the social sciences and sometimes even into the natural sciences, as well as into history. And Kautsky always, not only in his old age, found time to write substantial books that did not directly deal with matters of current concern. Thus, in an eight-year period (1906–14), when he was deeply involved in conflicts first over Revisionism and then over the mass strike, he wrote not only his lengthy historical treatise on the social bases of early Christianity, *Foundations of Christianity* (1908), but also books on ethics, population growth, and race.[78] In each of them, given his characteristic approach, the social sciences touch the natural sciences as he deals with the world of animals as well as that of men. During much of the same period Kautsky undertook the laborious task left to him by Engels of editing Marx's manuscript notes for a fourth volume of *Capital,* published in three volumes (1904–10) as *Theories of Surplus Value.*[79]

Kautsky was certainly a scholar, and even his most polemical writings display his total commitment to rational inquiry and argument;

but, in the tradition of the classical Marxism of his time, he also played an active part in politics as a writer and editor. Thus, all of his writings, even when he tried to keep them value-free, reveal his political and social values very clearly. These values are obvious and require no discussion at any length here. Still, in a consideration of what remains alive in Kautsky's thought, it is important to mention them.

Kautsky was not a pacifist, as he is often described because of his opposition to the SPD majority's support of the imperial government's war policy in World War I.[80] It is also true that, as does much literature on politics, including Marxist literature, he frequently employed terminology that is suggestive of violent conflict or warfare: in the class "struggle," the "fighting" proletariat, in its "fighting organizations," "battles" the class "enemy." But it is clear that Kautsky had a deep aversion to violence, both because he had no sympathy for irrationality and he saw violence as an irrational and costly way of settling conflict, and because he never forgot that physical injury and death cause pain to human beings.

This seems quite obvious, but in the German Empire Kautsky functioned in a society where war and bloodshed were constantly being glorified in the dominant culture. Socialists formed the one major opposition to this attitude, but, as became evident in 1914, not all of them were entirely immune to it. On the other hand, there was a tendency among some socialists to romanticize revolutionary violence, a tendency of which Kautsky was also quite free. He feared that proletarian victory could perhaps not be achieved in imperial Germany without violence provoked by the regime, but the point here is that he feared it and hoped to avoid it. Many have sneered at this attitude of Kautsky, for revolutionary élan and bravery are much more exciting than his caution, but I think he deserves credit for it. Kautsky lived long enough to witness the bloody violence inflicted on their opponents by both the Bolshevik and the Nazi regimes in the name of their revolutionary ideologies; he condemned it without reservation.

In *The Dictatorship of the Proletariat,* Kautsky wrote: "To be exact, socialism is not our final goal, but the latter consists of the abolition 'of every kind of exploitation and oppression, be it directed against a class, a party, a sex, or a race' (Erfurt Program)." The socialist mode of production appeared to be the only means of achieving this goal, but should it be proved to us that we are mistaken in this, that perhaps the emancipation of the proletariat and generally of mankind could be achieved only or most practically on the basis of private property in the means of production, . . . then we would have to throw socialism overboard without in the least giving up our final goal; indeed we would have to do it precisely in the interest of that final goal. . . . Democracy and socialism are both means to the same end.[81]

Kautsky, of course, never explained how socialism could bring about the emancipation of all mankind or even just what that concept meant, but the quotation from the Erfurt Program, which he was fond of, demanding the abolition of every kind of exploitation and oppression is a sweeping statement of his political values. Many of us today share Kautsky's ideal of a society or even a world without oppression, exploitation, and discrimination on the basis of class, party, sex, or race. For Kautsky, however, this ideal was not merely something to believe in and to profess; it actually guided all his work throughout his life.

Kautsky's commitment to the labor movement was based on this general humanism; it was in his view a commitment to improve the lot not merely of a class with its special interests but of all mankind. He frequently repeated the — somewhat dubious — argument (for example, in the passage from *The Dictatorship of the Proletariat* from which I just quoted) that, as the lowest class in society, the working class could not emancipate itself without doing away with all causes of exploitation and oppression.

What seems amazing today is the pairing of Kautsky's humanitarian values with his indomitable optimism. His writings are generally sober and unemotional, and he did not idealize even the future socialist order as one without conflict. In 1920 he said that "new contradictions, new problems, new struggles will arise in socialist society."[82] Yet he clearly did expect that all oppression and exploitation could and would be ended, not in some idealized distant age, but, at least in highly industrialized countries, in the quite foreseeable future.

Even a year after the Nazis had seized power in Germany, when he was nearly eighty years old, Kautsky could confidently write in a letter concerned with Nazism: "My time will come again, of that I am firmly convinced."[83] If "my time" referred to what he might have considered more "normal" times, he may have been right; if it referred to the victorious advance of the labor movement to power, he was, as we know by now, wrong; if it referred to the time of the realization of his goal of the end of all exploitation and oppression, we can only envy his optimism.

Rudolf Hilferding, an Austro-Marxist disciple of Kautsky who came closest to being his successor in the Weimar period as the principal Marxist theorist of the SPD, put it well when, with Hitlerism and Stalinism in mind, he emphasized Kautsky's commitment to knowledge and to humanism. In a letter to Kautsky in 1934, he called him the representative of a socialism "that is founded not on the belief in miracles performed by violence and the inspired dictator, but on insight and knowledge and the will to humanity."[84]

Notes

1. Werner Blumenberg, *Karl Kautskys literarisches Werk* (The Hague: Mouton, 1960), 32–104. The two of Kautsky's works that probably contributed most to the spread of Marxist thought, *The Economic Doctrines of Karl Marx* (1887) (New York: Macmillan, 1936; reprint; Westport, Conn.: Hyperion Press, 1979) and *Das Erfurter Programm* (1892) (*The Class Struggle,* New York: Norton, 1971) appeared, respectively, in twenty-six German editions and in over fifty editions in twenty languages, and in twenty German editions and in over forty editions in eighteen languages. See Blumenberg, *Karl Kautskys literarisches Werk,* 39–40, 47–48, with some recent additions. This standard bibliography of Kautsky's writings lists a lifetime total of 1,780 publications by him.

2. Hans-Josef Steinberg, *Sozialismus und deutsche Sozialdemokratie* (5th ed.; Bonn: J. H. W. Dietz, 1979); Gary P. Steenson, *Karl Kautsky. 1854–1938. Marxism in the Classical Years,* 2d ed. (Pittsburgh: University of Pittsburgh Press, 1991); Massimo Salvadori, *Karl Kautsky and the Socialist Revolution 1880–1938* (London: NLB, 1979); Ingrid Gilcher-Holtey, *Das Mandat des Intellektuellen: Karl Kautsky und die Sozialdemokratie* (Berlin: Siedler, 1986); Jürgen Rojahn, Till Schelz, and Hans-Josef Steinberg, eds., *Marxismus und Demokratie: Karl Kautskys Bedeutung in der sozialistischen Arbeiterbewegung* (Frankfurt: Campus Verlag, 1992).

3. As I mention in note 72 in chapter 2, below, Hans-Jürgen Mende, the author of *Karl Kautsky — vom Marxisten zum Opportunisten* (East Berlin: Dietz Verlag, 1985), a classic Leninist interpretation, has more recently changed his view of Kautsky. As late as 1988, another East German expert on Kautsky began and concluded a critical biographical sketch of Kautsky by pointing to the need for "a comprehensive Marxist-Leninist biography of Karl Kautsky." Annelies Laschitza; "Ich bin Redakteur und Parteimann, nicht blosser Privatgelehrter. Karl Kautsky," *Beiträge zur Geschichte der deutschen Arbeiterbewegung* 30, no. 5 (1988): 657, 676. Her wish is now not likely to be fulfilled.

4. V.I. Lenin, "Report on the Conference of the Extended Editorial Board of

Proletary," in *Collected Works,* 45 vols. (Moscow: Progress Publishers, 1960–70), 15:430.

5. I have sought to analyze the politics of "modernization from without" as distinguished from the Western pattern of "modernization from within" in a number of works. See especially my *Political Consequences of Modernization* (New York: John Wiley, 1972).

6. Beginning in 1914 Lenin constantly denounced Kautsky as a renegade, most notably in the title of his book *The Proletarian Revolution and the Renegade Kautsky,* in *Collected Works,* 28:227–325. When Georges Haupt, an outstanding historian of socialism in the period of the Second International, on a visit to a Canadian university, wondered why students always referred to "renegade Kautsky," he learned that they believed "renegade" was Kautsky's first name. Reported by Hans-Josef Steinberg, "Kautskys Stellung in der Geschichte der sozialdemokratischen Arbeiterbewegung und seine Bedeutung für die Gegenwart," in *Marxismus und Demokratie,* ed. Rojahn et al., 19. Given the reaction of many people when I am introduced to them, I can confirm that the word "renegade" and the name "Kautsky" are associated in many minds.

7. In 1988, at a conference on Karl Kautsky, Annelies Laschitza from East Berlin argued that Kautsky took a "revolutionary" position in 1905–1906 and in 1909, but suddenly abandoned it in 1910; however she then concludes her paper by stating more vaguely that "in a contradictory process, Karl Kautsky changed from 1905 to 1914, respectively, to 1917–18 from an internationally influential Marxist theoretician to the theoretical founder of centrism, an opportunistic current that is difficult to recognize and the existence of which is therefore again and again being doubted." Annelies Laschitza, "Karl Kautsky im Widerstreit zwischen Marxismus und Opportunismus 1905 bis 1914," in *Marxismus und Demokratic,* ed. Rojahn et al., 139.

8. Lenin, "Dead Chauvinism and Living Socialism," in *Collected Works,* 21:94.

9. Ibid., 97. I refer to Kautsky's position on "Millerandism" on p. 101, below.

10. Laschitza, "Karl Kautsky im Widerstreit," 136.

11. In roughly the same period, the population of Germany grew from 45,234,000 in 1880 to 64,926,000 in 1910 and 63,1818,000 in 1925 (when the country was smaller), but the economically active population in industry and construction nearly doubled—from 5,230,000 in 1882 to 9,043,000 in 1907 and 10,330,000 in 1925. B. R. Mitchell, *European Historical Statistics. 1750–1975,* 2d rev. ed. (New York: Facts on File, 1981), 30, 164. "Between 1871 and 1919 . . . the size of the central government budget . . . grew tenfold from 350 million marks to 3,500 million marks." W. L. Guttsman, *The German Social Democratic Party. 1875–1933: From Ghetto to Government* (London: Allen & Unwin, 1981), 52.

12. Rudolf Hilferding, *Finance Capital* (London: Routledge & Kegan Paul, 1981). On Kautsky's evolving theory of imperialism, see also Ursula Ratz, "Karl Kautskys Einschätzung von Krieg und Frieden im Zeitalter des Imperialismus," in *Marxismus*

und Demokratie, ed. Rojahn et al., 183–96, which emphasizes more clearly than I do Kautsky's changing views as to whether imperialism was an economic necessity of capitalism or merely a policy that could be abandoned without making capitalism impossible.

13. Lenin, *Imperialism, the Highest Stage of Capitalism,* in *Collected Works,* 22:185–304.

14. Kautsky, "Der Imperialismus," *Die Neue Zeit* 32/2 (1914): 908–22; "Zwei Schriften zum Umlernen," *Die Neue Zeit* 33/2 (1915): 33–42, 71–81, 107–16, 138–46. Lenin makes also one brief reference to Kautsky's pamphlet *Nationalstaat, Imperialistischer Staat und Staatenbund* (Nuremberg: Fränkische Verlagsanstalt, 1915).

15. Kautsky, "Zwei Schriften," 144–45. Two years later, Kautsky wrote: "It is by no means impossible that the present war will be ended by an agreement among the imperialists of the leading big powers on both sides on the division and exploitation of the world. . . . This is, of course, not meant to be a prediction. It is absolutely impossible today to tell how the war will end. An international agreement among the imperialists is only one among many other possibilities of a conclusion to the war." Kautsky, "Der imperialistische Krieg," *Die Neue Zeit* 35/1 (1917): 483.

16. Lenin, *Imperialism,* 271–73, 288, 293, 296.

17. Ibid., 294.

18. In a series of articles written in 1916 and then published separately, Kautsky attacked proposals for a Central European federation and wrote: "It is not impossible that [imperialism] will be followed by a new era of capitalism under conditions that make a federation of states, like the Central European ones, possible, on the basis of their members' joining voluntarily and gladly, and that would assure its lasting and productive functioning. This possibility is, however, very vague, uncertain, and not even very probable." Kautsky, "Mitteleuropa," *Die Neue Zeit* 34/1 (1916): 534; Kautsky, *Die Vereinigten Staaten Mitteleuropas* (Stuttgart: J. H. W. Dietz, 1916), 48.

19. How Kautsky saw his position after the German Revolution as consistent with the one he had maintained vis-à-vis Revisionism ten and twenty years earlier is well illustrated in a letter to his son Benedikt written on 31 July 1919, which happens to be the day when the Weimar constitution was adopted. The letter is quoted by Karl Kautsky, Jr. (Kautsky's second son) in his introduction to Karl Kautsky, Jr., ed., *August Bebels Briefwechsel mit Karl Kautsky* (Assen: Van Gorcum, 1971), xxxix–xl. "I regard the English manner of socialization as the most promising. Some consider this now as a capitulation to Bernstein. But whoever thinks so has forgotten (or never knew) what my conflict with Bernstein consisted of. He claimed that the Marxian prognosis of economic development was wrong, that the proletariat did not grow, and that therefore socialism was attainable only with the support of the socially inclined part of the bourgeoisie. He thought that part would grow if the class struggle were conducted in gentler forms and he declared that a revolution was everywhere useless or harmful. That I fought actively and in that I

remained right.

"People have never understood the distinction between the social and the political revolution. The latter can only be a sudden act and it was inevitable in Eastern Europe. Military monarchies could not be overcome in any other way. But that has now happened. Now the task everywhere is merely the social revolution — except in Asia and the colonies. But that revolution is possible only gradually and is thus on the surface often not at all recognizable as a revolution. It is impossible to tell exactly when and where capitalism began and so it is also impossible to say: now capitalism has come to an end, now socialism begins.

"That the social revolution will only be a gradual process is a conception I have always stood for, e.g. in the Erfurt Program. . . . I have therefore not changed my opinion on this."

20. See my introduction to Kautsky, *The Materialist Conception of History* (New Haven, Conn.: Yale University Press, 1988), li–liii.

21. See ibid., lviii–lxiv.

22. Kautsky, *Die proletarische Revolution und ihr Programm* (Stuttgart: J. H. W. Dietz, 1922), partially translated as *The Labour Revolution* (New York: Dial Press, 1925).

23. "Programm der Sozialdemokratischen Partei Deutschlands, beschlossen auf dem Parteitag in Heidelberg 1925," in *Programmatische Dokumente der deutschen Sozialdemokratie* ed. Dieter Dowe and Kurt Klotzbach (Bonn: J. H. W. Dietz, 1973), 206.

24. He stated this very bluntly himself in two letters to Bernstein, of 21 August 1897 and 1 August 1898, quoted in Steinberg, *Sozialismus,* 84, n. 251.

25. Bauer, in a passage disagreeing with Kautsky's view of Bolshevism as a mortal enemy of socialism, refers to him as "a man at whose feet we all sat as his disciples and from whom we all learned more than from anyone else among the living." Otto Bauer, "Der Kongress in Marseille," *Der Kampf* 18, no. 8–9 (August–September 1925): 284.

26. He did comment critically on the socialist uprising of February 1934 in Kautsky, *Grenzen der Gewalt: Aussichten und Wirkungen bewaffneter Erhebungen des Proletariats* (anonymously published; Karlsbad: Graphia, 1934).

27. Kautsky, *Krieg und Demokratie* (Berlin: J. H. W. Dietz, 1932); *Sozialisten und Krieg: Ein Beitrag zur Ideengeschichte des Sozialismus von den Hussiten bis zum Völkerbund* (Prague: Orbis, 1937); and *Erinnerungen und Erörterungen* (The Hague: Mouton, 1960).

28. *Die materialistische Geschichtsauffassung,* 2 vols. (Berlin: J. H. W. Dietz, 1927). I prepared an abridged edition in German (Bonn: J. H. W. Dietz, 1988) and in English translation, *The Materialist Conception of History.*

29. In my lengthy introduction to the abridged edition, I discuss this work as a contribution to social science. Abbreviated versions of my introduction appear as "Karl Kautskys 'Materialistische Geschichtsauffassung,' " in *Marxismus und Demokratie,* ed. Rojahn et al., 319–33, and as "Karl Kautsky's Materialist Conception of His-

tory," *International Journal of Comparative Sociology* 30, no. 1–2 (January–April 1989): 80–92, a journal issue also published as John H. Kautsky, ed., *Karl Kautsky and the Social Science of Classical Marxism* (Leiden: E. J. Brill, 1989).

30. Two years before the Stalin-Hitler Pact, which he did not live to see, Kautsky wrote: "Should it come to the point where [the present regime in Russia] reaches an understanding with Germany or Japan, then the Communists everywhere would become an auxiliary of fascism." Quoted in Andrea Panaccione, "Karl Kautsky in der Sozialistischen Arbeiter-Internationale — einige Bemerkungen," in *Marxismus und Demokratie,* ed. Rojahn et al., 314, from "Kommunismus und Demokratie," *Neuer Vorwärts,* 5 December 1937.

31. Kautsky, *The Materialist Conception of History,* 106.

32. Kautsky did not write very much about fascism. See especially his *Neue Programme: Eine kritische Untersuchung* (Vienna: Prager, 1933) and also "Einige Ursachen und Wirkungen des deutschen Nationalsozialismus," *Der Kampf* 26, no. 6 (June 1933): 235–45. Most of this article appeared in English translation as part of "Hitlerism and Social-Democracy," in *Socialism, Fascism, Communism,* ed. Joseph Shaplen and David Shub (New York: American League for Democratic Socialism, 1934), 53–73. For a summary of these and other relevant writings by Kautsky, see Salvadori, *Karl Kautsky,* 340-66, and for a thoughtful essay on Kautsky's analysis of fascism, see Till Schelz-Brandenburg, "Karl Kautskys Faschismus-Analyse," in *Marxismus und Demokratie,* ed. Rojahn et al., 233–47.

33. Kautsky, *Neue Programme,* 30–31.

34. Kautsky, "Die blutige Revolution," *Der Kampf* 26, no. 8-9 (August–September 1933): 361.

35. Kautsky's widow, Luise, was caught by the Gestapo at the age of eighty in Amsterdam and died in Auschwitz, where the infamous SS doctor Josef Mengele enjoyed lengthy conversations with her. Kautsky's youngest son, Benedikt, survived seven years in the concentration camps of Dachau, Buchenwald, and Auschwitz.

36. Kautsky, "Die Ausrottung der Besten," *Arbeiter-Zeitung,* 15 October 1933, quoted in Salvadori, *Karl Kautsky,* 352. Kautsky's reference is to Oswald Spengler.

37. Kautsky, *The Materialist Conception of History,* 394.

38. Kautsky, *Neue Programme,* 45.

39. Kautsky, *Sozialisten und Krieg,* vi.

40. On the bureaucratization of the SPD in the 1905–1909 period, see Carl E. Schorske, *German Social Democracy, 1905–1917* (Cambridge, Mass.: Harvard University Press, 1955), 116–45, and the long quotation from that source in my note 49 in chapter 3, below.

41. Letter from Kautsky to V. Adler of 26 September 1909, in Friedrich Adler, ed., *Victor Adler, Briefwechsel mit August Bebel und Karl Kautsky* (Vienna: Wiener Volksbuchhandlung, 1954), 501–2.

42. Kautsky, *The Dictatorship of the Proletariat* (Ann Arbor: University of Michigan Press, 1964; reprint; Westport, Conn.: Greenwood Press, 1981), 40.

43. Kautsky, *Der Weg zur Macht: Politische Betrachtungen über das Hineinwachsen in die Revolution* (Frankfurt: Europäische Verlagsanstalt, 1972), 68.

44. Ibid., 69.

45. Ibid., 16.

46. Ibid., 45. "The unification of the entire proletariat can only occur under the banner of our great final goal, which all proletarian strata have in common, not in the name of positive, practical day-to-day work, which is different for each proletarian stratum. As essential as this day-to-day work is, by itself alone it advances not the unification but the isolation of the various proletarian strata. It becomes a means of certain progress only when it is joined with the struggle for the final goal, with strong revolutionary feeling." Kautsky, "Ein neues Buch über die französische Revolution," *Vorwärts* (7 February 1909), quoted in Reinhold Hünlich, *Karl Kautsky und der Marxismus der II. Internationale* (Marburg: Verlag Arbeiterbewegung und Gesellschaftswissenschaft, 1981), 282–83, n. 249.

47. But see Max Weber's insightful remarks of 1907 on the bureaucratization of the SPD to a meeting of the German Association for Social Policy in *Schriften des Vereins für Socialpolitik*, vol. 125: *Verhandlungen der Generalversammlung 1907* (Leipzig: Duncker & Humblot, 1908), 296–97, quoted in Bo Gustafsson, *Marxismus und Revisionismus* (Frankfurt: Europäische Verlagsanstalt, 1972), 27–28.

48. Kautsky, like most European intellectuals of his time, had only a limited understanding of the politics of nonindustrialized countries and wrote little about them (except Russia). See my comments in my introduction to his *Materialist Conception of History,* lv–lviii.

49. See my comments on this in ibid., liii–lv.

50. I cite Kautsky's many comments on the rise of the new middle class, beginning with his book *Das Erfurter Programm* (1892), in a long note in Kautsky, *The Materialist Conception of History,* 398.

51. On the day I wrote this line, Bill Clinton accepted the Democratic presidential nomination "in the name of all those who do the work, pay the taxes, raise the kids and play by the rules, in the name of the hard-working Americans who make up our forgotten middle class." "Nominee Clinton Describes Vision of 'New Covenant,' " *Congressional Quarterly Report,* 50 (18 July 1992): 2128.

52. George Lichtheim, writing in 1971, thought that Kautsky's "gloomy vision" of ultra-imperialism, "of a global cartel linking all the industrially advanced centers of the world . . . first formulated in 1914 by the principal theorist of the Second International, looks remarkably modern today: more so than the productions of the rival Leninist school." George Lichtheim, *Imperialism* (New York: Praeger, 1971), 12; see also 109. A more recent author agrees: "From a present-day perspective it seems that Kautsky was right: Capitalism has in fact survived two great wars and has reached the phase of 'ultra-imperialism.' " Narihiko Ito, "Karl Kautsky und Rosa Luxemburg," in *Marxismus und Demokratie,* ed. Rojahn et al., 161.

53. Rojahn et al., eds., *Marxismus und Demokratie,* 7–8.

54. For summaries of Kautsky's anti-Communist writings, see Salvadori, *Karl Kautsky,* 251–318. A number of them are reprinted in Peter Lübbe, ed., *Kautsky gegen Lenin* (Bonn: J. H. W. Dietz, 1981). On Kautsky's role in the Socialist International with respect to the Soviet Union and Communist parties, see Panaccione, "Karl Kautsky," 305–15.

55. In a note to Kautsky, *The Materialist Conception of History,* 457, I refer to passages saying that the conditions for socialism did not yet exist in Russia in eight different works written by Kautsky before the October Revolution. See also my introduction to *The Dictatorship of the Proletariat,* pp. 207, 213–14, below.

56. Kautsky, "Die Aussichten der russischen Revolution," *Die Neue Zeit* 35/2 (1917): 13.

57. In 1925 Bauer wrote: "The Bolsheviks are a party unquestionably supported by a part of the Russian proletariat, unquestionably revolutionary and unquestionably socialist. Certainly their socialism is not ours. . . . It is the socialism of 'professional revolutionaries' who . . . subject the proletariat to a dictatorship of a bureaucracy dominating the means of production, not the socialism of the proletariat itself for whom socialism can only mean the workers' self-administration in the process of production. . . . But great as is the difference between their despotic and our democratic socialism, it is still socialism here and there. And out of this community of socialism there arises, in spite of all differences, a relative community of interest among us, which must not be forgotten no matter how sharply we stress all that separates us from Bolshevism." Bauer, "Der Kongress in Marseille," 284. For a summary of Kautsky's polemic with Bauer and others, see Salvadori, *Karl Kautsky,* 294–318.

58. Kautsky, *The Dictatorship of the Proletariat,* 6. See my introduction to that book, pp. 216–17, below.

59. Kautsky, *Terrorism and Communism* (London: National Labour Press, 1920; reprint, Westport, Conn.: Hyperion Press, 1973), 201–2.

60. In 1922 Kautsky had already said this of Lenin, not just of Stalin, in his *Labour Revolution,* 46–47. Later Kautsky recognized that "the analogy between the French Revolution since 1789 and the Russian one since 1917 proves nothing at all and is best not drawn at all." Kautsky, "Sozialdemokratie und Bolschewismus," *Die Gesellschaft* 8/1, no. 1 (January 1931): 55.

61. Kautsky, *Bolshevism at a Deadlock* (London: Allen & Unwin, 1931), 135–41. In the same book, Kautsky also compared the Soviet Communist Party to an aristocracy in a feudal system. Ibid., 97–98.

62. Kautsky, *The Materialist Conception of History,* 412.

63. Ibid., 413–14.

64. Kautsky, "Gedanken über die Einheitsfront," in *Kautsky gegen Lenin,* ed. Lübbe, 190. The article is reprinted from *Zeitschrift für Sozialismus* (April 1935), 825–38, and appeared in English translation as "The United Front," *The New Leader* (4, 11, 18, and 25 January 1936).

65. Kautsky, "Gedanken über die Einheitsfront," in *Kautsky gegen Lenin*, ed. Lübbe, 196. By seeing the Soviet regime as resting on a new class, Kautsky anticipated Djilas, who popularized the term two decades later, and also Rizzi and Burnham, who employed the concept a few years after Kautsky. Milovan Djilas, *The New Class* (New York: Praeger, 1957); Bruno Rizzi, *The Bureaucratization of the World* (1939) (New York: Free Press, 1985); James Burnham, *The Managerial Revolution* (New York: John Day, 1941).

66. Kautsky, "Gedanken über die Einheitsfront," in *Kautsky gegen Lenin*, ed. Lübbe, 196. Two years earlier, Kautsky had already equally clearly stated: "In Russia, capitalism was certainly smashed, but that is by no means tantamount to the construction of socialism." "Demokratie und Diktatur," *Der Kampf* 26, no. 2 (February 1933) : 53.

67. To help dispel this confusion is the goal of my forthcoming *Marxism and Leninism. not Marxism-Leninism*.

68. "Die Bolschewiki und wir, " *Sozialistische Auslandspolitik* 4 (13 March 1918) : 9, quoted in Susanne Miller, *Burgfrieden und Klassenkampf: Die deutsche Sozialdemokratie im Ersten Weltkrieg* (Düsseldorf: Droste Verlag), 357.

69. Kautsky, *Terrorism and Communism*, 202, 207.

70. Kautsky, *Von der Demokratie zur Staatssklaverei: Eine Auseinandersetzung mit Trotzki* (Berlin: Freiheit, 1921), 77.

71. Kautsky, *Bolshevism at a Deadlock*, 142–56.

72. Kautsky, "Demokratie und Diktatur," 55, 53–54.

73. Kautsky, *Bolshevism at a Deadlock*, 174–80.

74. The following are relatively recent evaluations of some of Kautsky's historical writings: Peter Schwartz, "Imagining Socialism: Karl Kautsky and Thomas More," *International Journal of Comparative Sociology* 30, no. 1–2 (January–April 1989): 44–56 (journal reprinted as John H. Kautsky, ed., *Karl Kautsky*) on *Thomas More and His Utopia* (1888) (London: Lawrence & Wishart, 1979).

   Beatrix Bouvier, "Kautsky und die französische Revolution," in *Marxismus und Demokratie*, ed. Rojahn et al., 350–60, on *Die Klassengegensätze von 1789* (Stuttgart: J. H. W. Dietz, 1889; 2d (1908) and later editions were entitled *Die Klassengegensätze im Zeitalter der Französischen Revolution*).

   Karl Kupisch, Introduction to *Der Ursprung des Christentums*, 16th ed. (Bonn: J. H. W. Dietz, 1977), vii–liii, on *Foundations of Christianity* (1908) (New York: Monthly Review Press, 1972).

   Hans Kloft, "Kautsky und die Antike," in *Marxismus und Demokratie*, ed. Rojahn et al., 334–49, on *Foundations of Christianity* and other writings on classical Greece and Rome.

   The introductions by Karl Kupisch to vol. 1, 8th ed. (vii–xxvii) and vol. 2, 9th ed. (vii–xxv) of *Vorläufer des neueren Sozialismus* (Bonn: J. H. W. Dietz, 1976). This work, partially translated as *Communism in Central Europe in the Time of the Reformation* (New York: A. M. Kelley, 1966), along with many other historical writings by Kautsky on socialist ideas and movements in ancient and medieval times and on pre-Marxian and Marxian modern socialism is also commented upon by Manfred Hahn, "Der Stammbaum: Karl Kautskys Entwurf der Geschichte des Sozialismus," in *Marxismus und Demokratie,* ed. Rojahn et al., 361–69.

For an earlier, brief, article praising the above mentioned writings by Kautsky, see O. Jenssen, "Karl Kautsky als marxistischer Historiker," *Der Kampf* 17, no. 10 (October 1924): 431–37, reprinted in a volume for Kautsky's seventieth birthday, *Karl Kautsky der Denker und Kämpfer* (Vienna: Wiener Volksbuchhandlung, 1924), 65–71.

75. Karl Marx, infinitely more than Kautsky, is frequently subjected to this unfair treatment by his would-be followers who expect to find answers in his writings to questions he could not even have been aware of.

76. I discuss Kautsky's approach to the explanation of social change with its merits and shortcomings in my introduction to Kautsky, *The Materialist Conception of History,* xxix–l.

77. On Kautsky's attempt at value-free social science, see ibid., xxix–xxx.

78. Kautsky, *Ethics and the Materialist Conception of History* (1906), 4th rev. ed. (Chicago: Charles H. Kerr, 1918; photocopy, Ann Arbor: University Microfilms International, 1977); *Vermehrung und Entwicklung in Natur und Gesellschaft* (1910), 3d ed. (Stuttgart: J. H. W. Dietz, 1921); *Are the Jews a Race?* (1914) (New York: International Publishers, 1926; reprint, Westport, Conn.: Greenwood Press, 1972).

79. Karl Marx, *Theorien über den Mehrwert,* 3 vols. (Stuttgart: J. H. W. Dietz, 1904, 1905, 1910).

80. In his *Sozialisten und Krieg,* Kautsky discussed circumstances under which socialist support for war was justified.

81. Kautsky, *The Dictatorship of the Proletariat,* 4–5.

82. Kautsky, "Gustav Mayers Engels-Biographie," *Archiv für die Geschichte des Sozialismus und der Arbeiterbewegung* 9 (1920): 346.

83. Letter to Gregor Bienstock of 15 January 1934, in IISG (Amsterdam), Kautsky Familienarchiv No. 5, quoted in Schelz-Brandenburg, "Karl Kautskys Faschismus-Analyse," 242, and also in Hans-Josef Steinberg, "Kautsky, Karl," in *Lexikon linker Leitfiguren* (Frankfurt a.M.: Büchergilde Gutenberg, 1988), 206.

84. Hilferding to Kautsky, 15 October 1934, IISG (Amsterdam), Kautsky-Nachlass D XIII, 662, quoted in Steinberg, *Sozialismus,* 86.

2

Lenin and Kautsky on the Role of Intellectuals in the Labor Movement: Different Conceptions in Different Environments

V. I. Lenin and Karl Kautsky are known as the principal representatives of two very different ideologies—Leninism and "orthodox" Marxism. Yet when Lenin, in one of his best-known passages, set forth a conception basic to the ideology of Leninism, he relied on a statement by Kautsky for support. To clear up any confusion that may result from this peculiar fact, the present essay seeks to demonstrate and then to explain the differences between Lenin and Kautsky on the subject in question.

In the following pages, I first note that Lenin quoted Kautsky to support his famous statement in *What Is to Be Done?* about socialism being brought to the labor movement by intellectuals, which has led to the misunderstanding that the two were in agreement. In section II, I speculate as to why Kautsky did not respond to the way Lenin used his words, and, in the next two sections, I show that Kautsky had already spelled out his views, which differed sharply from Lenin's, in earlier writings. Then I try to explain, in section V, why Lenin, though familiar with these writings, did not note Kautsky's disagreement with him; in sections VI and VII, why, in spite of that disagreement, misunderstanding Kautsky's "revolutionary" position, he did not break with him until 1914; and, in section VIII, why the break did occur then. In the final two sections, I argue that the two different conceptions of the proper role of intellectuals in the labor movement represented by Lenin

53

and Kautsky — I cannot here deal with the thought of Marx and of other Marxists on the subject — can best be explained as responses to two very different environments. In retrospect, we can see the Russian Revolution as one of many modernizing, intellectual-led revolutions in underdeveloped countries and Lenin's doctrine of intellectual leadership as appropriate to the politics of underdevelopment, while Kautsky's view corresponded to the more limited role of intellectuals in the politics of labor movements in industrialized societies.

I

The bitter conflicts between Karl Kautsky and Lenin carried on in open polemics after the outbreak of World War I and the Bolshevik seizure of power in Russia and the issues involved in these polemics are well known.[1] Here I shall deal with another issue, the one raised by Lenin in the following statement from *What Is to Be Done?*, written in late 1901 and early 1902, "the theoretical premises of which laid the foundations of the ideology of the Bolshevik Party."[2] Lenin said:

> Social-Democratic consciousness . . . would have to be brought to [the workers] from without. The history of all countries shows that the working class, exclusively by its own effort is able to develop only trade-union consciousness, i.e., the conviction that it is necessary to combine in unions, fight the employers, and strive to compel the government to pass necessary labour legislation, etc. The theory of socialism, however, grew out of the philosophic, historical, and economic theories elaborated by educated representatives of the propertied classes, by intellectuals.[3]

The conception expressed in this frequently quoted passage can be seen as the very basis of the principal features of Leninism in its relation to Marxism: the shift in its emphasis from proletarians to intellectuals, from the working class to the Party, from the mass to the leaders, from determinism to voluntarism.

The issue raised here underlies some of the issues involved in the later polemics between Lenin and Kautsky, but here, far from developing his position by attacking Kautsky, as he did beginning in 1914, Lenin implied that Kautsky agreed with him. Probably because the conflict was not openly fought out as such by the two protagonists, less attention has been paid to it in the literature than to the post-1914 polemics, though it is no less significant.

Given the later history of conflict between Kautsky and Lenin, it is striking and, at first sight, puzzling to find that Lenin could support his basic statement quoted above with a lengthy quotation from, of all people, Karl Kautsky. Lenin says:

> To supplement what has been said above, we shall quote the following profoundly true and important words of Karl Kautsky on the new draft programme of the Austrian Social Democratic Party: " ... [According to that program,] socialist consciousness appears to be a necessary and direct result of the proletarian class struggle. But this is absolutely untrue. Of course, socialism, as a doctrine, has its roots in modern economic relationships just as the class struggle of the proletariat has, and, like the latter, emerges from the struggle against the capitalist-created poverty and misery of the masses. But socialism and the class struggle arise side by side and not one out of the other; each arises under different conditions. Modern socialist consciousness can arise only on the basis of profound scientific knowledge. ... The vehicle of science is not the proletariat, but the *bourgeois intelligentsia* [K. K.'s italics]: It was in the minds of individual members of this stratum that modern socialism originated, and it was they who communicated it to the more intellectually developed proletarians who, in their turn, introduce it into the proletarian class struggle where conditions allow that to be done. Thus, socialist consciousness is something introduced into the proletarian class struggle from without [*von Aussen Hineingetragenes*] and not something that arose within it spontaneously [*urwüchsig*]."[4]

That Lenin could quote these words of Kautsky's, which are clearly strikingly similar to his own in some respects, has given rise to the misunderstanding that the two were, in fact, in agreement. Three examples of such a misunderstanding may be mentioned here. Neil Harding, having quoted part of the passage by Kautsky from Lenin's *What Is to Be Done?*, says that "Lenin's elaboration of this theme in *What Is to Be Done?* was but an exegesis of Kautsky."[5] Evidently solely on the basis of the one quotation from Kautsky selected by Lenin — Harding's text, notes, and bibliography refer to no writings by Kautsky other than the article from which Lenin quotes and in which only the one paragraph quoted by Lenin is concerned with the subject of consciousness — Harding concludes that "the writings of Kautsky" demonstrate that "the idea that socialism was a natural and spontaneous outgrowth of purely working-class experience ... was a profoundly mistaken idea."[6]

Iring Fetscher is another prominent writer who, because Lenin quotes Kautsky in *What Is to Be Done?*, ascribes a common "theory" to the two and even derives Stalin's "theory" and evidently his practice from that supposed Kautsky-Lenin theory, all without considering the different conclusions Kautsky and Lenin drew from their statements and the different political contexts that Kautsky, Lenin, and Stalin were responding to. Fetscher writes: "If in fact the consciousness of all ordinary citizens lags behind, they must be handed down the truth . . . from state officials (and Party officials) who have the privilege of anticipating and pointing the way. This Stalinist theory in turn can be traced back to a theory of Kautsky and Lenin." After citing *What Is to Be Done?* and Kautsky's statement quoted there, Fetscher concludes: "From this theory of the innate inability of the proletariat to arrive at a socialist consciousness without the stimulus and leadership of professional revolutionaries with Marxist training, there developed the doctrine of the Party as the guardian of true class consciousness, and finally the theory of the socialist Soviet State as the sole possessor of historical truth."[7]

Even a scholar who has written extensively on Kautsky, Dick Geary, summarizes Kautsky's thought in the language of Lenin and suggests that Lenin's theory was not only identical with Kautsky's but was simply taken from him. Geary says that to Kautsky

> revolutionary consciousness did not result from the sectional and economistic struggle of the unions but had to be instilled into the masses from *without,* by the party and revolutionary intellectuals. (When Lenin lifted this theory wholesale from Kautsky in *What Is to Be Done?,* he quoted Kautsky and *not* the revolutionary traditions of the Russian intelligentsia.)[8]

Whether Lenin believed that he was merely restating Kautsky's views or sought to mislead his readers into believing it, is a question I will touch on below. But, whatever his intentions may have been, he has in fact misled many of his readers down to the present and this would seem to make it worthwhile to attempt here to set the record straight and to indicate that Kautsky's views were a good deal more complex than the paragraph in question suggests.

In that paragraph, Kautsky certainly seems to agree with Lenin that socialist ideology was brought to workers "from without" by intellectuals. However, at least with respect to Marxism, that is no more than a historical fact, which both had to recognize, especially as Marx, Engels, and they themselves were intellectuals. Lenin's statement is important, however, not as a piece of historical analysis, but as the foundation for certain conclusions he drew from it. And these conclusions are clearly very different from Kautsky's views on the role of intellectuals in the labor movement. Their differences are generally reflected in their positions on both practical political issues, such as those of the organization and internal democracy of the labor party and of the trade unions and of their place in the larger society, and on questions of the philosophy of history, such as those concerning the role of individual leaders, of elites and of masses in history, and the complex issue of determinism.

I shall document at some length by reference to Kautsky's writings how his conclusions differed from the conclusions Lenin drew from the fact that they both noted in the same words. First, however, I need to dispose, as far as I can, of a relatively minor but intriguing question.

II

If Kautsky differed with Lenin, why did he not — and as far as I know, he indeed did not, at least in print — respond and object to the use Lenin made of his statement on the Austrian Social Democratic draft program? It is generally more difficult to explain why something did not happen than why something happened, and I have no definitely valid answer to this question. However, any one or a combination of several of the following considerations may help account for Kautsky's silence.

Lenin's statement appears in retrospect as of profound general significance when it is quoted out of its context, as it generally is and as I quoted it here. But Lenin embedded it in tedious polemics endlessly quoting, sneering at, and denouncing his opponents among Russian Social-Democrats. It is quite possible that Kautsky, who generally put a very high value on socialist unity, did not respond to Lenin because he did not want to become involved in these polemics. Had he objected to the way Lenin used his words to attack the Economists, he might have seemed to side with the latter. Kautsky might also have wanted to avoid giving this impression, for Lenin linked the Economists to Bernstein, with whom Kautsky was then engaged in the controversy over Revisionism.

Even after the Bolshevik-Menshevik split at the London Congress of 1903, Kautsky was reluctant to take sides openly with either of the two factions and kept urging them to reunite.[9] In 1904 Kautsky reprinted in *Die Neue Zeit* an article from *Iskra* by Rosa Luxemburg[10] that reviewed Lenin's *One Step Forward, Two Steps Back* and sharply attacked his "ultra-centralism," and in the next year Kautsky himself, in an article designed to inform German Social Democrats about the complex conflicts among Russian socialists, briefly mentioned Lenin as standing for "strict centralism with dictatorial authority for the central committee."[11] *What Is to Be Done?*, however, was ignored in *Die Neue Zeit.*

Kautsky also may not have mentioned Lenin in *Die Neue Zeit* until 1905 and may never have responded to the way Lenin used his words in *What Is to Be Done?* simply because Lenin and the disputes among Russian Social Democrats were perhaps not very important for him in 1902, before the Bolshevik-Menshevik split of 1903. Kautsky, then forty-seven years old, was at the height of his prominence in the Second International and in the German Social Democratic Party, then the largest socialist party in the world and the largest party in Germany. As the author of the SPD's Erfurt Program of 1891, which had come to serve as a model for other Marxist parties, he had become, after Engels's death in 1895, universally recognized as the leading authority in matters of Marxist theory, which he was now, beginning in 1899, defending against Revisionist attacks. Lenin, on the other hand, was a young man of not quite thirty-two when he published *What Is to Be Done?,* and he was to gain much of his prominence only as a result of having written this book. At the time he was merely one leader of a weak, divided party in a backward country that functioned primarily underground and in exile.

Given Kautsky's prominence and his involvement in the controversy over Revisionism, it stands to reason that he could hardly respond to all authors who quoted or interpreted or misinterpreted his words. He might well have ignored those who did so in a context of relatively little interest to him. To be sure, Kautsky was more interested in and better informed on Russian affairs than most Marxists in the West before World War I, but he had as yet published little on the subject and in the period in question was preoccupied with his conflict with Revisionism.[12]

Finally, it is also quite possible that Kautsky did not respond to

What Is to Be Done? simply because he had not read it and may not even have been informed about it in any detail in the period immediately following its appearance. The book was first published in March 1902 in Germany and, indeed, by Kautsky's own principal publisher, J. H. W. Dietz Nachf., in Stuttgart,[13] but only in Russian, which Kautsky did not read. Evidently, no translations into German, French, or English, the languages Kautsky did read, appeared until the 1920s.[14] Thus what eventually came to be known as a basic work of Leninism remained largely unknown in the non-Russian-speaking world until after its author came to power in Russia and even after his death.

III

Whatever the reasons for Kautsky's failure to reply to Lenin to spell out what he meant when he wrote that socialism was brought to the labor movement by intellectuals and to stress how the conclusions he drew from this fact differed from Lenin's, he had, in any case, already clearly stated his relevant views in earlier writings.

We may first note generally that Kautsky could never have agreed with the conclusion Lenin stated immediately after he quoted Kautsky:

Since there can be no talk of an independent ideology formulated by the working masses themselves in the process of their movement, the *only* choice is — either bourgeois or socialist ideology. . . . The *spontaneous* development of the working-class movement leads to its subordination to bourgeois ideology, . . . for the spontaneous working-class movement is trade-unionism, . . . and trade-unionism means the ideological enslavement of the workers by the bourgeoisie. Hence, our task, the task of Social-Democracy, is *to combat spontaneity, to divert* the working-class movement from this spontaneous, trade-unionist striving to come under the wing of the bourgeoisie, and to bring it under the wing of revolutionary Social-Democracy. The sentence . . . that the efforts of the most inspired ideologists fail to divert the working-class movement from the path that is determined by the interaction of the material elements and the material environment, *is* . . . *tantamount to renouncing socialism.*[15]

The notion that under capitalism the labor movement spontaneously tends to come "under the wing" of the bourgeoisie unless artificially diverted from this natural tendency by the Social Democratic Party and that the latter therefore represents an ideology opposed to the one spontaneously held by the labor movement would have struck Kautsky

as wholly incompatible with Marx's view of the inevitable development of capitalism, of the proletariat, and of the class struggle, as he
understood them all his life.

For Kautsky to think that socialism was brought to the labor movement by intellectuals was far from saying that, without the determined
efforts of intellectuals organized in a socialist party, the labor movement would move in a direction opposed to socialism. In fact, a careful
reading of Kautsky's words quoted by Lenin shows that he speaks
only of "modern" socialist consciousness arising on the basis of science and of "modern" socialism originating in the minds of individual
intellectuals. Clearly, this is a reference to "scientific socialism," that
is, to Marxism.

It is Marxism, then, that is brought to the workers from without, but
Kautsky does not, like Lenin, say that through their own efforts workers can develop only trade-union consciousness and not socialist consciousness, let alone class consciousness—though the first two sentences of his passage quoted above lend themselves to that interpretation. Thus, in 1893, he had written that the formation of an independent labor party "already presupposes a highly developed class consciousness in a part of the working class,"[16] thereby stating that class
consciousness, and not merely trade-union consciousness, as Lenin
thought, can exist without a socialist party. Kautsky had frequently
ascribed socialist consciousness to workers before they came under
Marxist influence[17] and therefore did not think that Marxists had to
divert the labor movement from its spontaneous striving when they
brought Marxism to it.

When Kautsky, writing in 1907–1908, poses the question: "How
does the proletariat come to socialism?," he does not give Lenin's
answer: by being diverted from its spontaneous striving by a socialist
party, but he says: "the doctrine of the class struggle provides the
answer: through the labor movement."[18]

To simplify the difference between Lenin and Kautsky: Lenin, in
What Is to Be Done?, suggests that the labor movement and socialist
intellectuals represent streams naturally flowing in different directions,
one bourgeois and one socialist, and that it is the task of the socialist
intellectuals to divert the labor stream to join theirs. To Kautsky, the
two streams, originating from the same capitalist source, are separate
but flow in the same direction and eventually merge. He regarded it as
one of Marx's and Engels' greatest achievements that they prepared

this merger by linking socialism and the labor movement in their theory, which earlier socialists had not been able to do.[19]

In his commentary of 1892 on the Erfurt Program, Kautsky had already written: "The militant proletariat is by far the most important and richest recruiting ground of Social Democracy,"[20] a belief that Lenin also held, though it may not be quite compatible with his other belief in the proletariat's spontaneous tendency to come under the wing of the bourgeoisie. Kautsky thought of the militant proletariat as a rich recruiting ground, because its political attitude necessarily resulted from the class struggle; that is, it reacted to capitalism. Kautsky's understanding rests on his conception of history, which sees ideology as a superstructure rising on a base of the relations of production, and which would therefore expect the ideology of the proletariat to be determined by its class position in capitalist society and hence to be hostile to the ideology of the bourgeoisie.[21]

Contrary to this conception of history, Lenin's view was that failure to divert the labor movement from the path "determined by the interaction of the material elements and the material environment" was "tantamount to renouncing socialism." Kautsky, on the other hand, directly contradicting Lenin, wrote in his book of 1899 against Bernstein: "Along with the proletariat, there arise with natural necessity socialist tendencies in the proletarians."[22] And, in a letter to Victor Adler, Kautsky stated: "A socialist drive or instinct or disposition or whatever one wants to call it is, of course, produced among the masses by their class position. That cannot be created by us. . . . The class position of the proletariat produces socialist *volition,* but not socialist *knowledge.*"[23]

Socialism, then, while it may have been originally separate from the labor movement, was never opposed to it. The labor movement is "spontaneously" receptive, rather than, as it should be in Lenin's view, resistant to socialist appeals, and socialism and the labor movements hence come to merge. Thus Kautsky continues in his book on the Erfurt Program:

Social Democracy is essentially nothing other than the part of the militant proletariat that is conscious of its goal. The militant proletariat tends to become more and more identical with Social Democracy. In Germany and Austria the two have, in fact, become one and the same.[24]

This passage can possibly still be interpreted as compatible with Lenin's conception insofar as the "militant proletariat" became, as Kautsky agreed, "conscious of its goal" only with the help of intellectuals acting "from without." But, clearly, Kautsky does not think of the Social Democratic Party as an outside force diverting the proletariat from its own goal. "To render the class struggle of the proletariat as conscious of its goal and as effective as possible, that is the task of Social Democracy,"[25] not to divert the proletariat from its spontaneous tendencies.

The following passages from *Das Erfurter Programm* directly contradict Lenin's already-cited notion that "the *spontaneous* development of the working-class movement leads to its subordination to bourgeois ideology":

> The interests of the proletariat and the bourgeoisie are of so contrary a nature that the political efforts of the two classes cannot be permanently harmonized. Sooner or later, in every country of the capitalist mode of production, the participation of the working class in politics must lead to its separation from the bourgeois parties and the formation of an independent party, the *labor party*. . . . Economic development brings this about with natural necessity. . . .

> Everything combines to make the militant proletariat extremely receptive to socialist teachings. . . . Wherever an independent labor party is formed, it must with natural necessity assume socialist tendencies; if this is not the case from the outset, it must finally become a *socialist* labor party, it becomes *Social Democracy*.[26]

These statements clearly point up the contrast between what can be seen as Lenin's voluntarist outlook and Kautsky's determinist one. Lenin expected the labor movement to become associated with a socialist party only as a result of being diverted from its "spontaneous, trade-unionist striving to come under the wing of the bourgeoisie." Kautsky, on the other hand, is convinced that under capitalism the working class must sooner or later separate itself from bourgeois parties, must form an independent labor party, which must become a socialist party. All of this happens with "natural necessity," the "necessity of nature" (*Naturnotwendigkeit*).

The point is not that Kautsky, unlike Lenin, thought that the process he described would take place without human intervention — a view of history that has sometimes been ascribed to him, though it is manifestly nonsensical. Rather, he believed that the human actions involved in the process were themselves determined as inevitable reactions to the development of capitalism.[27] These actions might — but, as the case of the British Labour Party shows, need not necessarily — include those of intellectuals bringing Marxism to a labor movement that was bound to become socialist. If they do, that, too, is a reaction to capitalism, for, as Kautsky had stated in the passage quoted by Lenin, "socialism, as a doctrine, has its roots in modern economic relationships."[28]

Of course, Lenin, too, might have argued that the "task" of combatting spontaneity that he ascribed to Social Democracy would inevitably and with necessity be fulfilled. Thus, the contrast between Kautsky and Lenin on this point is not quite as sharp as the words "determinism" and "voluntarism" might suggest. Perhaps the contrast is rather one between optimism and pessimism or, if not pessimism, at least, an optimism tempered by realism.

The indomitable optimism that pervades all of Kautsky's work and that must strike us as incredible in retrospect was conditioned by what he had witnessed: the rapid and seemingly irresistible progress in the latter half of the nineteenth century of industrialization and capitalism, of labor movements and socialist parties, especially in Germany, and, to some degree there and even more in Western Europe, of democracy. Lenin, on the other hand, responded to conditions in an underdeveloped country in the early stages of industrialization, a country with no long history of democratic strivings by an urban petty bourgeoisie and bourgeoisie, with what seemed before 1905 to be a still powerful autocratic regime, with a huge peasantry that could not be trusted to be revolutionary, and with a still relatively tiny working class that Lenin evidently did not quite trust either. No wonder he could not share Kautsky's faith in a mass socialist labor party necessarily and inevitably arising in response to capitalism.

IV

It was not only with respect to his conception of history and of the class struggle that Kautsky had expressed views distinctly different from Lenin's before the publication of *What Is to Be Done?*. The same was true with respect to his ideas on the organization and leadership of the Party, the area where Lenin is usually credited with what can variously be described as his most significant contribution to, revision of, or deviation from Marxist thought.

Lenin stressed that intellectuals originate the theory of socialism and bring it to the labor movement, in order to conclude that they are also the ones to lead and control that movement, which then becomes the basis of his conception of the Party as a small elite of "professional revolutionaries" who serve as the "vanguard" or "shock troops" of the proletariat. It was this conception that was set forth in his *What Is to Be Done?*[29] and that eventually became the ideological justification of the role of the Communist Party in the Soviet Union and in other countries.

Kautsky drew none of these conclusions, as is generally obvious from the assumption underlying all his thinking that the Social Democratic party was and ought to be a mass labor party (though he recognized, of course, that it could not function openly as such in tsarist Russia). His specific differences with Lenin become very clear in a brief article on "Academics and Proletarians," written in April 1901 just before Lenin wrote *What Is to Be Done?*, that is worth quoting at some length in our context.

Kautsky begins, like Lenin, with the assertion that

> only through socialism, that is, through a revolutionary final goal, can the proletariat become politically independent. . . . A vital socialism cannot be created by the proletariat with its own resources; it must be brought to it by thinkers who, armed with all the aids of bourgeois science, place themselves on the proletarian standpoint. . . . Thus it has been predominantly elements out of the bourgeoisie that turned the unconscious class movement of the proletariat into a conscious and independent one and thereby prepared the ground for and finally founded Social Democracy. . . . It is, then, above all, the task of the scientifically trained bourgeois elements, the intellectuals or "academics," in our party to develop and diffuse insight into the major social interrelationships, a far-sighted socialist knowledge that rises above the interests of the moment, that is, a revolutionary spirit in the best sense of the word.[30]

But having said all this, with which Lenin could readily agree, Kautsky immediately adds bluntly:

> It is for the knowledge of the goal that the proletariat needs the academics, but it does not need them for the leadership of its class movement. Thus, how to organize trade unions, how to win strikes, how to organize cooperatives, even how to draft and to advocate labor-protective legislation in parliaments, workers experienced in the movement know better than any academic; to the extent that the latter understand something of it, they learned it from the workers.[31]

What does this passage suggest other than what Lenin would consider surrender of the leadership of the labor movement to the trade-unionist spontaneity that he feared and despised? This spontaneity rested, according to Lenin, on trade-union consciousness defined as "the conviction that it is necessary to combine in unions, fight the employers, and strive to compel the government to pass necessary labour legislation," as if he had taken his examples from Kautsky's listing of the activities of the "class movement."

While Lenin felt that to keep the labor movement from following its spontaneous tendencies the intellectual elite had to concern itself not only with theory but also with the day-to-day elements of labor politics ("*Kleinarbeit*"), Kautsky stressed that

> for the daily *Kleinarbeit*, the academics are superfluous. . . . Indeed, how are they superior to workers in day-to-day work, except with respect to a certain superficial facility in the use of the pen, sometimes also of the tongue, a knowledge of the proper use of dative and accusative?[32]

Far from ascribing spontaneous bourgeois striving to the proletariat from which intellectuals must divert it, Kautsky concludes his article by saying, as he had elsewhere, that the proletariat "has and must have ideals . . . that it produces out of its class position," and "intellectuals in the Party are called upon . . . to develop and support these ideals scientifically. That is their historical task; thereby they become an important element of Social Democracy."[33] The intellectuals do not, as they do for Lenin, set the goal and the ideal of the labor movement in opposition to the workers' "spontaneity"; their task is the far more modest one of recognizing the workers' ideals and developing them scientifically. They have, as Kautsky wrote in a letter to Victor Adler, "only one task in our party: to spread clarity. Everything else is better taken care of by the proletarians themselves."[34]

It is possible to conclude, then, that Kautsky was to some degree inconsistent in his thought or, at any rate, imprecise in his use of words, particularly the all-too-vague term "socialism." On the one hand, he saw a socialist "tendency," "instinct," or "volition" naturally developing in and along with the labor movement. On the other hand, he insisted that, at least in the early decades of the nineteenth century, workers were incapable of developing socialist insights and knowledge (perhaps as distinguished from tendencies and instincts) by themselves[35] and that socialism, particularly in the sense of modern social-

ism or Marxism, had been brought to labor from without by intellectuals. Neither of the two views, if they differ much at all, agrees with
Lenin's, however, for neither sees labor moving spontaneously away
from socialism and both see the role of Marxist intellectuals, like
Kautsky himself, merely as bringing "scientific" clarity to the labor
movement, not as producing or changing its socialist nature.

V

There can be no question that Lenin was familiar with the writings
just quoted where Kautsky drew conclusions very different from Lenin's
from the fact that socialism is brought to workers by intellectuals,
which he had noted in the passage Lenin quoted so prominently in
What Is to Be Done?. It goes without saying that Lenin was thoroughly
familiar with Kautsky's commentary on the Erfurt Program, for it
"organized the thoughts and the efforts of socialists not only in Germany but wherever socialist parties existed."[36] Moreover, "according to
the memoirs of Lenin's brother, Dimitrii Ul'ianov, Lenin himself
translated the *Erfurter Programm* during the summer of 1894."[37]

Similarly, it can be assumed that Lenin had read Kautsky's article
on "Akademiker und Proletarier."[38] *Die Neue Zeit* was popular among
Russian socialists and relatively widely, though only illegally, available in Russia,[39] but Lenin had, in any case, left Russia for the West at
the end of July 1900, well before Kautsky's article appeared in April
1901. It was quite as available to him, living in Munich as he did until
March 1902, as the article of October 1901 that he quoted in *What Is to
Be Done?*[40]

Why, then, did Lenin quote Kautsky at length to show that the two
agreed that socialism (or at least "modern" socialism) had been brought
to workers from without, but did not note that Kautsky did not agree —
and thus implied that he did agree — with the conclusions Lenin drew
from this on the role, organization, and leadership of the Party?

The simplest and, no doubt to many, the most obvious answer to
this question, that by withholding Kautsky's conclusions Lenin deliberately sought to deceive his readers, or at least did not mind if they
were in fact deceived, cannot be ruled out. As is amply clear from
What Is to Be Done?, Lenin was engaged in a very bitter dispute and
deeply believed that the fate of his Party and of the coming Russian
Revolution depended on its outcome. He was single-minded and, in-

deed, ruthless in the pursuit of his revolutionary goals. Like other Russian Marxists, he had immense respect for Kautsky and believed that he could greatly strengthen his case by invoking Kautsky's authority on its behalf.[41] Had he quoted the passages from Kautsky that I just quoted, he would have weakened his case (or, at any rate, he could have expected that effect) and thereby, as he saw it, weakened the cause of the revolution. Thus, being a passionately engaged politician rather than a dispassionate scholar, Lenin may have quite deliberately misrepresented Kautsky's position by quoting one relevant passage and omitting several others from Kautsky's writings that he knew very well.

Still, while politicians have been known to practice deliberate deception, more often than not their sins of commission or omission against the truth can, I suspect, be better explained by giving them credit — or blame — for deceiving themselves as well as others. Obvious as his differences with Kautsky are, Lenin may not have been clearly aware of them because he did not want to be. After all, he managed all his life to remain unaware of his major departures from the thought of Marx and Engels[42] and, just as he considered himself to be and wanted to be their faithful disciple, so, in the period in question, he considered himself to be and wanted to be a faithful disciple of Kautsky.[43] On the other hand, he was a practical politician who responded in his thinking to the existing Russian environment to which much in the thought and writings of Kautsky — as in those of Marx and Engels — was irrelevant. He could only resolve this dilemma by taking from Kautsky — as well as Marx and Engels — and perhaps by reading into them what he needed and ignoring what did not fit his needs.

If this process of selection involves deception, as distinguished from self-deception, it is probably a matter of degree. To some degree it seems almost inevitable that a reader reacting to a particular environment would misread the thought, especially the political thought, of an author responding to a very different environment. Kautsky surely did this in some ways with respect to the thought of Marx and Engels, and those who read their works now, in a world even more different from theirs, are even more likely to do so. Lenin's misreading of Kautsky may or may not have been more conscious and deliberate than this kind of misreading, which most of us are often unavoidably guilty of.

In any case, my principal aim here has not been to establish Lenin's motivation but to show that he did indeed misinterpret Kautsky when he suggested that the two were in agreement on his line of reasoning in *What Is to Be Done?* on the role of intellectuals in the Social Democratic Party and the labor movement.

VI

Whether Lenin, or for that matter Kautsky, was aware of it or not, there were, then, profound and clear differences between the two on the questions at issue here, at least from the time of *What Is to Be Done?*, and, indeed, before that to the extent that Lenin earlier held the views that he put forth in that book. These differences, then, antedate the Bolshevik-Menshevik split of 1903, Kautsky's relative shift from the Left to the "Center" of the SPD in 1910, his position at the outbreak of World War I in 1914, and his attacks on the new Bolshevik regime in Russia beginning in 1918.

What changed in the course of the quarter-century history of the Kautsky-Lenin relationship was not the existence of differences between them, but their awareness of these differences. For quite a long time, it may not have mattered very much to Kautsky whether Lenin agreed with him or not. To Lenin, on the other hand, Kautsky's agreement was always of crucial importance. As long as he thought he enjoyed that agreement, he repeatedly relied on it for support, as he regarded Kautsky as the greatest living authority on Marxism. When, during the last decade of his life, their differences had become too obvious to be concealed, he went very far to discredit Kautsky.

This interpretation of their relationship as one of persistent, long-standing disagreement seems to be contradicted by the drastic change in Lenin's attitude toward Kautsky, from deep respect bordering on adulation to bitter hatred and contempt. A temptingly simple explanation of this change — that at least one of the two thinkers must have changed his views — cannot be accepted. Lenin, always the practical revolutionary politician and hence sometimes described as an opportunist, certainly did change his thinking on major questions over the years, but he remained remarkably consistent on the leading role of intellectuals, that is, of his Party, in the revolutionary movement. Kautsky, while not as rigid as the picture often drawn of him as the high priest of Marxian orthodoxy suggests, was wholly consistent, through his nearly six decades as a Marxist writer, on the importance of democracy in the labor movement as well as in government, both before and after the proletarian conquest of power.[44]

Kautsky was never a Leninist, then, nor was Lenin, at least after *What Is to Be Done?*, a Kautskyist. Why, then, were "his writings, until the outbreak of World War I, filled with an infinite number of Kautsky quotations,"[45] and why did he think of himself and clearly want to be thought of as a follower of Kautsky? I believe that Lenin's self-image — and also Kautsky's image of him — as an orthodox Marxist was a misunderstanding, part of the much larger misunderstanding generally prevailing down to the present, that sees the Bolsheviks in Russia and then Communists in other underdeveloped countries as a part or at least a branch of a single movement that also comprises Western labor parties and holds a single ideology called "Marxism."[46]

The complex phenomenon that, for the sake of simplicity, I crudely label a "misunderstanding" turns primarily on the concept of revolution. The principal element in Marx's Marxism that has appealed to modernizing intellectuals, like Lenin, in underdeveloped countries has been its emphasis on revolution and its promise, supposedly resting on science, of ultimate revolutionary success. To be sure, to be adapted to conditions of industrial backwardness, that element had to be divorced to a greater or lesser extent, from another element with which it was inextricably linked in Marx's thought, that of the industrial proletariat as both the maker and the prime beneficiary of the revolution: to a lesser extent in countries like turn-of-the-century Russia, where there was a small, new industrial proletariat that modernizing intellectuals could appeal to for support; to a greater extent in countries like Afghanistan, Ethiopia, or Angola, where there is no social class Marx could have recognized as proletarian at all.

In areas like late-nineteenth-century and early-twentieth-century Western and Central Europe with advancing industry and growing labor movements, the element in Marx's Marxism that appealed to some leaders of these movements and, especially, to some intellectuals in sympathy with them was the prediction of the inevitable rise of labor from suffering, degradation, and impotence to well-being and power. However, in countries with nonrepresentative, aristocratic-bureaucratic-militaristic regimes — as well as powerful labor movements — like Austria and, especially, Germany until the end of World War I, where Kautsky's thought was shaped, the concept of revolution, too, was retained by Marxist thinkers because it served a certain function to be noted now.

To Lenin, operating in autocratic Russia, the meaning of the word "revolution" was simple and straightforward: it stood for the violent overthrow of the tsarist regime and the removal of its bases in the landed aristocracy, the bureaucracy, and the military. The function of the term was to mobilize those discontented with prevailing conditions. The matter was not so simple for Kautsky, associated as he was with a movement of workers who had made great economic and political advances and were not ready to go to the barricades, yet still were and felt severely discriminated against by a deeply hostile regime they could not expect to remove by peaceful and constitutional means.[47]

For one thing, Kautsky used the term "revolution" in connection with the final goal of "socialism."[48] It always remained ill-defined, but it was a "revolutionary" goal to Kautsky, because it would come about only as a result of a drastic change from the existing society, of a social "revolution" rather than of mere "reforms" within the existing system. For Kautsky, no doubt responding to the exclusion of Social Democracy from state and society under the Bismarckian and Wilheminian regimes, the term "revolution" in this sense served the function of emphasizing that the Social Democratic Party was sharply different from all other parties in that its goal went beyond relatively minor changes in the existing society.[49] Belief in that goal, in turn, was to assure still alienated workers that they could look forward to a wholly different and better society and was thus to help maintain and strengthen the unity and class consciousness of the labor movement in preparation for what Kautsky regarded as labor's inevitable assumption of power.

On the question of how the labor movement would come to power in Wilheminian Germany, Kautsky remained vague. He hoped the process would be a peaceful one, but, much as he favored pro-labor reforms, he did not share Bernstein's belief in a gradual growth into socialism by mere trade-union pressure and reforms granted by the regime. On the other hand, he did not share Rosa Luxemburg's underestimation of the bureaucratic, military, and popular strength of the regime and her overestimation of the workers' willingness to confront it. Fearing defeats and serious setbacks, he hoped to avoid, or at least to postpone violent confrontations with the regime.

In a situation in which it was, indeed, difficult to see how Social Democracy could gain power, even if the Party did win a majority of votes in an election, Kautsky advocated what he called an

"Ermattungsstrategie," a strategy designed to wear out the enemy, and what Dieter Groh called a policy of *"revolutionärer Attentismus,"* of waiting for and expecting the revolution.[50] At any rate, Kautsky's goal was clearly the replacement of the existing regime by a democratic parliamentary republic, a goal that could well be called "revolutionary" in the imperial German context. Thus, Kautsky stood not only for a distant, gradual, and peaceful social "revolution," but also for a political "revolution" that would necessarily be less distant, probably less gradual, and possibly even less peaceful.

I might add a comment here on Kautsky's often-quoted phrase that "Social Democracy is a revolutionary but not a revolution-making party."[51] When one considers the complex set of meanings the term "revolution" had for Kautsky, as well as his determinist tendencies — he was fond of referring to Engels' statement "that revolutions are not made intentionally and at will, but that they were everywhere and at all times the necessary consequence of circumstances that are entirely independent of the will and the conduct of particular parties and of entire classes"[52] — Kautsky's dictum, striking as it may be, hardly seems to involve an attempt at quibbling or obfuscation on his part, as is frequently said of it.[53]

Kautsky's passage is preceded by this paragraph:

> We are revolutionaries and not only in the sense in which the steam engine is revolutionary. The social revolution we strive for can only be attained by means of a political revolution, by means of the conquest of political power by the militant proletariat. And the particular constitutional form in which alone socialism can be realized is the . . . democratic republic.

Kautsky then adds that, since Social Democracy can no more make the revolution than its opponents can prevent it, "it does not even occur to us to want to start or prepare a revolution" — a point Lenin overlooked when he associated himself with Kautsky's view of revolution — and "we cannot say anything about when, under what conditions, and in what form the revolution will occur." It seemed to him, though, that, more than was the case in the revolutionary struggles of the bourgeoisie, the "means of economic, legislative, and moral pressure" would predominate over those of "physical violence." When Kautsky's dictum about Social Democracy being revolutionary but not revolution-making is not, as it usually is, taken out of this context, it can be seen to be much less ambiguous than it is often held to be.

VII

Much as Kautsky's concept of revolution differed from Lenin's with respect to both methods and objectives, the two concepts were so indistinct and the differences were so obscured by the use of the same term, "revolution," for both of them that Lenin, who wanted to associate himself with Kautsky in any case, could not only rightly believe that Kautsky, too, favored the violent overthrow of the tsarist regime in Russia, but he could also wrongly assume that the two shared the same concept of revolution.

This was particularly true in the period when Lenin wrote *What Is to Be Done?*. He then saw Kautsky — as, indeed, Kautsky saw himself — as the defender of orthodox "revolutionary" Marxism against "reformist" Revisionism. In *What Is to Be Done?*, Lenin repeatedly identifies his opponents among Russian Marxists, especially the "Economists," with what he calls the "Bernsteinians." In a note to the first page of the book, he states explicitly that "German Bernsteinians and the Russian Critics" as well as English Fabians and French Ministerialists "all belong to the same family" engaged in an "international battle with . . . international revolutionary Social-Democracy." Lenin thus identifies himself by implication with Kautsky in the latter's conflict with Bernstein and, quite explicitly, sees his cause and Kautsky's as the same "revolutionary" one.

Lenin especially admired Kautsky's *Road to Power* of 1909,[54] above all because of its emphasis on "revolution." He overlooked the fact that Kautsky did not call for a revolution to be made, but merely predicted a revolutionary situation. The goal of the political revolution that Kautsky advocated and had predicted all along, but that he now saw as an early prospect, was equal suffrage in Prussia and parliamentary government in Germany[55]; it was simply political democracy. As of 1909 Lenin, in this respect not unlike Kautsky, had a clearer idea of what the revolution was to destroy than of what it was to create, but, beginning in 1917 it became quite evident that his revolutionary goal differed from what Kautsky had advocated and expected.

In the period of the controversy over Revisionism, Lenin saw himself as siding with Kautsky's "Left" against Bernstein's "Right" because he thought that he shared Kautsky's view of revolution. It may seem more surprising that he continued to identify himself with Kautsky when the latter moved from the SPD Left to the "Marxist Center," not so much because he had changed his position[56] but because a new radicalism had arisen on his left, represented most notably by Rosa Luxemburg. Though she attacked Kautsky and the Party leadership, especially on the issue of the political mass strike, for being insufficiently "revolutionary," much as Lenin did later, he did not take her side.[57]

Indeed, on a key issue in the Kautsky-Luxemburg controversy of 1910, Lenin was even more opposed to Luxemburg's position than was Kautsky. While Kautsky wanted to rely on the workers organized in the Party and the trade unions for political and strike action, Luxemburg, distrustful of the Party and union bureaucracy and under the influence of the 1905 revolution in Russia, glorified the unorganized "masses" and thus relied on the very spontaneity and decentralization that Lenin feared. To be sure, at the bottom of Lenin's belief that a small, well-organized group, primarily of intellectuals, could call on the masses to make a revolution lies the same confidence that Luxemburg had in the masses' ever-present readiness to engage in revolutionary activity.[58]

VIII

It was not until the outbreak of World War I, more than a dozen years after he had written *What Is to Be Done?*, that Lenin became aware of his differences with Kautsky. He was deeply shocked and surprised by the support that the majorities of the socialist parties in the belligerent countries gave to the war policies of their respective governments in August 1914, and he was particularly furious with the German Social Democrats and especially with Kautsky, in whom he had had so much faith. Actually, Kautsky opposed the Majority Social Democrats' support of the imperial government,[59] but he also considered Lenin's demand that the War not be ended as quickly as possible but be turned into a revolutionary civil war in both the Allied and the Central Powers as wholly unrealistic.[60]

Lenin saw the position both of "Social Chauvinists" and of Kautskyist "Centrists" as a betrayal of the cause of revolutionary socialism, as he had understood it.[61] His explanation of this betrayal showed the same distrust of labor movements as he had voiced in *What Is to Be Done?*, when he referred to their spontaneous tendency to come under the wing of the bourgeoisie. He now argued, notably in his book *Imperial-*

ism, the Highest Stage of Capitalism, that sections of labor had been bribed by the high profits of imperialism and hence had become "opportunist."[62] His solution to the problem was the same as it had been for Russia in *What Is to Be Done?*: the leadership of labor movements had to be in the hands of revolutionary intellectuals like himself, but now not only in Russia but also in the West.

Kautsky regarded World War I as a disastrous interruption — but only an interruption — of the inevitable forward march of proletarian socialism. He was particularly upset about the divisions it had caused within socialist parties and in the Socialist (Second) International, and he looked forward with passionate dedication to their reunification after the War. Lenin drew more far-reaching and very different conclusions from the position taken by the socialist parties in August 1914. To apply the principles of *What Is to Be Done?,* he moved to split these parties and the International and came to favor the creation of a new, Third (Communist) International and of new parties, to be called "Communist," if the old ones did not accept his principles and join his International.[63]

Thus the differences between Kautsky and Lenin on the role of intellectuals in the labor movement that have occupied us here were now at last coming into the open, and their wider implications were becoming apparent even to the two protagonists, who had been reluctant to see them earlier. As long as Lenin's commitment to intellectual leadership of the labor movement was confined to Russia, it could seem to Kautsky to involve only a relatively insignificant question of organization in the endless quarrels among Russian revolutionaries.[64] Lenin, on the other hand, could associate himself with German Social Democracy in general and with Kautsky in particular and maintain his trust in them, because they were, after all, "revolutionary." All this changed in 1914, and Kautsky, who had all along held a very different position from Lenin on the proper role of intellectuals, now suddenly turned in Lenin's eyes into an opportunist and a renegade.[65] When Lenin seized power in Russia and Kautsky, within a few weeks, attacked him for disregarding the absence of the prerequisites of a socialist revolution and for violating democratic principles[66] and thereby injuring the cause of the proletariat, the break between them became irreparable.[67]

That there was, in 1914, an abrupt and drastic change in Lenin's attitude toward Kautsky is obvious. However, it seems that politicians, particularly if they appeal for mass support and do not wish to confuse and possibly lose their followers, are generally reluctant to admit that they changed their views. Lenin therefore asserted that it was Kautsky who had changed. In time, however, it must have seemed incredible even to him that Kautsky, who had for Lenin for two decades been the most reliable Marxist champion of revolution, had literally overnight, on 3 August 1914, turned into a renegade. So in 1917, in his *State and Revolution,* he set out "to investigate how Kautsky drifted into the morass of unbelievably disgraceful confusion and defense of social-chauvinism" and he now discovered retrospectively and sought to demonstrate at some length in Kautsky's anti-Revisionist writings, which he had earlier greatly admired, "his systematic deviation towards opportunism precisely on the question of the state," a question Kautsky "again completely avoided" even in his *Road to Power.*[68]

The change in Lenin's attitude is well illustrated by the shift in his treatment of Kautsky's *Bernstein und das Sozialdemokratische Programm.* When he received it in 1899 he regarded it as so important that, as Krupskaia recalls, he and she set everything aside to translate it in two weeks,[69] and he wrote a long, wholly positive review of it.[70] In 1917 he found in the same work a refusal to analyze "the utter distortion of Marxism by opportunism," "a surrender to opportunism," and the "fraudulent" substitution of one question for another.[71]

I mention Lenin's claim that Kautsky more or less suddenly converted to "opportunism" because it initiated what became a dominant theme in much of the literature about Kautsky for most of the following seventy-five years, not only of Communist literature,[72] but also of many non-Communist and more or less scholarly treatments. However, different authors differ — as did Lenin's own views — as to just when Kautsky became a renegade and how the change manifested itself. Some see it, as Lenin did at first, in 1914; others place it in 1910 or even in the period 1906–10, when Kautsky assumed his Centrist position against Rosa Luxemburg; and some even put Kautsky, along with Bernstein, in the camp of Revisionism.

In the face of this line of analysis, I would maintain that Kautsky did not become a renegade. I hope to have shown that, on the issues of concern to us here, which were basic to his conflict with Lenin, he remained consistent. Had Kautsky been more familiar with Lenin's writings, notably with *What Is to Be Done?,* had Lenin not been so eager to associate himself with Kautsky, and had both of them not been deceived by their common Marxist revolutionary vocabulary into believing that they held similar views, the differences between them would have been obvious to both of them all along, and there would have been no occasion for Lenin's sudden shift vis-à-vis Kautsky in August 1914 or for his assertion that Kautsky had shifted.

IX

The fact that Lenin and Kautsky each saw the other as a traitor to Marxism implies that either could have chosen not to betray it: that Kautsky was free to become an advocate of violent revolution and a dictatorship of intellectuals, or that Lenin was free to rely on the growth of a mass labor movement and on electoral and parliamentary methods to achieve his goal. Of course, it was not impossible for either of them to adopt such ideas. There were people in Germany who looked to Lenin and the new Soviet regime for their inspiration, and there were disciples of Kautsky in Russia, especially among the Western-oriented Mensheviks. But it is significant that when the chips were down at the end of World War I and revolutions occurred, the "Leninists" in Germany and the "Kautskyists" in Russia failed, because in each case their model was derived from an environment that proved irrelevant in their own environment.[73]

Given the position each one held in his country, it was, indeed, impossible for Kautsky to become a Leninist or for Lenin to become a Kautskyist. As a Leninist, Kautsky could not have become or remained the principal theoretician or ideologist of a mass labor movement in an industrialized country.[74] As a Kautskyist, Lenin could not have become the leader of a revolution and then of a revolutionary government in an underdeveloped country. Yet it is because they served these functions that Kautsky's and Lenin's thoughts are of so much interest. In each case, function and thought went together and, since in very different environments and conditions they had to serve very different functions, they held very different thoughts.

In the Eurocentric view of Kautsky's and Lenin's generation of intellectuals, there was the "civilized" world, consisting of Europe, including Russia, and overseas territories settled by Europeans, and there was the rest of the world, of which they knew little and to which they paid little attention and which was therefore, at least by implication, presumed to be uncivilized.[75] Today we can see the world as divided differently, into industrialized countries that had been modernized from within and underdeveloped areas being modernized from without. We can then perceive Lenin's Russian environment as an underdeveloped country under the impact of modernization from without and in the throes of early industrialization.

In such societies, intellectuals typically play a key role in politics. They are students and professional people who have been exposed to and have adopted some Western values, like material progress and greater equality, values that are revolutionary in the context of their still traditional or colonial social and political order. They regard themselves as champions of the lower classes, the peasants and workers, and appeal to them for support. To carry out their program of rapid modernization, they need to capture control of the government and then to use the government to control agriculture and existing and future industry, policies they typically think of as land reform and socialization in the interest of the lower classes.

The revolutionary intellectuals' attitude to these lower classes is ambivalent. On the one hand, they revere them as the true "people" who are to govern in the future society they dream of. On the other hand, they look down on them with some contempt and distrust, frustrated by the fact that they are difficult to mobilize by their would-be champions sunk, as peasants are, in traditional isolation, impotence, and apathy; and concerned, as miserable, poor workers are, with immediate benefits rather than with dreams of a wholly different, new society.[76]

Lenin's function in history can be better understood as that of a revolutionary, modernizing intellectual in an underdeveloped country than as a Marxist leader of a socialist labor party in an industrialized country. He saw himself as linked to Marx and Engels, to Kautsky and Bebel, but we can appreciate him better as fulfilling a historical function like that of the Communists Mao, Ho, and Castro, but also of non-Communists like Sun and Kemal, Nehru and Sukarno, Nassser and Nkrumah. Of course, we are not accustomed to seeing Lenin in that light because he was a European and he had a more coherent ideology, which was couched in Marxian terminology. But his revolution, like those of other revolutionaries in underdeveloped countries, was not only led by but represented the views and interests of modernizing intellectuals, not of a labor movement, and relied heavily on peasant support. The regime he founded was more successful than other revolutionary regimes in underdeveloped countries, but like them was committed to the rapid industrialization of a backward society, not the conversion of a capitalist society into a workers' socialist society, as Marxists envisaged it.

The role Lenin assigned to intellectuals and hence his differences with Kautsky on this point reflect his implicit recognition — explicit recognition would have been incompatible with his self-image as a Marxist — that, in an underdeveloped country like Russia, revolutions are made not by the industrial proletariat and its organizations but by intellectuals, a recognition since confirmed by the experience of dozens of underdeveloped countries with their revolutionary single-party movements and regimes led by intellectuals. The change brought by Lenin to Marxism is not a minor tactical or organizational one, at least not if we hold the social groups that a movement is composed of and that an ideology represents to be an essential element characterizing that movement and ideology. Movements composed of different groups are different movements; ideologies representing different groups are different ideologies. Seen in this light, Leninism is and has been from its beginnings a different ideology from Marxism.

The depth of the difference between Marxism and Leninism becomes clear when it is realized that once the core of the revolutionary movement has been shifted from the proletariat to the intellectuals, the former is merely one possible support group for the latter, to which others can be added and which can be replaced or abandoned altogether.[77] Lenin himself already added the peasants to the workers; Mao added not only the petty bourgeoisie but even the capitalist "national" bourgeoisie to them to form his "bloc of four classes" and effectively forget the proletarian class struggle. Nowadays, modernizing intellectuals, "Marxist" and non-Marxist alike, tend to ignore class categories altogether and simply appeal to the "masses" or the "people." What remains constant is intellectual leadership — precisely the point on which Lenin disagreed with Kautsky.

Kautsky refused to have his Party appeal to peasants and to "convert German Social Democracy from a Party of the militant proletariat into a mishmash of all the discontented."[78] To appeal to all the discontented, including even capitalists, is precisely a policy that makes sense in an underdeveloped country, where members of different classes can be united against a traditional regime or a foreign colonial power, a policy that can be pursued by a Leninist party of intellectuals.[79] For a labor party fighting the class struggle of the proletariat, as Kautsky saw the SPD, it would be nonsensical to claim to represent the interests of capitalists or even of peasants.

X

In underdeveloped Russia, Lenin's thought was more concerned with a revolutionary than with a labor movement, though, having generally adopted the Marxian vocabulary, he stressed the latter. In industrialized Germany and Western Europe, Kautsky was involved with actual labor movements. It is, then, anything but surprising that they held very different conceptions of the role of intellectuals in the labor movement.

In late-nineteenth-century Russia, the great majority of intellectuals were oppositional or even revolutionary in their attitude toward the then existing regime, as is not unusual in prerevolutionary underdeveloped countries. The industrial working class was small, weak, and poorly organized. In late-nineteenth-century Germany, the great majority of intellectuals more or less favored the Bismarckian and Wilheminian regimes, and those who did have sympathy for the rapidly growing and already well organized labor movement often sought to reconcile it with the regime. No wonder that, at roughly similar points in their careers, Lenin, in *What Is to Be Done?*, put his faith in intellectuals and showed his distrust of workers, while Kautsky took exactly the opposite position. In a letter to Bebel in 1885, Kautsky wrote: "Our workers base themselves on the *Communist Manifesto,* our intellectuals do not,"[80] and as late as 1894 he went so far as to say, in a letter to Heinrich Braun: "intellectuals are always unreliable."[81]

The difference in the positions held by intellectuals in German and Russian society to which Kautsky and Lenin reacted is also indicated by the fact that Kautsky frequently discussed the intellectuals in the context of analyses of the rise of the new white-collar middle class and, indeed, often did not clearly distinguish between intellectuals and white-collar workers.[82] The development of this new class, which Kautsky recognized quite early, had, as a phenomenon of advancing industrialization, not yet occurred in Russia and was, therefore, of no interest to Lenin. To some extent, the intellectuals Kautsky and Lenin had in mind were not the same kind of people at all.

Kautsky's and Lenin's different conceptions of the proper role of intellectuals in the labor movement were also very much a result of the quite different positions intellectuals in fact occupied in the German labor movement and the Russian revolutionary movement. In tsarist Russia, under conditions of illegality and police repression, the revolutionary movement had, apart from intellectuals, no professional party leaders or parliamentarians, no professional party editors and propagandists, no professional party organizers and bureaucrats, no professional labor organizers and trade-union bureaucrats. Intellectuals did not have to share power with such people; to the extent that these positions existed at all, they were filled by intellectuals — whom Lenin wanted to be "professional revolutionaries." The position held by intellectuals in a revolutionary movement in an underdeveloped country, as Lenin correctly perceived it, is one of nearly uncontested power.

In industrialized societies with openly functioning mass parties, intellectuals can and do play some role in party politics, usually as consultants to politicians and as writers, propagandists, and ideologists, but power is mostly in the hands of politicians who are mostly not intellectuals and who hold offices in the government or in the bureaucracy of their party. Kautsky's role as a party intellectual was actually an exceptionally powerful one,[83] but it was limited, and he knew it and wanted it to be limited.[84]

The German Social Democratic Party was a party with huge numbers of leaders and officials at the national and various local levels; with parliamentarians in the legislatures of the Reich, the Länder and the localities; with delegates to national and local Party congresses; with numerous affiliated organizations, each having its own leaders and officials; and with close ties to the powerful trade unions which also had their own leaders and bureaucracies. It was a party so different from the Russian Social Democratic Party or its Bolshevik faction that to apply the same descriptive noun "party" to both of them really tends to be quite misleading.

Corresponding to his position in such a party, Kautsky believed in a division of labor between "practical politicians" and "theoretical politicians."[85] The function of intellectuals seemed very important and, indeed, crucial to Kautsky, but also, as it was not to Lenin in his underdeveloped environment, quite limited. As I quoted Kautsky above, the function of intellectuals was to provide "knowledge of the goal" and a scientific basis for the workers' ideals and instincts, but not "leadership" for the labor movement or involvement in its *Kleinarbeit*.

In his succinct words to Victor Adler, the intellectuals' only task in the Party was "to spread clarity."

Just as Lenin's theory of the intellectuals' role corresponded to their position in the revolutionary politics of underdeveloped countries under the impact of modernization from without,[86] so Kautsky's theory of the intellectuals' much more limited role corresponded to the situation in industrialized Germany, where blue-collar and white-collar workers could occupy many leading positions in the labor movement. In contrast to Lenin's, Kautsky's "theory of the intellectuals does not end in the demand that the philosophers had to be kings, for the subject of history had a historical dynamic of its own and had to carry out its task itself."[87]

Kautsky's and Lenin's conceptions of the intellectuals' role were not merely responses to their respective external environments. They were inevitably also influenced by their own roles as intellectuals in their movements, as they played them and as they wanted to play them, roles that were, of course, also constrained by their environments. On the other hand, the role each played must in part have been shaped by his conception of the role.[88] To be sure, each man's personality and talents also helped shape his role and hence presumably his conception of it. Thus, Lenin was a decisive and, when he thought it necessary, ruthless tactician, while Kautsky could say of himself in a letter: "I am too inclined to be critical to be able to make decisions easily at crucial moments. I seek first to think through all possible consequences and generally finish with that only when the debate is over."[89] Kautsky's role, which hardly has any parallel today, required a passionate commitment to "theory" and to scholarship; Lenin's, as a comparison with many revolutionary leaders in underdeveloped countries will show, required a combination of iron will, political flexibility, and "charisma."

Leninism, with its emphasis on the key role of intellectuals in revolutionary movements of underdeveloped countries, became irrelevant in the industrialized Soviet Union, but it may retain its relevance for intellectuals in industrially more backward countries, like Ethiopia. Kautsky's conception of the role of intellectuals in the labor movements of industrialized countries has lost its relevance, as these movements are no longer in need of a "theory" or a "final" goal of socialism to give them hope, strength, and unity.[90] But whatever their present-day relevance, Kautsky's and Lenin's conceptions of the role of intellectuals can be seen as important elements in the evolution of the two very different ideologies of Marxism and Leninism. An explanation of the differences between these conceptions in terms of the different environments in which they arose, such as I have at least hinted at here, should help make the point that Marxism and Leninism are, indeed, two distinct ideologies. This should not be obscured by the way Lenin quoted Kautsky in *What Is to Be Done?*, though Lenin was all too successful in concealing it from himself and from many in his own and subsequent generations.

Some thirty years ago, my friend, Morris Watnick, urged me to write a note on Lenin quoting Kautsky in *What Is to Be Done?*. Now that I have at last got around to doing that and a bit more, I wish he could still be among those who read and helpfully commented on the draft of this article. They are Moira Donald, Jack Knight, Alfred Meyer, Bernard Morris, Leo van Rossum, Peter Schwartz, Sanjay Seth, and Gary Steenson. I am grateful to all of them and to Morris Watnick.

Notes

1. See especially Lenin's extensive direct attacks on Kautsky in his works *Imperialism, the Highest Stage of Capitalism* (1916); *The State and Revolution* (1917); and *The Proletarian Revolution and the Renegade Kautsky* (1918), in V. I. Lenin, *Collected Works,* 45 vols. (Moscow: Progress Publishers, 1960–70), 22:185–304; 25:385–497; 28:227–325; and Kautsky, *The Dictatorship of the Proletariat* (1918) (Westport, Conn.: Greenwood Press, 1981); *Terrorism and Communism* (1919) (Westport, Conn.: Hyperion Press, 1973); *The Labour Revolution* (1922) (New York: Dial Press, 1925), 22–89.

2. "Preface" to vol. 5 of Lenin, *Collected Works,* 5:11.

3. Lenin, *What Is to Be Done?*, in *Collected Works,* 45 vols. (Moscow: Progress Publishers, 1960–70), 5:375. All quotations from Lenin in this chapter are taken from this edition. For a discussion of Lenin's thought on "consciousness," drawing on many of his writings, see Alfred G. Meyer, *Leninism* (New York: Praeger, 1962), 19–56.

4. Lenin, *What Is to Be* Done?, 383–84. The quotation is from Karl Kautsky, "Die Revision des Programms der Sozialdemokratie in Österreich," *Die Neue Zeit* 20/1 (1901) : 79–80. Lenin himself provides the German word *"urwüchsig"*, which means "originally," and thus points up his own questionable translation of it as "spontaneously," which he prefers, because it fits into his argument against "spontaneity" that is central to his analysis in *What Is to Be Done?*.

5. Neil Harding, *Lenin's Political Thought* (New York: St. Martin's Press, 1977), 1:169. Oddly, Harding asserts, in his note 17 on pp. 323–24, that the first half of the passage by Kautsky, which I quoted above, was not quoted by Lenin, though it

is in fact quoted in the source that both he and I use, that is, the edition of Lenin's *Collected Works* that is a translation of the fourth Russian edition.

6. Harding, *Lenin's Political Thought,* 285.

7. Iring Fetscher, *Marx and Marxism* (New York: Herder & Herder, 1971), 103. Kautsky is also described as "a precursor of Lenin's party and organization theory" by Kurt Lenk, *Theorien der Revolution,* 2d ed. (Munich: Wilhelm Fink, 1981), 146, on the basis of the same passage that Lenin quoted from Kautsky (and which Lenk wrongly ascribes to Kautsky's article "Akademiker und Proletarier," to which I will refer below). I am indebted to Reinhold Hünlich, *Karl Kautsky und der Marxismus der II. Internationale* (Marburg: Verlag Arbeiterbewegung und Gesellschaftswissenschaft, 1981), 96–97, for calling my attention to the statements by Fetscher and Lenk that I have quoted. He refers to their line of thought as representing a "legend."

8. Dick Geary, "Max Weber, Karl Kautsky and German Social Democracy," in *Max Weber and his Contemporaries,* ed. Wolfgang J. Mommsen and Jürgen Osterhammel (London: Allen & Unwin, 1987), 357. In support, Geary cites (in a note) *Die Neue Zeit* 19/2 (1901): 80–90, presumably to refer to Kautsky's "Akademiker und Proletarier" on pp. 89–91 of this volume of *Die Neue Zeit.* The passage just quoted also appeared in another, largely identical article by Dick Geary, "Karl Kautsky and German Marxism," in *Rediscoveries: Some Neglected European Thinkers,* ed. John A. Hall (Oxford: Clarendon Press, 1986), 176. In his book *Karl Kautsky* (Manchester: Manchester University Press, 1987), 30, Geary refers to "the theory of 'consciousness from without' " as "perhaps Kautsky's most important contribution to Marxist theory" and repeats that "when Lenin lifted it wholesale in *What is to be done?* (1902), it was Kautsky, not the Russian revolutionary tradition, which he quoted." In an earlier review article, Geary had written that Kautsky "elaborated the theory of 'consciousness from without' – the idea that the working class would only come to revolutionary politics with the aid of the bourgeois intelligentsia – which became the basis of Lenin's revolutionary strategy." Dick Geary, "Karl Kautsky and 'Scientific Marxism,' " *Radical Science Journal* 11 (1981): 130.

George Lichtheim, in his classic work *Marxism: An Historical and Critical Study* (New York: Praeger, 1961), 336–37, merely says of Lenin's view of workers' socialist consciousness as an "extraneous element" that, "though decked out with appropriate quotations from Kautsky, this notion was at best of dubious orthodoxy." An author whose more recent book comments on Lenin quoting Kautsky but who clearly understands the difference between the two, is Axel van den Berg, in his *Immanent Utopia* (Princeton: Princeton University Press, 1988), 124–27. For other comments, see Martin Seliger, *The Marxist Concept of Ideology* (Cambridge: Cambridge University Press, 1977), 92–94.

9. For two articles, based largely on unpublished letters, that throw light on Kautsky's attitude, see Dietrich Geyer, "Die russische Parteispaltung im Urteil der deutschen

Sozialdemokratie, 1903–1905," *International Review of Social History* 3 (1958): 195–219, 418–44; and Abraham Ascher, "Axelrod and Kautsky," *Slavic Review* 26, no. 1 (March 1967): 96–106. See also Peter Lösche, *Der Bolschewismus im Urteil der deutschen Sozialdemokratie, 1903–1920* (Berlin: Colloquium Verlag, 1967), 28–66.

10. Rosa Luxemburg, "Organisationsfragen der russischen Sozialdemokratie," *Die Neue Zeit* 22/2 (1904): 484–92, 529–35; (unreliably) translated into English in Rosa Luxemburg, *The Russian Revolution* and *Leninism or Marxism?* (Ann Arbor: University of Michigan Press, 1961), 81–108.

11. Kautsky, "Die Differenzen unter den russischen Sozialisten," *Die Neue Zeit* 23/2 (1905): 70.

12. In the twelve months following the publication of *What Is to Be Done?*, Kautsky published *The Social Revolution* and two smaller brochures as well as ten articles in *Die Neue Zeit* and several contributions to German and foreign newspapers; none of these writings was concerned with Russia. Werner Blumenberg, *Karl Kautskys literarisches Werk* (The Hague: Mouton, 1960), 63–68. It was principally only in later years, especially in 1905–1906 and from 1917 on, that Kautsky wrote a lot on Russian developments.

13. According to S. V. Utechin's "Preface" to his edition of *V. I. Lenin's What Is to Be Done?* (Oxford: Clarendon Press, 1963), v, it was first published as a separate pamphlet (in Russian) in Geneva in 1902.

14. "For two decades [*What Is to Be Done?*] remained completely unknown outside the Russian-language-speaking world." Friedrich Adler, "Karl Kautsky," *Der Sozialistische Kampf* (Paris) no. 12 (5 November 1938): 270. According to the bibliography *Lenins Werk in deutscher Sprache* (East Berlin: Dietz Verlag, 1967), 64, the first complete German translation, *Was Tun?*, appeared in 1929 in Lenin, *Sämtliche Werke* (Vienna: Verlag für Literatur und Politik), 4/2:125–346, and excerpts had been published by the same publisher in 1924, 1925, and 1927. The first French translation to which I found a reference, *Que faire?*, appeared in 1925 (Paris: Librairie de l'humanité); the first English one was published in 1929 (London Martin Lawrence; and New York: International Publishers; also in 1929 in *Collected Works of V. I. Lenin,* 4: "The Iskra Period," book 2, New York: International Publishers).

15. Lenin, *What Is to Be Done?*, 384–85. Italics in this quotation and all subsequent ones appear in the original. Lenin repeats, ibid., 426, that "trade-unionist politics of the working class is precisely *bourgeois politics* of the working class," and, on p. 437, he states: "*any* subservience to the spontaneity of the mass movement and *any* degrading of Social-Democratic politics to the level of trade-unionist politics mean preparing the ground for converting the working-class movement into an instrument of bourgeois democracy. The spontaneous working-class movement is by itself able to create (and inevitably does create) only trade-unionism, and working-class trade-unionist politics is precisely working-class bourgeois poli-

tics." On p. 475, Lenin writes: "the spontaneous struggle of the proletariat will not become its genuine 'class struggle' until this struggle is led by a strong organization of revolutionaries." A year earlier, Lenin had written: "Isolated from Social-Democracy, the working-class movement . . . inevitably becomes bourgeois." "The Urgent Tasks of Our Movement," Lenin, *Collected Works,* 4:368.

16. Kautsky, *Der Parlamentarismus, die Volksgesetzgebung und die Sozialdemokratie* (Stuttgart: J. H. W. Dietz, 1893), 134.

17. In 1892 in his book on the Erfurt Program Kautsky spoke of pre-Marxian "proletarian socialists," their "violent revolutionary socialism," and "original working-class socialism." *Das Erfurter Programm,* 19th ed. (Bonn: J. H. W. Dietz, 1974), 226. The English translation of this work, *The Class Struggle* (New York: Norton, 1971), is incomplete and unreliable. Indeed, in 1895 in his *Communism in Central Europe in the Time of the Reformation* (New York: Russell & Russell, 1959), 28, 53–77, 121–54, 190–215, 256–62, 293, and also in 1888 in his *Thomas More and His Utopia* (New York: Russell & Russell, 1959), 189–90, Kautsky had ascribed socialist or "communist" consciousness to the lower classes in the German Peasant War and among heretical sects, like the Taborites and the Anabaptists, already at the beginnings of capitalism in the sixteenth century, and later, in 1908, in his *Foundations of Christianity* (New York: Monthly Review Press, 1972), he ascribed socialist consciousness even to the early Christians. I am indebted to the doctoral dissertation by Alan M. Shandro, "Orthodox Marxism and the Emergence of Lenin's Conception of Revolutionary Hegemony" (University of Manchester, 1983), for calling my attention to the relevance of Kautsky's writings on religious movements to the distinction between his and Lenin's concepts of socialist consciousness.

18. Kautsky, *Die historische Leistung von Karl Marx,* 2d ed. (Berlin: Buchhandlung Vorwärts, 1919), 35.

19. Ibid., ch. 5: "Die Vereinigung von Arbeiterbewegung und Sozialismus." In this chapter, Kautsky restates what he had said in the passage quoted by Lenin about the separate origins of the labor movement and socialism, and then he adds that "Marx always . . . claimed that the only power capable of bringing about the success of socialism was the working class. In other words, the proletariat can emancipate itself only by its own strength. Which by no means says that only proletarians are able to point its way in this direction." Ibid., 28. Kautsky adds that it was today obvious "that socialism is nothing, if it is not carried by a strong labor movement, [but] that the labor movement can develop its full strength only if it has comprehended and accepted socialism," because only socialist theory points out the community of interest of the different proletarian strata vis-à-vis capitalism. Ibid., 28–29.

20. Kautsky, *Das Erfurter Programm,* 208.

21. As Kautsky put it quite generally in an article in 1896: "The standpoint from which the mass of members of a particular class approaches a specific problem is essentially given, and thus the direction in which it seeks the solution to the

problem is also given for that class. This standpoint can be traced back to the specific economic conditions of society." Kautsky, "Was will und kann die materialistische Geschichtsauffassung leisten?," *Die Neue Zeit* 15/1 (1896): 235.

22. Kautsky, *Bernstein und das sozialdemokratische Programm: Eine Anti-Kritik,* 3rd ed. (Bonn: J. H. W. Dietz, 1979), 53.

23. Kautsky to Adler, 25 October 1901, in Friedrich Adler, ed., Victor Adler, *Briefwechsel mit Karl Kautsky und August Bebel* (Vienna: Wiener Volksbuchhandlung, 1954), 375.

24. Kautsky, *Das Erfurter Programm,* 208. See also Adam Przeworski, *Capitalism and Social Democracy* (Cambridge: Cambridge University Press, 1985), 51–55.

25. Kautsky, *Das Erfurter Programm,* 230. Kautsky's 1899 definition of Social Democracy tends to distinguish it from the labor movement, but not so as to have it divert the latter: "Social Democracy is the party of the militant proletariat; it seeks to enlighten it, to educate it, to organize it, to expand its political and economic power by every available means, to conquer every position that can possibly be conquered, and thus to provide it with the strength and maturity that will finally enable it to conquer political power and to overthrow the rule of the bourgeoisie." "Zum Parteitag von Hannover," *Die Neue Zeit* 18/1 (1899): 13.

26. Kautsky, *Das Erfurter Programm,* 218–19, 222. See also Kautsky, *Der Parlamentarismus,* 111.

27. Kautsky himself says: "When one speaks of the irresistibility and natural necessity of social development, one obviously presupposes that men are men and not dead puppets; men with certain needs and passions, with certain physical and mental powers that they seek to use in their own interest. . . . We consider the collapse of present-day society inevitable, because we know that economic development produces, with natural necessity, conditions that compel the exploited to fight against private property." Kautsky, *Das Erfurter Programm,* 102.

28. According to Kautsky, Marx and Engels had proved that socialism was the "naturally necessary [*naturnotwendige*] consequence of economic development." Ibid., 230. More generally, Kautsky always considered it a key element of his materialist conception of history that the human mind could not, on its own, originate anything new, but could only react to changes in its environment. See, for example, Kautsky, *The Materialist Conception of History,* abridged ed. (New Haven, Conn.: Yale University Press, 1988), 38–40, 168–70, 213–16.

29. Especially *What Is to Be Done?,* 464.

30. "Akademiker und Proletarier," *Die Neue Zeit* 19/2 (1901): 89–90.

31. Ibid., 90. Six years earlier, in an article exploring the question of which intellectuals might become Social Democrats, Kautsky had similarly written that "students should participate in the class struggle of the proletariat not as *teachers* and not as *fighters* but as *learners.* . . . They should come to us to *learn,* to get to know our *literature,* but also our *movement.* To attain a complete understanding of socialism . . . they must . . . come to know the proletariat, . . . the *working* and

fighting proletariat." Kautsky, "Die Intelligenz und die Sozialdemokratie," *Die Neue Zeit* 13/2 (1895): 79.

32. Kautsky, "Akademiker und Proletarier," 90. Engels had made a similar point about dative and accusative when, in a letter to Bernstein, he blamed Liebknecht for drawing narrow-minded petty bourgeois (spiessbürgerliche) elements into the Party, thinking that "nothing worse could happen than that a worker might sometime confuse "mir" and "mich" in the Reichstag." Engels to Bernstein, 27 February 1883, in Karl Marx, Friedrich Engels, *Werke,* 35 (East Berlin: Dietz Verlag, 1967), 443.

33. Kautsky, "Akademiker und Proletarier," 91.

34. Kautsky to Adler, 4 April 1903, in Friedrich Adler, ed., Victor Adler, *Briefwechsel,* 415.

35. This is spelled out very clearly in Kautsky, *Die historische Leistung von Karl Marx,* 26–27.

36. Przeworski, *Capitalism,* 48.

37. Moira Donald, "Karl Kautsky and Russian Social Democracy before the First World War," in *Marxismus und Demokratie: Karl Kautskys Bedeutung in der sozialistischen Arbeiterbewegung,* ed. Jürgen Rojahn, Till Schelz, Hans-Josef Steinberg (Frankfurt: Campus Verlag, 1992), 253. The reference is to *Vospominaniia o V.I. Lenine* (Moscow: Izd-vo polit. lit-ry, 1979), 1:117 Lenin had also translated Kautsky's book against Bernstein and, in *What Is to Be Done?,* 481, had quoted from Kautsky, *Der Parlamentarismus,* two other books cited above as disagreeing with Lenin.

38. Ernest Mandel even asserts that the way Kautsky here formulated the thought that socialist consciousness is introduced into the labor movement from without "directly inspired Lenin's *What Is to Be Done?"* Ernest Mandel, "Lenin und das Problem des proletarischen Klassenbewusstseins," in Paul Mattick et al., *Lenin: Revolution und Politik* (Frankfurt: Suhrkamp, 1970), 150, n. 1.

39. Cf. Donald, "Karl Kautsky," 252–53, and B. Nikolajewsky, "Karl Kautsky in Russland," in *Ein Leben für den Sozialismus: Erinnerungen an Karl Kautsky,* ed. Benedikt Kautsky (Hanover: J. H. W. Dietz, 1954), 93.

40. In 1901 in "The Agrarian Question and the 'Critics of Marx,' " *Collected Works,* 5:103–222, Lenin quotes at length (on pp. 152–53) from a minor article by Kautsky, "Tolstoi und Brentano," *Die Neue Zeit* 19/2 (1901): 20–28, which appeared only two weeks before "Akademiker und Proletarier," and he sharply attacks (on pp. 147–48) a Russian critic of Kautsky for ignoring a passage published by the latter in late 1899 in "Zwei Kritiker meiner Agrarfrage," *Die Neue Zeit* 18/1 (1899): 292–300, 338–46,363–68, 428–36, 470–77. This suggests that Lenin read *Die Neue Zeit* very carefully in the period before and when he wrote *What Is to Be Done?*

41. "Shortly after the 1903 split in the Russian Social Democratic Party both the Mensheviks and the Bolsheviks tried to win Kautsky's approval, on the assumption that the German's prestige in the international socialist movement was so

great that the side he supported would emerge victorious." Ascher, "Axelrod," 96.

42. Marx's and Engels's thought on the subject of proletarian socialist consciousness is beyond the scope of this article. It may be noted, however, that they tended toward the belief that class consciousness develops in the course of the class struggle without being brought to the workers from without. The statement by Marx most explicitly contradicting Lenin's contempt for trade unionism and spontaneity is probably the following one made by him in Hanover on 30 September 1869 to J. Hamann, an official of the General German Metalworkers Union as reported by the latter: "The trade unions . . . must never be connected with or made dependent on a political organization. . . . The trade unions are the schools for socialism. . . . The greater mass of workers has attained the insight that their material condition must be improved. . . . But if the worker's material condition is improved, then he can devote himself more to the education of his children, his wife and children need no longer go to the factory, he himself can better cultivate his mind and look after his body, he becomes a socialist without having an inkling of it [*ohne dass er es ahnt*]." *Volksstaat* (Leipzig) no. 17 (27 November 1869), quoted by August Bringmann, *Geschichte der deutschen Zimmererbewegung* (Stuttgart: J. H. W. Dietz, 1903), 1:364, and by Kautsky, "Sekte oder Klassenpartei?," *Die Neue Zeit* 27/2 (1909): 7. Another English translation of the full statement appears in Frederic L. Bender, ed., *Karl Marx: The Essential Writings,* 2d ed. (Boulder: Westview Press, 1986), 496–97. See also the editorial note in Marx, Engels, *Werke,* 16 (East Berlin: Dietz Verlag, 1964), 734, which claims, without presenting any evidence, that the report of the interview in the *Volksstaat* is distorted.

The contrast is also striking between, on the one hand, Lenin's view quoted above that "the task of Social-Democracy is *to combat spontaneity, to divert* the working-class movement" from its spontaneous striving, and, on the other, these words of Marx written in 1866: "It is the business of the International Working Men's Association to combine and generalize the *spontaneous movements* of the working classes, but not to dictate or impose any doctrinary system whatever." Karl Marx, "Instructions for Delegates to the Geneva Congress," in Karl Marx, *The First International and After* (New York: Vintage Books, 1974), 90.

43. By 1901 Lenin had written wholly favorable reviews (*Collected Works,* 4:94–99, 193–203) of Kautsky's two major works of 1899, *The Agrarian Question,* 2 vols. (London: Zwan, 1988) — Lenin called it "the most important event in present-day economic literature since the third volume of *Capital*" — and *Bernstein und das Sozialdemokratische Programm* as well as two lengthy articles wholly or partly in defense of *The Agrarian Question* ("Capitalism in Agriculture," *Collected Works,* 4 :105–159, and "The Agrarian Question and the 'Critics of Marx,' " ibid., 5:103–222). Here Kautsky is, like Marx and Engels, invariably treated as an unfailing fountain of unquestionable truths, and those who disagree with him are savagely attacked and ridiculed.

It should be noted, however, that a few years later, when Lenin responded to comments by Kautsky on Russian Social Democratic Party factionalism, his remarks were anything but admiring. In reply to Kautsky's article "Die Spaltung der russischen Sozialdemokratie" in the *Leipziger Volkszeitung* of 15 June 1905, he wrote that Kautsky's "picture of the relations that exist in the Russian Social-Democracy is a highly distorted one" and he added: "Kautsky has no right to speak about his impartiality. He has always been partial as regards the present struggle within the Russian Social-Democracy. This is his right, of course. But one who is partial would do better not to speak too much of impartiality, if he does not want to be accused of hypocrisy." "Open Letter to the Editorial Board of the *Leipziger Volkszeitung*," *Collected Works*, 8:531, 532. In December 1913, still some months before his break with Kautsky, Lenin referred to a speech by Kautsky on Russian party affairs at the International Socialist Bureau as a "monstrous statement" and "a sad curiosity," and to Kautsky's "stupendous" confusion, "his most deplorable ignorance of Russian Party life" and his "unpardonable mistake." But he blamed "irresponsible emigré coteries" and "liquidator whisperers" for misleading foreign comrades. "A Good Resolution and a Bad Speech," *Collected Works*, 19:528–30, and "Kautsky's Unpardonable Error," ibid., 20:63–64.

44. That consistency is stressed by Massimo Salvadori, *Karl Kautsky and the Socialist Revolution 1880–1938* (London: New Left Books, 1979). He says: "[T]hroughout his activity, or at least from the beginning of the 1890s to his death in 1938, Kautsky maintained a 'consistent' conception of the modern state, of the role of parliament, of the function of the political and civil liberties bequeathed by bourgeois liberalism, . . . and of the importance of political democracy as an instrument for assuring knowledge of society and ascertaining the will of its citizens. Kautsky's point of view on all such problems remained remarkably constant." Ibid., 11–12; see also 251–55. "There was never any real 'apostasy' or 'betrayal.' Rather two antithetical conceptions of socialism had taken the field against each other." Ibid., 255.

45. Lösche, *Der Bolschewismus*. 16. "Anyone who takes the trouble to collect the quotations concerning Kautsky in Lenin's pre-war writings will soon be convinced that Lenin regards this man as no less than an oracle." Franz Borkenau, *World Communism: A History of the Communist International* (Ann Arbor: University of Michigan Press, 1962), 50.

46. It is neither possible nor necessary to stress here that labor movements in industrialized countries and modernizing revolutionary movements in underdeveloped countries, which sometimes call themselves "Communist" or "Marxist," are quite different, even if they confuse themselves and others by using a similar vocabulary. I develop the sociology-of-knowledge argument that the two kinds of movements have two very different ideologies in my forthcoming book *Marxism and Leninism, not Marxism-Leninism*.

47. For an interpretation of post-1890 Social Democratic policy as a response to this

situation, see Guenther Roth, *The Social Democrats in Imperial Germany: A Study in Working-Class Isolation and National Integration* (Totowa, N.J.: Bedminster, 1963), especially 163–71, 184–92.

48. In his famous statement that the "final goal of socialism . . . is nothing at all to me, the movement is everything" (Eduard Bernstein, "Der Kampf der Sozialdemokratie und die Revolution der Gesellschaft," *Die Neue Zeit* 16/1 [1898]: 556), Bernstein showed an awareness that Kautsky lacked of the difference between myth and reality. He failed to see, however, that the myth of the final goal may be needed for the movement to function or even to exist, the assumption on which Kautsky acted.

49. On the SPD policy of "separation," "official self-differentiation," and irreconcilable "non-participating opposition," see Peter Nettl, "The German Social Democratic Party 1890–1914 as a Political Model," *Past and Present* no. 30 (April 1965): 65–95, who refers to Kautsky as "the champion of social isolation." Ibid., 66–67, 82.

50. Dieter Groh, Negative *Integration and revolutionärer Attentismus: Die deutsche Sozialdemokratie am Vorabend des Ersten Weltkrieges* (Frankfurt: Ullstein-Propyläen, 1973), especially 36.

51. Kautsky, "Ein sozialdemokratischer Katechismus," *Die Neue Zeit* 12/1 (1893): 368.

52. Friedrich Engels, "Grundsätze des Kommunismus" in Marx, Engels, *Werke*, 4 (East-Berlin: Dietz Verlag, 1964), 372.

53. Hobsbawm is wrong, I think, when he refers to it as "Kautsky's embarrassed redefinition of the SPD," but, more important in our context, he is quite right in saying that it "could not but be meaningless for Lenin." Eric Hobsbawm, "Preface" to Georges Haupt, *Aspects of International Socialism, 1871–1914* (Cambridge: Cambridge University Press, 1986), xiv.

54. Kautsky, *Der Weg zur Macht: Politische Betrachtungen über das Hineinwachsen in die Revolution* (Frankfurt: Europäische Verlagsanstalt, 1972). See my article on this book below.

55. Kautsky, *Der Weg zur Macht*, 12, 91–92, 109–10.

56. Kautsky felt that both Revisionist and radical policies had to be opposed as impatient, and hence un-Marxian, attempts to bring the proletariat to power before it and the "material conditions" had sufficiently developed. See Kautsky, *Der politische Massenstreik* (Berlin: Vorwärts, 1914), 215–22, 247.

57. On 21 July 1910 Trotsky wrote to Kautsky that Lenin was "of the opinion that you are quite right in your judgment as to the present political situation," and Trotsky added: "I at any rate have not met a single Comrade — even among the Bolsheviks — who has come out openly for Luxemburg." Quoted in J. P. Nettl, *Rosa Luxemburg* (London: Oxford University Press, 1966), 1:433. See also Marek Waldenberg, "Kautskys Marx-Rezeption," in *Marxismus und Demokratie*, ed. Rojahn et al., 36.

    In the same year, Lenin referred to "the differences which had arisen between Luxemburg and Kautsky" as "not of prime importance." "Two Worlds," *Collected*

Works, 16:312. See also his "The Historical Meaning of the Inner-Party Struggle in Russia," ibid., 383.

On 31 January 1911, that is, after the Kautsky-Luxemburg controversy, Lenin wrote an extremely friendly letter to Kautsky, asking him for an article for his journal *Mysl.* "Needless to say, we shall be happy to receive any article from you on any subject." He also asked for advice as to articles he might write for *Die Neue Zeit.* Lenin, "To Karl Kautsky," *Collected Works,* 43:263–65, and, in German, in *International Review of Social History,* 9/2 (1964): 259–62.

58. Lenin's failure to support Rosa Luxemburg against Kautsky may also have been due to the fact that he remembered her attacks on his "ultra-centralism" in 1904. He was, moreover, involved in a bitter conflict with her over the organization and unity of the Polish Social Democratic Party.

59. At the meeting of the SPD Reichstag caucus [*Fraktion*] on 3 August, which decided that the Party should vote the war credits to the government the next day, Kautsky, not a member of the Reichstag himself, proposed that such a vote be made contingent on a promise by the government to conclude the war without any annexations or reparations. He felt sure that the government would refuse to make such a promise, which would then permit the SPD deputies, in spite of pro-war pressure from their patriotic constituents, to vote against the war credits, or at least to abstain. This is how Kautsky describes his proposal and his motivation in his *Sozialisten und Krieg* (Prague: Orbis, 1937), 446–57. For a more critical scholarly analysis, see Jürgen Rojahn, "Kautsky im Ersten Weltkrieg," in *Marxismus und Demokratie,* ed. Rojahn et al., 199–219. See also Susanne Miller, *Burgfrieden und Klassenkampf: Die deutsche Sozialdemokratie im Ersten Weltkrieg* (Düsseldorf: Droste Verlag, 1974), 64–65. In 1917 Kautsky joined the Independent Social Democratic Party (USPD) upon its formation to oppose the government's war policy. On his attitude, see his *Sozialisten und Krieg,* 468–76, and his *Mein Verhältnis zur Unabhängigen Sozialdemokratischen Partei* (Berlin: Breitscheid, 1922).

60. Kautsky, *Sozialisten und Krieg,* 464–68, 491–92, 500, 547. Lenin's views appear in many pieces of writing in volume 21 of his *Collected Works.*

61. This, too, is evident from his writings in volume 21 of *Collected Works.*

62. Lenin, *Collected Works,* 22:301.

63. As early as 1 November 1914, Lenin wrote: "The Second International is dead, overcome by opportunism. . . . Long live the Third International, purged not only of 'turncoats' . . . but of opportunism as well." "The Position and Tasks of the Socialist International," *Collected Works,* 21:40.

64. See, for example, Kautsky's letter of 1904 to M. Liadov (Lydin), published by R. Abramowitsch, "Karl Kautsky und der Richtungsstreit in der russischen Sozialdemokratie," in Benedikt Kautsky, ed., *Ein Leben,* 87.

65. "The fanatical personal hatred with which Lenin pursued Karl Kautsky after August 1914 cannot be explained simply on grounds of differences of opinion. Such

hatred can only be entertained by a person who has formerly loved greatly. After 1914 Lenin sought to revenge himself upon Kautsky for having mistakenly admired his ideas and organization for twenty years past." Arthur Rosenberg, *A History of Bolshevism* (Garden City, N.Y.: Doubleday, 1967), 76–77. "[F]rom 1914 till his death, Lenin poured more abuse [on Kautsky] than upon any other single adversary; which means much, in view of the unscrupulous forms of abuse which Lenin, as other fanatics, consistently used in his polemics." Borkenau, *World Communism*, 53.

66. Insistence on the presence of certain prerequisites for a socialist revolution to be possible—as well, as I noted, insistence that democracy was a necessity in the workers' organizations and in the state, both before and after the socialist revolution—were recurrent themes in Kautsky's writings decades before the Bolsheviks made them major controversial issues. A characteristic passage occurs in *The Road to Power* (1909), which Lenin so admired: "While [Blanqui] believed that he could capture the government by a conspiracy, a coup d'état of a small minority, and to make it serve proletarian interests, Marx and Engels recognized that revolutions cannot be made at will, but that they necessarily arise under certain conditions and remain impossible as long as these conditions, which develop only gradually, are not present. Only where the capitalist mode of production is highly developed is it economically possible to transform through the government the capitalist property in the means of production into social property. On the other hand, the possibility of conquering and holding on to the government arises for the proletariat only where it has grown into a great mass that is economically indispensable, is in large part firmly organized, and understands its class position as well as the nature of the state and of society." Kautsky, *Der Weg zur Macht*, 16. In the same book, Kautsky also quoted a 1904 article of his, saying: "A revolution in Russia could not, for the present, establish a socialist regime. For that the economic conditions of the country are too immature. It could at first only create a democratic regime." Ibid., 25, quoted from "Allerhand Revolutionäres," *Die Neue Zeit* 22/1 (1904): 625.

67. This is obviously not the place to deal with the post-1917 Kautsky-Lenin polemics. Salvadori, *Karl Kautsky*, 251–93, devotes a chapter to summarizing Kautsky's major and a few minor writings against the Bolsheviks, and Peter Lübbe, ed., *Kautsky gegen Lenin* (Bonn: J. H. W. Dietz, 1981) conveniently reprints a dozen of the latter. Here I may simply provide references to some passages in Kautsky's post-1917 writings that deal with the role of intellectuals: *The Dictatorship of the Proletariat*, 49–50; *Terrorism and Communism*, 189–91; *Die proletarische Revolution und ihr Programm* (Stuttgart: J. H. W. Dietz, 1922), 37–39; *The Materialist Conception of History*, 397–400, 408; *Bolshevism at a Deadlock* (London: Allen & Unwin, 1931), 124–26.

68. Lenin, *Collected Works*, 25:482, 487. Lenin also finds here (p. 489) that "Kautsky completely abandoned the Marxist position and went over wholly to opportunism" in "Die neue Taktik," *Die Neue Zeit* 30/2 (1912): 654–64, 688–98, 723–33, an ar-

ticle against Pannekoek, who was close to Rosa Luxemburg on the issue of the mass strike.

69. Donald, "Karl Kautsky," 254. She refers to *Vospominaniia o V.I. Lenine*, 1:232.
70. Lenin, *Collected Works*, 4:193–203.
71. Ibid., 25:483–84.
72. A fairly recent example is Hans-Jürgen Mende, *Karl Kautsky — vom Marxisten zum Opportunisten* (East Berlin: Dietz Verlag, 1985). It may be noted that after the revolution of 1989–90 in East Germany, the same author called for a positive reevaluation of Kautsky's work in his "Nachwort" to two volumes reprinting the Kautsky-Lenin-Trotsky polemics of 1918–21. Hans-Jürgen Mende, ed., *Demokratie oder Diktatur?* (Berlin: Dietz Verlag, 1990), 2: 285–301.
73. In his controversy with Rosa Luxemburg, Kautsky stressed that the Russian Revolution of 1905 could not be a model for Germany. He was fond of quoting Marx's dictum (from the preface to the first edition of *Capital*) that "the country that is more developed industrially only shows, to the less developed, the image of its own future," but he did not see that that dictum has not proved accurate beyond Western Europe, in underdeveloped countries, and that Germany therefore could be no model for Russia, any more than Russia could be one for Germany.
74. That he did not retain this position after 1914 as a "Kautskyist" is another story. On it, see the insightful article by David W. Morgan, "The Eclipse of Karl Kautsky, 1914–1924," *International Journal of Comparative Sociology* 30, no. 1–2 (January–April 1989): 57–67.
75. Lacking the model of revolutions in underdeveloped countries so amply available to us, especially since the end of World War II, they thought of the Russian Revolution, both before and when it occurred, as paralleling the French Revolution and the Paris Commune. Even when two of the greatest revolutions in underdeveloped countries — the Mexican and the Chinese — broke out a few years before 1917, European Marxists, including Russian Marxists, virtually ignored them. Lenin wrote two very brief and quite superficial articles offering hardly any analysis at all of the Chinese Revolution (*Collected Works*, 18:163–69, 400–401) and none on Mexico. Kautsky wrote nothing on either revolution, though his *Neue Zeit* published two substantial articles on the Chinese Revolution (29/2 [1911]: 37–42, 80–84; and 30/1 [1911–12]: 372–85, 494–506, 557–70) and one on the Mexican Revolution 29/2 [1911]: 396–402).
76. I analyzed the patterns of revolutionary politics in underdeveloped countries and stressed the role of intellectuals in them at greater length in earlier writings, especially in *The Political Consequences of Modernization* (New York: John Wiley, 1972). In particular, I interpreted Russian and Communist history in terms of these patterns in *Communism and the Politics of Development* (New York: John Wiley, 1968) and in *Patterns of Modernizing Revolutions: Mexico and the Soviet Union.* Sage Professional Papers in Comparative Politics, vol. 5, series no. 01–056 (Beverly Hills: Sage Publications, 1975).

77. Franz Borkenau had already seen and briefly noted this in 1939, when he wrote: "Lenin's revolution is essentially not a proletarian revolution, it is *'the* revolution' of the intelligentsia, of the professional revolutionaries, but with the proletariat as their chief ally. Allies, however, are exchangeable. The course of the Russian dictatorship has proved that instead of the proletariat other groups could step in." Borkenau, *World Communism,* 44.

78. Kautsky, "Die Breslauer Resolution und ihre Kritik," *Die Neue Zeit,* 14/1 (1895): 186.

79. As Lenin himself wrote in *What Is to Be Done?*: "our task is to utilise every manifestation of discontent, and to gather and turn to the best account every protest, however small. . . . Indeed, is there a single social class in which there are no individuals, groups, or circles that are discontented with the lack of rights and with tyranny and, therefore, accessible to the propaganda of Social-Democrats?" *What Is to Be Done?,* 430.

80. Kautsky to Bebel, 14 February 1885, in Karl Kautsky, Jr., ed., *August Bebels Briefwechsel mit Karl Kautsky* (Assen: Van Gorcum, 1971), 27. Kautsky also expressed his dislike for intellectuals in a letter to Bebel of 8 November 1884, ibid., 24, and in letters to Engels of 31 May 1882, 14 September 1883, and 29 May 1884, in Benedikt Kautsky, ed., *Friedrich Engels' Briefwechsel mit Karl Kautsky* (Vienna: Danubia, 1955), 58, 81, 118.

81. From a letter to Heinrich Braun, 17 January 1894, quoted by Alfred G. Meyer, *The Feminism and Socialism of Lily Braun* (Bloomington: Indiana University Press, 1985), 43. In the same letter Kautsky wrote: "You have always sought to draw the 'intelligentsia' into our movement, while in my opinion it has always been our most important task vis-á-vis the literary people and students who seek to approach us to view them with mistrust and to let no one who has not proved himself occupy a position of trust." Quoted by Julie Braun-Vogelstein, *Heinrich Braun: Ein Leben für den Sozialismus* (Stuttgart: Deutsche Verlags-Anstalt, 1967), 131.

82. For references to Kautsky's many relevant writings, see my note in my abridged edition of Kautsky, *The Materialist Conception of History,* 398.

83. For an excellent explanation of Kautsky's role as a party intellectual, see Ingrid Gilcher-Holtey, *Das Mandat des Intellektuellen: Karl Kautsky und die Sozialdemokratie* (Berlin: Siedler, 1986).

84. As Kautsky said (and as Lenin could never have said of himself): "I myself felt not the least qualification to be the leader of the Party. I was always very happy if there was a man in the Party who did have that qualification and to whom I could give my confidence and my support." Kautsky, *Erinnerungen und Erörterungen* (The Hauge: Mouton, 1960), 325. And to Victor Adler he wrote: "I always feel insecure in practical and tactical matters." Kautsky to Adler, 13 February 1914, Friedrich Adler, ed., Victor Adler, *Briefwechsel,* 592.

85. Kautsky "Der Parteitag in Lübeck," *Die Neue Zeit* 20/1 (1901): 19-20.

86. "In *What Is to Be Done?* Lenin strode a step closer to his ultimate goal of trans-

forming Marxism into a revolutionary doctrine for backward nations." James E. Connor, "Introduction" to Connor, ed., *Lenin on Politics and Revolution* (New York: Pegasus, 1968), xxi. "By vigorously asserting the legitimacy of the activist interpretation, Lenin took the first step in transforming Marxism into an ideology for underdeveloped areas." Ibid, xx. For an insightful analysis of the relevance of Leninism to the politics of underdevelopment, see Meyer, *Leninism,* 257–73.

87. Gilcher-Holtey, *Das Mandat,* 261.

88. Gilcher-Holtey sees Kautsky's theory of the intellectuals as linked to his image of his own role in the SPD. Ibid., 253–62.

89. Kautsky to Adler, 28 November 1914, Friedrich Adler, ed., Victor Adler, *Briefwechsel,* 605.

90. That Kautsky's conception may yet gain relevance for new labor movements in the industrialized successor states of the Soviet Union and the industrialized countries of Eastern Europe, as they emerge from Communist single-party rule, is at any rate imaginable. If something like this were to happen, however, that conception would probably have to be couched in a different vocabulary from Kautsky's, for terms like "Marxism" and perhaps "socialism" would be associated by workers with their unattractive past rather than with an attractive future.

3

The Road to Power

I

Karl Kautsky's *Road to Power*[1] of 1909 is substantially a book on revolution. Its very title can be seen as a synonym for "revolution," and in his preface to its first edition Kautsky describes his work as a supplement to his brochure *The Social Revolution,*[2] published in 1902. The word "revolution" occurs throughout, as do the virtually equivalent German terms *"Umwälzung"* and *"Machtverschiebung"* (that is, shift in power relations), and the book culminates in a chapter entitled "A New Age of Revolutions." Kautsky used the term "revolution" throughout his six decades as a socialist writer, but perhaps he did so most emphatically and saw the revolution closest at hand in *The Road to Power.*

Lenin, misled by the Marxian vocabulary he shared with Kautsky, misinterpreted and therefore liked *The Road to Power.*[3] Given his perspective of a revolutionary in underdeveloped tsarist Russia, he failed to understand what Kautsky, writing in the context of the industrialized German Empire, meant by "revolution." This is worth mentioning here because, due to the prominence of Lenin's view of Kautsky, it has resulted in a widespread double misunderstanding that, I hope, the following pages will dispel. On the one hand, *The Road to Power* is often seen as Kautsky's closest approach to Leninism because it is a "revolutionary" work; on the other hand, Kautsky is often accused of abandoning that revolutionary position shortly after writing *The Road*

This essay is a slightly modified version of the introduction I wrote for a new translation of *The Road to Power* to be published by Humanities Press in 1994.

to Power and thus becoming a renegade, which is to explain Lenin's later break with him.[4]

What does Kautsky mean by "revolution"? *The Road to Power* provides some quite clear answers, but Kautsky's conception of revolution can only be understood as a response to the environment he confronted. It will be misunderstood if it is implicitly assumed that this environment was the same as either the one confronted by Lenin in Russia then or the one we face in the West today. Imperial Germany at the beginning of the twentieth century was not, like the tsarist empire, an underdeveloped country in the early stages of industrialization, populated overwhelmingly by peasants living in the isolation of their village communities and governed by a brutally repressive aristocratic-bureaucratic autocracy. Those who hoped for a social and political order drastically different from the existing one were not, as in Russia, tiny groupings or conspiracies of intellectuals hoping for the support of unorganized, potentially revolutionary masses of peasants or of workers in the very few cities.

On the other hand, in the first decade of this century imperial Germany was not, like Britain even at that time or like Germany today, a parliamentary democracy. Its Social Democratic Party (SPD) could not, like the British Labor Party then in its beginnings or the German Social Democrats today, hope to come to power merely by winning elections and gaining parliamentary majorities.

Kautsky was keenly aware of the differences between Germany and Britain and between Germany and Russia, and he argued that the strategy of his Party had to be different from that of the British socialists and that of Russian revolutionaries. When in 1898 Bernstein, who had been living in England and may have been influenced by the Fabians,[5] began to advocate a strategy of gradual "growth into socialism," Kautsky stressed that in Germany, unlike in Britain, the bourgeoisie did not stand for democracy. "I admit that the road taken by the English proletariat is better and demands fewer sacrifices and that we must wish we could take the same road; the course of history is, however, not determined by pious wishes but by facts, and these tell us that the English road is impassable for us, that the victory of democracy can be brought about only through the victory of the proletariat."[6] Earlier the same year, Kautsky had written to Bernstein: "I completely agree with you that in England the road to the development of a socialist society is open without a revolution. . . . Things are different in Germany. In Germany, a political revolution is needed to get to where the English are."[7]

In 1910, the year after Kautsky wrote *The Road to Power,* when Rosa Luxemburg, who had participated in the Russian Revolution of 1905, advocated that the SPD in Germany support the kind of spontaneous economic and political strikes of unorganized workers that characterized that revolution, he responded that the conditions for mass strikes in Prussia were different from those in Russia: "As far as the Russian model is concerned, the first successful mass strike there took place . . . under such conditions as do not exist in Prussia today: a war disgracefully lost, the army disorganized, all classes of the population full of hatred and contempt for the government."[8] A few months later Kautsky elaborated on this theme, stressing that "in Russia in 1905 the government was completely isolated. In Prussia today the proletariat is isolated whenever it undertakes an action that is to attack existing conditions energetically."[9] He interpreted the strikes of the 1905 Revolution as a result of Russian backwardness, a model that could not and should not be followed in a country like Germany, with its highly developed capitalist industry and powerfully organized working class.[10]

By the standard of its time, imperial Germany was a highly industrialized country. Except in the period of Bismarck's Anti-Socialist Law (1878–90), its labor movement benefited from far-reaching freedom of association, of speech, and of the press and could develop a huge organizational apparatus. By 1905 the largest trade union federation in the country, which was closely linked to the Social Democratic Party, had nearly a million and a half members. The Party grew rapidly; it won 124,700 votes in 1871, in the first election to the new Reichstag; 3,259,000 votes in 1907, in the last election before *The Road to Power* was written; and 4,250,400 votes in 1912, in the last election in imperial Germany.

On the other hand, as Kautsky stresses in chapter 8 of *The Road to Power,* the SPD was drastically underrepresented in the Reichstag as a result of the failure to redraw electoral district lines any time during the forty-eight-year history of the Empire, a period of rapid urbanization. In Prussia, which included nearly two-thirds of the population of the Empire, the SPD held no seats at all in the legislature until 1908 (and only a tiny percentage thereafter), and the Conservative Party was firmly ensconced in power (and was therefore powerful in Germany) as a result of the three-class system of suffrage. This system divided the electorate into three equally represented classes, each paying one-third of the direct taxes, making the (not secretly cast) vote of a member of the first class sixteen to twenty-six times as valuable as the vote of a member of the third class.[11] Furthermore, the imperial government was constitutionally not responsible to the Reichstag, and the governing regime was in fact one of the higher bureaucracy and the military, which responded to the interests of the agrarian Prussian Junkers and of the big industrialists in their famous marriage of iron and rye.

The regime did, however, enjoy a great deal of popular support, especially from the middle classes of the shrinking petty bourgeoisie and of the growing white-collar and professional strata as well as from the still numerous peasantry. While the Social Democrats had become the single largest party in Germany by 1890, they polled only 28.9 percent of the popular vote in 1907 and 34.8 percent in 1912, and all the other major parties more or less supported the imperial government. As the only major party consistently opposed to the government, the SPD, though quite legal, was widely regarded as subversive, disloyal, and unpatriotic.

> The formal prohibition of socialist activities had ended in 1890 but legal prosecutions, economic pressure and intimidation continued. And, less easily defined but none the less real was the general animosity which bourgeoisie and official society showed towards all those who identified with Social Democratic politics. During the period of the German empire to be a Social Democrat was to be regarded both as dangerous and amoral.[12]

Had the SPD ever seemed likely to acquire a popular majority, a coup d'état limiting the suffrage or the powers of the Reichstag was far more probable and more imaginable than that the emperor would appoint a Social Democrat as imperial chancellor.

The politically ambiguous environment of the German Empire, different from that of autocratic tsarist Russia and that of parliamentary-democratic Britain yet containing elements of both autocracy and parliamentary democracy, accounts for the character of Kautsky's concept of revolution as it appears in his *Road to Power*. On the one hand, like most Social Democrats at the time, impressed by the growth of the labor movement, he was absolutely certain that his Party would come to power, that is, that the revolution would take place. On the other hand, he was quite uncertain as to when and especially how this would occur; he did not know how the obstinate opposition of a powerful regime and its supporters could be overcome—perhaps because, in fact, it could not be overcome.

Kautsky opens *The Road to Power* by stating that the Social Democratic Party is a revolutionary party, both because it is committed to the social revolution of replacing capitalism with socialism and because, in order to carry out the social revolution, it seeks to obtain political power, that is, to make a political revolution. He proceeds to explain how Marxian theory, confirmed by the actual development of capitalism and the labor movement, proves that the proletarian revolution is inevitable. On this conviction rests the indomitable optimism that pervades all of Kautsky's writings and that could not even be shaken at the end of his life by the rise of the Nazis to power in Germany and in Austria.

In *The Road to Power* Kautsky takes the inevitability of the proletarian revolution for granted. Here he is concerned with how the proletariat, that is, his Party, can come to power, but especially with how it cannot come to power. As the word *"Hineinwachsen"* in its subtitle suggests, his book is an attack on Revisionism—his last one, as it turned out—whose reformist policies he had by then for a decade opposed in his role as the chief defender of "orthodox" Marxism in the SPD and the Second International.[13] In particular, Kautsky objected to the Revisionists' hope to form a coalition government with relatively leftist "bourgeois" parties and to their confidence in continuing gains in social and labor protective legislation and in advances by cooperatives and especially by trade unions that would constitute a gradual growth into socialism without any drastic changes in the political order.

While not opposed to limited socialist cooperation with left liberal parties, like the Progressives or *Freisinnige* in the German Empire, to form electoral alliances in runoff elections, once the question arose—when Millerand joined the Waldeck-Rousseau cabinet in France in 1899—Kautsky had opposed socialist participation in bourgeois coalitions under "normal circumstances." Still, "in Switzerland and in England, such participation seems possible to me; in Germany it is out of the question."[14] There, the class antagonism between proletariat and bourgeoisie would make fruitful collaboration of the Social Democrats with bourgeois parties in a coalition government impossible. Joining a bourgeois coalition would tend to discredit the Party with its working-class following (p. 20). The proletariat "can accomplish the *conquest of political power* only *by itself,* only when it is strong enough to take up the struggle with the entire bourgeois world victoriously."[15]

Especially during the first decade of this century, when he was engaged in his dispute with Revisionism, Kautsky had also argued that in imperial Germany, in contrast to Britain, merely economic growth into socialism without major political changes was impossible. The passage directed at Bernstein quoted above, which said that in Germany the victory of democracy could only be brought about by the victory of the proletariat, ends with the following words: "Is there anyone who believes that this victory is possible without a catastrophe? I desire it, but I do not believe it."[16] As capitalism develops, the power of both the proletariat and capital grows, "and the end of this development can be nothing but a great decisive struggle that cannot end until the proletariat has achieved victory."[17] Furthermore, "the proletariat cannot be emancipated without the conquest of political power; all practical achievements attained through social reform and the organization of the proletariat strengthen the latter but do not reduce its antagonism to the capitalist class, which, rather, grows ever more until political power is wrested from that class in a great showdown."[18]

Long before he wrote *The Road to Power,* then, Kautsky had insisted on the inevitability of a political revolution in the German Empire, but his references to a "catastrophe," a "great decisive struggle," a "showdown" had always been very general. Time and again, he had insisted that it was impossible to predict when the political revolution would break out or what form it would take. In *The Road to Power,* he came a little closer than before to doing just that. Why the change?

II

In an autobiographical sketch written in 1923, Kautsky notes that the 1905 Revolution in Russia had

> reinforced the power of the struggle for the suffrage in Prussia. Together with the armament race, it created a state of insecurity in Europe that promised to bring the most surprising catastrophes. I developed this point in 1909 in my book *The Road to Power.*[19]

In this book itself, Kautsky refers explicitly to various factors that impressed him as leading to a revolutionary situation, like growing expenditures for colonialism and armaments and the threat of a world war, the failure of trade unions to score successes and of welfare policies to expand, rising food prices, and growing corruption. In addition, some specific developments not mentioned by Kautsky affected the situation in which he wrote *The Road to Power,* particularly the Reichstag elections of 1907, the *Daily Telegraph* Affair, and the Harden-Eulenburg scandals. Kautsky hints at these last two when he refers to "struggles against the personal regime and constitutional questions" in the first sentence of his preface to the first edition and to the possibility of "moral collapse of the ruling regime" at the end of chapter 6.

A constitutional crisis had developed over the "personal regime" of William II, when in October 1908 the London *Daily Telegraph* published an article reporting an interview with the emperor that demonstrated that he had personally carried on inept and indiscreet foreign policy discussions in England.[20] The prestige of the monarchy was also gravely damaged and the position of the emperor and his chancellor, Prince Bülow, was weakened by three trials in the period 1907–1909, involving charges of homosexuality, slander, and perjury, that resulted from attacks by the writer Maximilian Harden on Prince Eulenburg, a close friend and confidant of the emperor.[21]

One event that had certainly affected the position of the Social Democratic Party in the Empire and prevailing attitudes in the Party was the Reichstag election of 1907, the so-called Hottentot election. Fought by the government parties in the "Bülow Bloc" on the issue of support for German colonialism, "on a wave of nationalist sentiment and in a mood of all-out attack on the SPD"[22] for its lack of patriotism, the election resulted in the loss of thirty-eight of the eighty-one seats the SPD had held in the Reichstag. This loss was due primarily to the failure of the left liberals (*Freisinnige*), who supported the government in this election, to vote for Social Democrats in runoff elections.

In less than a quarter of a century, the SPD's popular vote had steadily risen and had increased nearly tenfold (from 312,000 votes in 1881 to 3,010,800 in 1903), and its share of the popular vote had grown more than fivefold (from 6.1 percent in 1881 to 31.7 percent in 1903). In 1907 the SPD's popular vote still grew, but only by a quarter of a million over its 1903 level, the smallest increase since 1887, and the Party's share of the popular vote dropped by nearly 3 percent as against 1903, the first decrease since 1881, when the Party had been handicapped by the Anti-Socialist Law. The outcome of the 1907 election shook the SPD's faith in the inevitability and irresistibility of its electoral growth.[23]

The Revisionists reacted with renewed emphasis on their policy of gradual reforms through trade-union advances and coalition politics because "in the foreseeable future, no period of revolutionary development is to be expected in Germany."[24] It was in response to this view, as expressed by Max Maurenbrecher, that Kautsky wrote the article that grew into *The Road to Power.*

In an article written five days after the first round of the 1907 election,[25] Kautsky explained the SPD's defeat by two factors. One was "the loss of some hundreds of thousands of fellow travellers from the intermediate strata" of the petty bourgeoisie and the new middle class of white-collar workers and professionals, who, suffering from the rise in food prices, had supported the SPD in 1903 because of its opposition to protective tariffs, but who now turned against labor's attempt to raise wages. Kautsky was not displeased that his Party's electorate had thus assumed a more exclusively proletarian character and demanded that this character must not be obscured in order to attract the intermediate strata, who would, in any case, in good part return to the SPD sooner or later.

The second factor that, in Kautsky's view, accounted for the great increase in the number of nonsocialist voters and of 1903 nonvoters who voted in 1907 — turnout increased by more than 15 percent — was fear of Social Democracy and "the attractiveness of the colonial idea in bourgeois circles. . . . The fact that the colonial state of the future fascinated the entire bourgeois world . . . is closely linked to the growing fear of the state of the future of Social Democracy." But Kautsky predicted that German colonialism would merely result in higher taxes, more armaments, the isolation of Germany, and growing danger of a world war. And he concluded that the effects of this policy could "tremendously accelerate the course of development" and that it was therefore "not impossible that our defeat, which at first sight seems to have the effect of significantly postponing our victory, becomes a means to bring it about more quickly than we ourselves had suspected."[26]

Diametrically opposed to the Revisionist view, it was this prediction of the development of a revolutionary situation resulting from growing class antagonism between working class and bourgeoisie that

Kautsky elaborated in his *Road to Power*. Here Kautsky repeats several times (on pp. 30, 76, 95, 98, 100) that imperialism offers the only, the last, hope for nonsocialists for the future, that it serves the bourgeoisie as an ideal counterposed to socialism,[27] and he stresses the great costs imposed on the proletariat by ever growing expenditures for the army and navy (pp. 97–98, 100), which would be further increased by attempts to overcome growing native resistance in the colonies (pp. 102–4).

Kautsky also notes the regime's virtually complete failure to enact social and labor-protective legislation since the early 1890s. He cites as the only change the reduction, in 1908, of the working day for female workers from the eleven hours set in 1891 to ten hours and notes that male workers remained entirely unprotected (p. 77).[28] The proletariat's standard of living was further threatened by food prices that had been rising since the turn of the century, partly as a result of protective tariffs favoring agrarian interests (pp. 83–84).

In addition to these relatively long-term trends that had been aggravated by the depression beginning in 1907, Kautsky emphasizes, above all, changes that, as he saw it, had become apparent only more recently. No doubt they account for the somewhat more radical tone of *The Road to Power,* although these changes seemed to Kautsky merely to confirm the correctness of his objections to the Revisionist advocacy of policies relying on a gradual "growth into socialism," objections he had been voicing for a decade.

Revisionist hopes and predictions in this regard had rested on the growth of the working class and its organizations, which Kautsky also emphasizes (pp. 32–33, 63–69), and especially on the very real advances made by the trade unions from the 1890s to about 1907 (pp. 8, 77–79). Kautsky argues that it was exactly labor's advances, the result of what the Revisionists called "positive work," that aroused growing bourgeois resistance, which made further advances more difficult.[29] Now, he claims, these advances were becoming rarer and more difficult to achieve, especially with respect to real wages, because of the resistance of rapidly growing cartels and, even more important, of increasingly powerful employers' associations (pp. 80–81, 84).

In this connection, Kautsky also deals with the arrival in industry of cheap labor from agrarian areas (pp. 81–82), an aspect of the more general problem of the migration of rural people from underdeveloped countries into urban areas, both within these countries and in industrial countries, a problem that has become prominent in the latter half of the twentieth century and that will remain so in the twenty-first.

Finally, the situation that provoked Kautsky into writing *The Road to Power* allowed him to argue more strongly than ever that Social Democrats should not pursue a policy of coalitions with bourgeois parties.[30] He held that the 1907 election and its aftermath, in which the left liberal parties supported the government, made this obvious.[31] He writes that 1907 marked "the total collapse of German democracy" (p. 26), that is, of nonsocialist supporters of democracy. Petty bourgeois, peasant, and bourgeois democrats are not even an opposition party any more (p. 63); only the Social Democrats still oppose militarism and armaments (pp. 76, 95–96).

Kautsky explains why the petty bourgeoisie and the peasantry have become more and more hostile to the working class (pp. 93–95) and that the latter cannot rely on them as allies, though he speculates that much of the petty bourgeoisie might one day, responding to high taxes and the corruption of the militarist regime, join the proletariat and thereby assure its victory (pp. 106–109). For the present, though, Kautsky argues in *The Road to Power* that the proletariat was isolated (p. 96), and he even says that the concept of the "reactionary mass," which, following Marx, he had always rejected as a dangerous over-simplification, had now become reality.[32] Pursuit of a policy of coalition with bourgeois parties would now constitute political and moral suicide for Social Democracy (p. 111).

Kautsky's analysis led him to conclude that, with the progress of the working class having come to a halt — or threatening to come to a halt — Germany was entering "a period of general insecurity" (pp. 109, 112) and more specifically of growing class antagonism and therefore "a new era of revolutions." A revolution could no longer be regarded as premature when the proletariat "has drawn as much power from the existing governmental base as could be taken from it, when a transformation of this base has become a condition for its further advance" (p. 105). Once it has become clear that changes in the political power relations and institutions are necessary if the proletariat is to continue its economic advance, political struggles are inevitable in which "the proletariat must grow mightily; it cannot be victorious in them, it cannot achieve its . . . goals of democracy and the removal of militarism without itself attaining a dominant position in the state" (p. 92).

III

To Kautsky, then, the political revolution is the achievement of political power by the proletariat, that is, by the Social Democratic Party. In *The Road to Power* that revolution is perhaps more clearly defined with respect to its immediate goals than in his previous writings, but as far as its timing and duration and especially its forms are concerned, Kautsky cannot be much more definitive than he was earlier.

The goals of the revolution involved first of all constitutional changes, including the attainment of the secret ballot and of equal suffrage through the abolition of the three-class system in Prussia and Saxony and the equalization of the electoral districts for Reichstag elections. The Reichstag must be strengthened by making the executive responsible to it and thus creating "a real parliamentary regime" (p. 89), but also by strengthening the national government vis-à-vis the German states and particularly Prussia.

These changes would give the proletariat access to legislation, but not the means to enact social reforms, for these means were then consumed by military expenditures. Kautsky therefore also demands the abolition of the standing army and disarmament, which, in turn, require an end of colonial and imperialist policies (pp. 89–90). In the preface to the second edition, he thus summarizes the immediate goals of the revolution:

> To overcome the policy of armaments and the domination of the state by the *Krautjunker* and *Schlotjunker* [the big landowners and the big industrialists], that is, the democratization of the country, these are the most important practical tasks of the German proletariat. They must be accomplished if its advance is to continue." (P. 12)

When does Kautsky expect the revolution to occur? He already stresses on the second page of *The Road to Power* that the proletarian revolution cannot be made at will,[33] that it will be a response to certain conditions, which the development of capitalism creates. It follows, as Kautsky saw it and as he said in an article of 1893,[34] which he quotes at great length in *The Road to Power* (pp. 52–60), that the Social Democratic Party was "a revolutionary but not a revolution-making party" (p. 52). This statement has often been cited as illustrating the quibbling or ambiguous nature of Kautsky's or of his Party's revolutionism, as showing that they were only "pseudo-revolutionaries" and merely verbally radical,[35] but, as the context makes quite clear, it merely says that the Party is committed to both the social and the political revolution, but that the revolution will come only when its prerequisites have matured, no sooner and no later.

To Kautsky, this did not mean that, as is often suggested, he minimized or ignored the "subjective factor" in history, that he held the literally nonsensical view that will played no role in the revolution, that men would go to the barricades or the ballot box without wanting to do so. In chapter 4 of *The Road to Power,* "Economic Development and Will," he argues that the human will is the driving force of the economy and of politics, but that this will is not free; rather, it is conditioned "in the last analysis" by economic development.

As Kautsky could not predict just when conditions would be ripe for the revolution — is not a successful revolution the only clear indicator of their ripeness? — he stressed in his 1893 article that "we cannot say anything at all about when, under what circumstances, and in what forms it will occur" (p. 52), and he repeats in 1909 that the "forms and duration" of the revolution are unpredictable (pp. 61, 112). As to the timing of the revolution, however, Kautsky now feels that conditions have changed and that a period of struggles for governmental institutions and governmental power has begun that would "very probably, already in the foreseeable future, bring about major shifts in power in favor of the proletariat, if not already its sole rule in Western Europe" (p. 61). Kautsky suggests that his Party might come to power as a result of "the moral collapse of the ruling regime" (p. 70) or — and here he proved right — of the defeat of that regime in a war (p. 105).

But even with respect to the forms to be assumed by the revolution, Kautsky is not as uncertain in *The Road to Power* as he sometimes professes to be. It is surely significant that he reprints several pages of his 1893 article with their heavy emphasis on "the democratic-proletarian method . . . of class struggle that limits itself to the nonmilitary means of parliamentarism, strikes, demonstrations, the press, and similar means of pressure" (p. 54), "at least in countries with reasonably democratic institutions," including "freedom of association, freedom of the press, and universal suffrage" (p. 53), all of which did exist in imperial Germany.

Far from seeing "nonmilitary" methods as nonrevolutionary, Kautsky argues that it was precisely the workers' belief in "the revolutionary character of our Party," their "revolutionary enthusiasm," that made them adhere to these "civilized forms of struggle" rather than the more "brutal" ones of anarchism (p. 59). The possibility of an armed uprising is not even considered in *The Road to Power.* Kautsky also implies that the revolution will be a gradual process when he suggests that the coming struggles for power "may drag on through various changes of fortune through decades" (p. 61) and even that the new revolutionary period might last as long as that of the bourgeoisie, which, he says, extended from 1789 to 1871 (p. 112).

A major new emphasis in *The Road to Power* is on the political role of the trade unions. Kautsky states repeatedly that the obstacles he sees as now blocking the continued advance of the working class "cannot be overcome by purely trade-union methods but only through political struggle" (p. 12), that the unions could no longer expect "to advance the proletariat as mightily through purely trade-union methods as they could in the past dozen years" (p. 84). He says that they now have more and more "political tasks" (p. 87), but he does not spell out what these tasks are beyond mentioning that strikes in industries dominated by the powerful employers' associations assume an ever more political character and that social reform and labor-protective measures can only be achieved through political action (pp. 87–88).

Kautsky also notes, however, that more and more often "in purely political struggles, for example struggles for the suffrage, the weapon of the mass strike can be successful" (p. 87). When at the end of his book he lists the immediate goals of the proletariat as the democratization of Germany and the fight against militarism, he adds: "Equally clear as these tasks are the means that are available to us for their solution. To those we have applied in the past, the mass strike has been added" (p. 110).

Though barely made explicit in *The Road to Power,* Kautsky's call on the trade unions to accept the political mass strike as a weapon is an important element in his book.[36] In his preface to its second edition, Kautsky writes that one task he undertook in his book was to direct the attention of the trade unions "to the new functions that arise for them in addition to the purely trade-union ones and that thus increase the importance of the trade unions" (p. 14).[37] Here he is quite outspoken when he says that only *mass action,* that is, the action of *organized* masses, can move us forward today. . . . But proletarian mass organization and mass action means *trade-union* organization and action. . . . We cannot win political victories without the help of strong trade unions, capable of struggle and conscious of their strength" (P. 13)

Yet in April 1910, just two months before he wrote this preface, Kautsky, in a long article, rejected Rosa Luxemburg's call for a mass strike.[38] She wanted the party to turn the massive street demonstrations that had been held in February–April 1910 against the Prussian three-class suffrage into political strike actions. Following the model of the Russian Revolution of 1905 and in response to the negative attitude of the trade unions, she emphasized the role of the unorganized workers.[39] Kautsky, as I just quoted him, insisted that mass action had to be trade-union action, and he had stated in *The Road to Power* that the mass strike was "not effective in every situation" and "that it would be foolish to want to apply it under all circumstances" (p. 110). With the union and Party authorities opposed to calling for mass strikes and given the power of the regime, he feared that the political mass strike was likely to fail and to endanger achievements and organizations of the Social Democratic Party and the trade unions.

Kautsky argued that the Party should not risk defeat just when, he felt certain, it would win a great victory in the next Reichstag election, which would be "nothing less than a catastrophe for the entire ruling system of government."[40] In reaction to such a defeat, or possibly even before the election order to avoid defeat, the regime was likely to resort to measures of brutal repression and a coup to abolish universal suffrage.[41] Such actions, Kautsky thought, would mobilize a mass response, "a mass strike under *such* circumstances could very well be capable of sweeping the existing regime away."[42] The political revolution would then be a reply to the unconstitutional, violent action of the regime and be legitimated by the support of a majority of the population. As the author of an insightful study of Kautsky's role in the SPD says: "The postponement of the political mass strike was thus not an expression of mere opportunism or weakness on Kautsky's part, but was determined by the concern with democracy that had always characterized Social Democracy and also determined Kautsky's thought."[43]

IV

The Road to Power is certainly an important work among Karl Kautsky's many writings, particularly because he argued in it that the situation in the German Empire had changed so that the trade unions would have to become more directly involved in politics if they were to continue to advance the workers' welfare. And having in the past avoided predictions as to when the inevitable political revolution would occur, Kautsky now considered it "highly probable" that major shifts in power in favor of Social Democracy would take place or at least begin "in the foreseeable future."

The Road to Power does not, however, mark a major departure from positions Kautsky had taken earlier, as has often been asserted,[44] nor did he abandon the positions he took in this book when he turned against Rosa Luxemburg's advocacy of the mass strike. Both interpretations, one of which sees Kautsky as more radical than he was and even, quite wrongly, as somehow similar to Lenin, and the other of which sees him as more moderate than he was and even, quite wrongly, as a renegade, ignore the fact that at different times he faced different circumstances from the same position, which he therefore expressed with different emphases.

That the working class, through a socialist party, would have to come to power in industrialized countries sooner or later, that is, that there would be a political revolution, had been an article of faith for Kautsky all along. And he had stated many times that in Germany this would have to consist of the replacement of the imperial regime by a parliamentary republic with universal suffrage.[45] Indeed, Kautsky had already bluntly made one of the principal points of *The Road to Power* in a letter in 1893: "The struggle for a real parliamentarism will, in my opinion, become the decisive struggle for the social revolution in Germany, for in Germany a parliamentary regime is tantamount to the political victory of the proletariat and also *vice versa.*"[46] With respect to the nature and immediate goals of the revolution, then, *The Road to Power* says nothing new, except to make more explicit, in response to current German policies, the additional goal of putting an end to colonial expansionism and militarism.

Kautsky had never predicted just what form the revolution would take and he did not do so in *The Road to Power.* Here, as he had earlier, he suggested that it would probably be peaceful and gradual, though he always thought the imperial regime might provoke a violent confrontation. Some drastic political change toward democracy would certainly have to occur. By the time *The Road to Power* was published, Kautsky had been denouncing for a decade the Revisionist hopes for imperceptible growth into socialism without any such change in imperial institutions.

What had changed by 1909 was, however, not only the political situation in Germany, especially through and after the 1907 election, but also the political situation in the Social Democratic Party, whose right wing had grown stronger, partly due to the SPD's loss of seats in that election. The trade unions had grown more powerful in the Party as they had grown in strength and had won more successes, and were particularly cautious in a period of economic depression. Their leaders bitterly resented Kautsky's prediction that they would not be able to advance in the future by mere trade-union methods as a reflection on their past achievements, and they also interpreted his hope that they would turn to political methods as implying that the unions should be subordinated to the Party. The trade-union leadership attacked Kautsky in its central organ,[47] and Kautsky responded in his preface to the second edition of *The Road to Power*.[48]

The trade unions had never had much use or respect for Kautsky, because he was a "theorist," but he had enjoyed considerable influence and respect with the Party leadership, at least since he wrote the SPD's Erfurt Program in 1891. He was cast in the role of something like the principal official Party theorist, not because all Party leaders or intellectuals always agreed with him but mostly because of his long-lasting close political relationship to August Bebel, the unquestioned Party leader. With the huge growth of the Party and its many auxiliary organizations, it had become bureaucratized and, partly also due to Bebel's being ill, the leadership and Kautsky's relation to it had changed. To many full-time Party functionaries and leaders, he must have seemed to be an impractical theorist and troublemaker.[49]

This change became strikingly apparent when the Party Executive Committee (*Parteivorstand*), with only one dissenting vote (by Luise Zietz), after the first appearance of *The Road to Power,* prohibited its further distribution by the official Party publishing house Vorwärts.[50] The cautious Executive Committee[51] was or claimed to be concerned that the public prosecutor might charge Kautsky with high treason, though in fact nothing of the sort happened. Always worried about the legal status of the Party, some of the executive committee members, probably including Bebel, may have feared renewed repression after their losses in the 1907 election to the Bülow bloc. Also, as Bebel wrote to Victor Adler, [52] as one Marxist practical politician to another, *The Road to Power* could provide an occasion for attacks on the SPD, which the regime could use to distract attention from its own troubles, a tactical consideration for which he said Kautsky had no appreciation.

Gary Steenson, the best biographer of Kautsky, lists as "an additional possible source for the hostility" of the Executive Committee "Kautsky's powerful assertion that without theory, both as a consciousness-raising tool and as a source of direction, the mundane work of the movement would lead nowhere. This struck deeply into the heart of the growing socialist bureaucracy and attacked the basic rationale for its existence."[53] And Kautsky expressed his resentment of the Executive Committee for their resentment of him as an intellectual when he wrote to Adler: "the louts want the intellectual [*den Literaten*] to feel their power; they want to show him that he is merely their coolie and has to shut up when they command."[54]

Finally, as Kautsky notes in a letter to Hugo Haase, [55] there were also rumors that a "Revisionist intrigue" was behind the order to withdraw his book, and according to Clara Zetkin the Executive Committee was afraid of the Revisionists, who had threatened to split the Party if Kautsky's "scandalous brochure" was given official sanction by its publication by the Party publishing house.[56]

It would, indeed, be surprising if the principal reason for the opposition to *The Road to Power* had not been objections to its radical message and its radical tone. As a sophisticated student of German Social Democracy wrote: "At a time when the party executive had de facto reconciled itself to the existing order of state and society, the publication of Kautsky's theses about the political revolution were bound to meet with resistance from the responsible party authorities. . . . The executive regarded Kautsky's book as an offense against the peaceable tactics of the party."[57]

The bitter conflict ended in a compromise, by which the Party Executive Committee permitted the publication by Vorwärts of a second edition of *The Road to Power,* in which Kautsky had made certain changes from the first edition. Since Kautsky had proposed these conditions himself at the beginning of the controversy, he accepted the compromise. As his legal adviser in the matter, Hugo Haase, then a prominent Social Democratic defense lawyer in East Prussia and later chairman of the SPD and, beginning in 1917, of the Independent Social Democratic Party (USPD), wrote to Kautsky: "Substantively, you are not giving anything away; the Party Executive Committee offers you what you demanded to begin with. You are not subjecting yourself to any decision of the Party Executive Committee, but help the Party Executive Committee out of a messy situation. This is how I see the matter."[58]

The verbal changes Kautsky made in the text of the first edition of *The Road to Power* were minor, indeed, and did not significantly affect the substance or even the tone of his work.[59] Kautsky also agreed, however, to add a new final paragraph to his preface to the first edition in which he stressed that he alone, and not his Party, was responsible for what he had written, "in so far as it did not rest on our Party program and decisions of our party congresses." This latter clause may have been meant by Kautsky to suggest that in some or much of what he said he was still speaking for his party even as he complied with the party Executive Committee's wish that he assume personal responsibility for *The Road to Power*.

Ingrid Gilcher-Holtey, whose entire book is a sensitive analysis of Kautsky's role as a Party theorist, is undoubtedly right in saying that the real question at issue in the controversy over the publication of *The Road to Power* was whether the analysis of the situation and the strategy for the Party proposed there should be recognized as "official" ones by the Party. She concludes that in fighting the conflict over the issue of his freedom of opinion as a writer rather than over the political issue, Kautsky gave up his claim "as a theorist to provide to the Party a binding value and action orientation."[60] However that may be, it must be understood that Kautsky had always in his role as a theorist left the making of political decisions to the practical politicians,[61] and it is also clear from his letters in the controversy that he was anxious not to have the Party, which was, after all, *his* Party and not his enemy, placed in an embarrassing position.

In any case, Kautsky's role in the Party had clearly changed. "He could no longer control the Party's policy alternatives, and the Party no longer needed him to interpret the times."[62] *The Road to Power* may have differed at most in tone and not in substance from what Kautsky had been saying repeatedly for some time, but under new circumstances it was received differently. That reception, and particularly the attack directed at it by the now more powerful trade unions and the reformist wing of the SPD, gave more prominence to the radical character of the work.

Similarly, it was the situation and not Kautsky's position that had changed when he opposed Rosa Luxemburg on the question of the mass strike in 1910. The new situation was created by the emergence of a new radical wing on the left of the Party, which advocated political mass strikes that were quite different, especially with respect to their reliance on unorganized workers, from the ones Kautsky had in mind in his *Road to Power*.

Kautsky's emphasis in his response to Rosa Luxemburg on the coming Reichstag election and on the use of the mass strike to defend universal suffrage and to defeat any attempt by the regime to weaken or abolish existing electoral and parliamentary institutions is very much in line with his emphasis in *The Road to Power* on the importance of universal suffrage and parliamentarism, an emphasis that remained consistent through Kautsky's political writings for half a century.[63]

Thus, Kautsky's statement in *The Road to Power* that "it has been the successful struggles for the control of parliaments and in parliaments that have mightily raised the sense of power and the power of the proletariat" (p. 46) is reminiscent of what he had already written in 1892, in his commentary on the Erfurt Program of 1891, which he himself had drafted with Engels' approval:

When the proletariat participates as a self-conscious class in the struggles for control of parliament (particularly in electoral campaigns) and within parliament, parliamentarism . . . ceases to be a mere means of domination of the bourgeoisie. It is just these struggles that prove to be the most powerful means to awaken those strata of the proletariat that are still indifferent and to give them confidence and hope; they prove to be the most powerful means to weld the various proletarian strata ever more firmly into a united working class; and finally they also prove to be the most powerful means at present available to the proletariat to influence the government and to extract from it those concessions that, depending on the circumstances, can for the present be extracted at all; in short, these struggles are among the most effective levers by which to raise the proletariat out of its economic, social, and moral degradation.

The working class has, then, not only no reason to stay away from parliamentary activity, it has every reason to be decisively active everywhere to strengthen parliament vis-à-vis the executive and to strengthen its own representation in parliament through an independent socialist labor party.

Besides *freedom of association* and *freedom of the press, universal, equal, and direct suffrage* and the *secret ballot* are a *vital condition* for the sound development of the proletariat.[64]

When, in *The Road to Power*, Kautsky speaks (on p. 87) of the growing political tasks of the trade unions and specifically of the mass strike, he stresses in italics that, in contrast to the antiparliamentarism of Syndicalism, "the 'direct action' of the trade unions can effectively occur only to *supplement* and to *strengthen*, not to *take the place* of the parliamentary activity of the labor parties."

Kautsky had also already written in *The Road to Power* what he said in 1910, that "we must be prepared for our next great electoral victory to bring us an attack on the existing suffrage for the Reichstag" (p. 47; see also p. 88). He had quoted his own article of 1893 stressing the danger that the ruling classes would, in response to the growing strength of the working class, resort to violence, and counseling Social Democracy to postpone a confrontation, if it should be inevitable, as long as possible and "to avoid and, indeed, to fight everything that would constitute a pointless provocation of the ruling classes" (pp. 55–56).

In opposing Luxemburg, Kautsky took a position he himself called that of the "Marxist Center," for he felt that the greater threat to Marxism now came from the "rebellious impatience" of the radical Left than from the "statesman-like impatience" of the Revisionists.[65] Kautsky's shift from the Left of the Party to the Marxist Center was thus only relative; it was due to the rise of a new force to the left of him. His position did not change, as has often been asserted.[66] Kautsky had always been a "centrist," for Marxism — as distinguished from what later came to be known as Marxism-Leninism — occupied a centrist position opposing both reformism and revisionism on the right and doctrines and movements like anarchism, Blanquism, and Syndicalism on the left.

The Road to Power was Kautsky's last major work against Revisionism, and as such it sounded relatively radical, especially as his opponents on the Right described it. "Was nun?" and Kautsky's subsequent polemics on the mass strike against Luxemburg and Pannekoek were his first writings against the new radical Left, and as such they sounded relatively moderate, especially as his opponents on the Left described them. In fact, though differing in tone and emphasis, both relatively radical and relatively moderate works were, absolutely, written from the same point of view of the Marxist Center.

There is some disagreement in Communist literature as to whether Kautsky abandoned Marxism in 1910, when he became a "centrist," or in World War I, beginning in 1914, when he opposed the SPD majority's support for the imperial government's war policies but also opposed Lenin's policy of turning the war into a civil war. But there is no question among Communists that by 1920 Kautsky had become a renegade, for he had attacked the new Bolshevik regime in Russia from its beginnings.[67]

Yet when Kautsky in 1920 wrote a lengthy new preface to a third edition of *The Road to Power*,[68] he could claim that he could reprint that book in unchanged form "because I still subscribe to every sentence in it today." He conceded only that his language had changed:

> Anyone who, by referring to my *Road to Power,* wants to discover a shift in my position since the revolution has not read or not understood my work of 1909. I maintain the same position today as then. Only my language has become different since then. There are times of discouragement, when one must encourage and spur on those who lose heart, and there are times of blind rush, when one must admonish the deluded and the fanatics to be prudent. But these changes in language are indicative only of a change in the historical situation, not in principled conception.[69]

Kautsky can then present a dozen quotations from his book stating that he did not favor revolution "at any price"; that a violent revolution was neither desirable nor probable "except in Russia"; that socialism could be realized only in a "democratic republic"; that Russia was economically too "immature" for a revolution to establish a socialist regime; that, except in Russia, small minorities could no longer seize and maintain power; that only a party representing "the great majority of the population" could do so. And he keeps repeating that no "revolutionary Marxists" disagreed with him in 1909; if they did so now, it was they who had changed. Kautsky says:

> I assumed then that I spoke in the name of revolutionary Marxism. And none of the Marxist revolutionaries disavowed me, neither Rosa Luxemburg nor Clara Zetkin, neither Lenin nor Trotsky. They then all shared with me the same democratic convictions.[70]

The Road to Power is a historical document important for an understanding of the history of German Social Democracy and of Kautsky's role in it. But as a historical document, it can itself be understood only with reference to its historical context in the German Empire. Kautsky's position in the Marxist Center between Bernstein's Revisionism and Luxemburg's Radicalism corresponds, in a sense, to the location of the Empire, not only geographically but politically, between Britain, where, it seemed to Kautsky, Bernstein's policy was appropriate, and tsarist Russia, where, he thought, Luxemburg's approach was suitable.

As in Britain, the socialist party had reason to hope for an electoral victory in the German Empire, but, as in tsarist Russia, there was every reason to doubt that it could come to power under the existing regime. Corresponding to this situation, Kautsky's concept of the political revolution involved great emphasis, on the one hand, on electoral participation and the reforms and the political education that would strengthen the workers' party in elections and, on the other hand, on extra-parliamentary pressures, especially through the mass strike, to protect and extend the workers' right to vote and to defeat any attempt to limit or destroy what parliamentary institutions there were.[71]

Political action by the Social Democratic Party and by the trade unions, in ways not clearly specified in *The Road to Power,* electoral victories and, if necessary, mass strikes were to serve to bring about parliamentary democracy in Germany. That goal is very clearly specified there, for to Kautsky the achievement of parliamentarism and of working-class power through a parliamentary majority was the content of the socialist political revolution, which he considered the inevitable and necessary prerequisite of the future social revolution; it was to him the road to power.[72]

I would like to thank Gary Steenson for his perceptive comments on an earlier draft of this chapter.

Notes

1. Kautsky, *Der Weg zur Macht: Politische Betrachtungen über das Hineinwachsen in die Revolution* (Frankfurt a.M.: Europäische Verlagsanstalt, 1972). Page numbers in parentheses appearing in the text refer to this edition. The only English translation, *The Road to Power* (Chicago: Samuel A. Bloch, 1909), is often inexact and does not contain the important preface to the second edition of 1910.

2. Kautsky, *The Social Revolution* 3d ed. (Chicago: Charles H. Kerr, 1916).

3. Even after his open break with Kautsky in 1914, Lenin described *The Road to Power* as "a most complete exposition of the tasks of our times," which expressed "the undisputed opinion held by all revolutionary Social-Democrats." "Dead Chauvinism and Living Socialism," Lenin, *Collected Works*, 45 vols. (Moscow: Progress Publishers, 1960–70), 21:94, 98. See also "Under a False Flag," ibid., 147. In 1917 Lenin still called *The Road to Power* "the last and best of Kautsky's works against the opportunists," which "should serve as a measure of comparison of what the German Social-Democrats *promised to be* before the imperialist war and the depth of degradation to which they — including Kautsky himself — sank when the war broke out." "State and Revolution," *Collected Works*, 25:486, 487.

4. For example, Georg Fülberth, in his introduction to the most recent German edition of *The Road to Power,* refers to it as Kautsky's "last 'revolutionary' piece of writing, shortly before his open shift to 'centrist' positions in 1910." *Der Weg zur Macht,* xvii. As recently as 1988, Annelies Laschitza, an East German Communist scholar, wrote: "Kautsky's *Road to Power* constituted a convincing summary of the conception of revolutionary theory championed by the Marxists in the Party. . . . But when, with the rise of a mighty suffrage movement in 1910, a political crisis began to mature, Kautsky lost his courage and placed himself de facto in conflict with the theoretical views he had just propagated." Annelies Laschitza, "Karl Kautsky im Widerstreit zwischen Marxismus und Opportunismus 1905 bis 1914," in *Marxismus und Demokratie. Karl Kautskys Bedeutung in der sozialistischen Arbeiterbewegung,* ed. Jürgen Rojahn, Till Schelz, and Hans-Josef Steinberg (Frankfurt: Campus Verlag, 1922), 132, 135.

5. On the question of Fabian influence on Bernstein, see Bo Gustafsson, *Marxismus und Revisionismus* (Frankfurt a.M.: Europäische Verlagsanstalt, 1972), 127–80.

6. *Protokoll über die Verhandlungen des Parteitages der Sozialdemokratischen Partei Deutschlands abgehalten zu Stuttgart vom 3. bis 8. Oktober 1898* (Berlin: Vorwärts, 1898), 129.

7. Letter of 18 February 1898, International Institute of Social History (IISG, Amsterdam), Kautsky Nachlass, C 180, quoted in Hans-Josef Steinberg, *Sozialismus und deutsche Sozialdemokratie* (4th ed., Bonn: J. H. W. Dietz, 1976), 80. In the same letter Kautsky stressed that the proletariat's political revolution that he considered inevitable in Germany would be a revolution not for socialism but for democracy, which Marx had associated with the bourgeoisie: "As the only opposition party, we have to fulfill the historical tasks of the bourgeoisie, not of the proletariat, to establish not the state of the future but the present-day English state."

8. Kautsky, "Was nun?," *Die Neue Zeit* 28/2 (1910): 36.

9. Kautsky, "Eine neue Strategie," *Die Neue Zeit* 28/2 (1910): 368.

10. Ibid., 364–74, and Kautsky, "Zwischen Baden und Luxemburg," *Die Neue Zeit* 28/2 (1910): 656–67, See also Kautsky, *Der politische Massenstreik* (Berlin: Vorwärts, 1914), 198–203.

11. A similar system prevailed until 1909 in Saxony, the other major industrial state in the German Empire. On the Prussian and Saxon suffrage and its results, see Gerhard A. Ritter, *Wahlgeschichtliches Arbeitsbuch* (Munich: C. H. Beck, 1980), 132–49, 163–82.

12. W. L. Guttsman, *The German Social Democratic Party 1875–1933. From Ghetto to Government* (London: Allen & Unwin, 1981), 132. See also 4, and, for some striking illustrations, 132–41; and also my remarks in my article on Kautsky and Eurocommunism on pp. 174–75, below.

13. See also Kautsky, *Bernstein und das sozialdemokratische Programm* (1899) 3d ed. (Bonn: J. H. W. Dietz, 1979) and Kautsky, *The Social Revolution* (1902). *The Road to Power* grew out of a polemic with the Revisionist Max Maurenbrecher, and chapters 3 and 4 and part of chapter 2 reproduce much of Kautsky's article "Reform und Revolution," *Die Neue Zeit* 27/1 (1908): 180–91, 220–32, 252–59.

14. Kautsky, "Die sozialistischen Kongresse und der sozialistische Minister," *Die Neue Zeit,* 19/1 (1900): 37.

15. Ibid., 44. See also Kautsky, "Zum Parteitag," *Die Neue Zeit* 21/2 (1903): 732–34, and Kautsky, "Bürgermeister und Minister," *Die Neue Zeit* 19/2 (1901): 796. Once the German Empire had been replaced by the parliamentary Weimar Republic with the SPD as its strongest supporter, but not strong enough to govern alone, Kautsky favored socialist participation in coalition governments, as he wrote in 1922, "not as a substitute for the proletarian revolution . . . , but as an introduction to and preparation of this revolution, that is, the political rule by the proletariat alone through a purely socialist government supported by a proletarian majority [Übermacht]. . . . Those who still reject the policy of coalitions on principle today are blind to the signs of the times in Germany." Kautsky, *The Labour Revolution* (New York: Dial Press, 1925), 53–54.

16. *Protokoll,* 129.

17. Kautsky, *The Social Revolution,* 82–83.

18. Kautsky, "Allerhand Revolutionäres," *Die Neue Zeit* 22/1 (1904): 590.

19. Kautsky, "Karl Kautsky," in *Die Volkswirtschaftslehre der Gegenwart in Selbstdarstellungen,* ed. Felix Meiner (Leipzig: Felix Meiner, 1924), 22; reprinted as "Mein Lebenswerk," in *Ein Leben für den Sozialismus: Erinnerungen an Karl Kautsky,* ed. Benedikt Kautsky (Hanover: J. H. W. Dietz, 1954), 25.

20. Johannes Ziekursch, *Politische Geschichte des Neuen Deutschen Kaiserreiches,* (Frankfurt: Frankfurter Societäts-Druckerei, 1930), 3:191–96; Geoff Eley, *Reshaping the German Right* (New Haven, Conn.: Yale University Press, 1980), 285. For more detailed studies, see Wilhelm Schüssler, *Die Daily-Telegraph-Affaire; Fürst Bülow, Kaiser Wilhelm und die Krise des Zweiten Reiches 1908* (Göttingen: Musterschmidt, 1952), emphasizing the role of the chancellor and the emperor; and Theodor Eschenburg, *Das Kaiserreich am Scheideweg* (Berlin: Verlag für Kulturpolitik, 1929), 131–75, and Erich Eyck, *Das persönliche Regiment Wilhelms II* (Erlenbach-Zurich: Eugen Rentsch, 1948), 492–503, emphasizing political and

constitutional issues.

21. "The conviction grew in the population at large that their Kaiser had for years been under the influence of psychologically unbalanced and intellectually incompetent court advisers. In Kautsky's view this element of corruption would raise the revolutionary potential of the peasantry and lower middle class." Carl F. Schorske, *German Social Democracy. 1905–1917* (Cambridge, Mass.: Harvard University Press, 1955), 113. Both the Daily Telegraph Affair and the Harden-Eulenburg scandals are briefly discussed in Alex Hall, *Scandal, Sensation, and Social Democracy* (Cambridge: Cambridge University Press, 1977), 160–67.

22. Guttsman, *The German Social Democratic Party,* 90.

23. The membership of the free trade unions, that is, those close to the SPD, which had (with a minor exception in 1901) grown steadily from 223,530 in 1893 to 1,865,506 in 1907, actually declined slightly to 1,831,731 in 1908 and 1,832,667 in 1909 . The membership of the much smaller "Christian" and "Hirsch-Duncker" trade unions also declined from 1907 to 1908, but grew again beginning in 1909. Wolfgang Hirsch-Weber, *Gewerkschaften in der Politik* (Cologne: Westdeutscher Verlag, 1959), 145–47.

24. Max Maurenbrecher, "Offener Brief an den Genossen Kautsky," *Die Neue Zeit* 27/1 (1908): 149, and Max Maurenbrecher, "Wo stehen wir?," *Die Neue Zeit* 27/1 (1908): 395. Guttsman says: "The election of 1907, which reduced the size of the party's representation by thirty-eight, did not abate the strength of the belief in the values of reform within the group of deputies as against the greater radicalism of the party at large. Yet the response to a policy of coalition or mere collaboration was not really forthcoming from the Liberal parties." Guttsman, *The German Social Democratic Party,* 298.

25. Kautsky, "Der 25. Januar," *Die Neue Zeit* 25/1 (1907): 588–96.

26. Ibid., 589, 596.

27. Kautsky had already emphasized the attraction of imperialism to nonproletarian strata in his first major article on imperialism, "Aeltere und neuere Kolonialpolitik," *Die Neue Zeit* 16/1 (1898): 812, and also in "Die kommenden Kongresse," *Die Neue Zeit* 18/2 (1900): 715 . At the 1907 Stuttgart Congress of the Second International, he had opposed German and other advocates of colonialism under capitalism and, in the future, under socialism. For references, see note 46 to my article "J. A. Schumpeter and Karl Kautsky," below. After the outbreak of World War I, Kautsky again attacked socialists who could not resist imperialist ideas. Kautsky, "Imperialistische Tendenzen in der Sozialdemokratie," *Die Neue Zeit* 34/1 (1915): 98; and also Kautsky, *Sozialisten und Krieg* (Prague: Orbis, 1937), 657. See also Hans-Christoph Schröder, *Sozialistische Imperialismusdeutung* (Göttingen: Vanderhoek & Ruprecht, 1973), 59–61.

28. According to Guttsman, *The German Social Democratic Party,* 142, "up to 1900 a twelve-hour day was still quite common and . . . by 1914 . . . a ten-hour day and six-day week were general."

29. Kautsky, "Positive Arbeit und Revolution," *Die Neue Zeit* 27/2 (1909): 325–26, 337.
30. As he wrote in response to Ludwig Quessel, a Revisionist critic of his book: The Revisionists still expect that "the rule of the proletariat will be preceded by a victory of bourgeois democracy. . . . A new great revolution is still possible only as a *proletarian* revolution, a revolution carried from the *beginning* by the proletariat, even if it does not from its beginnings appear as a *socialist* revolution." Kautsky, "Ludwig unter den Propheten," *Die Neue Zeit* 28/1 (1909): 206.
31. After the 1903 Reichstag election, in which the SPD was exceptionally successful and the left liberals registered losses, Kautsky had already written: "Imperial Germany is anything but a state governed by parliament. The conflicts between Social Democracy and the conservative parties become ever sharper. The dream of a 'great party of the Left,' which was to form a mass capable of governing, is definitely over. The bourgeois Left has been decimated and stands in decided opposition to Social Democracy. . . . Class interests are stronger than party interests. The political party interests of bourgeois and proletarian democrats may share ever so many points, the class antagonism between bourgeoisie and proletariat becomes ever deeper and drives the former the more into the camp of the opponents of democracy the stronger the proletarian democrats become. . . . It is simply impossible that strong bourgeois and proletarian democrats exist side by side. The one excludes the other." Kautsky, "Zum Parteitag," *Die Neue Zeit* 21/2 (1903): 734.
32. For an outspoken statement by Kautsky in an earlier period attacking the "principle" of opposition to one reactionary mass and advocating a policy of compromise and of electoral agreements with appropriate other parties, see his letter to Victor Adler of 5 May 1894 in Friedrich Adler, ed., Victor Adler *Briefwechsel mit August Bebel und Karl Kautsky* (Vienna: Wiener Volksbuchhandlung, 1954), 152–54.

   For Kautsky's strong advocacy of SPD participation in elections to the Prussian parliament, which the Party was then boycotting, and in electoral agreements with left liberals, see Kautsky, "Umsturzgesetz und Landtagswahlen in Preussen," *Die Neue Zeit* 15/2 (1897): 275–82, where he wrote that his Party should not "declare war on any compromise in practical politics [nor] reject any planned cooperation agreed upon with neighboring parties on a particular occasion against a common enemy." Nonparticipation "might have seemed practical as long as we were a small party that had no influence on actual developments. This is different today; we are now the largest party in Germany, and our passivity has equally practical effects as our activity." Ibid., 279, 280. See also Kautsky, "Die preussischen Landtagswahlen und die reaktionäre Masse," *Die Neue Zeit* 15/2 (1897): 580–90, on the same subject, where Kautsky sharply attacks the concept of the "one reactionary mass" and emphasizes conflicts among the opponents of Social Democracy.

   Twenty years later, Kautsky again attacked the concept of one reactionary mass in "Der imperialistische Krieg," *Die Neue Zeit* 35/1 (1917): 450–54. There he quotes at length Engels's letter to him of 14 October 1891, which also appears in Benedikt Kautsky, ed., *Friedrich Engels' Briefwechsel mit Karl Kautsky* (Vienna: Danubia,

1955), 309–11. See also Kautsky, "Imperialismus und reaktionäre Masse," *Die Neue Zeit* 35/2 (1917): 102–15, where Kautsky emphasizes the complexity of class interests and of their expression in the form of political tactics.

It is interesting to note that in rejecting a "bourgeois-proletarian bloc regime as a means to the development of proletarian power," Kautsky (on p. 20 of *Der Weg zur Macht*) refers to the Marxian "word" of the dictatorship of the proletariat and interprets it as involving not a special form or style of government, but simply "the political *Alleinherrschaft* [sole rule] of the proletariat as the only form in which it can exercise political power."

33. His words are close to Engels's in "Grundsätze des Kommunismus," in Marx, Engels, *Werke*, 4 (East Berlin: Dietz Verlag, 1964), 372.

34. Kautsky, "Ein sozialdemokratischer Katechismus," *Die Neue Zeit*, 12/2 (1893): 368. The title of this piece does not suggest that Kautsky presented a Social Democratic catechism, but that he critically commented on a publication by that title.

35. Reinhold Hünlich, *Karl Kautsky und der Marxismus der II. Internationale* (Marburg: Verlag Arbeiterbewegung und Gesellschaftswissenschaft, 1981), 284, could, in his note 260, cite six works published between 1967 and 1975 using the passage in this manner. See also Marek Waldenberg, "Kautskys Marx-Rezeption," in Marxismus und Demokratie, ed. Rojahn et al., 39–40, and my comments on the passage in my article on Lenin and Kautsky on p 71, above.

36. For an excellent summary discussion of the evolution of Kautsky's thought on the mass strike in the context of debates on the subject among German Social Democrats, see Ingrid Gilcher-Holtey, *Das Mandat des Intellektuellen: Karl Kautsky und die Sozialdemokratie* (Berlin: Siedler, 1986), 184–204, 211, 219–22, 234. See also Dick Geary, *Karl Kautsky* (Manchester: Manchester University Press, 1987), who confuses Kautsky's failure to advocate specific tactics with fatalism and the advocacy of inaction.

For a convenient collection of Kautsky's earlier statements on the political mass strike going back to 1891 (when he was the first German Marxist to see that strikes could serve to achieve political ends), see Kautsky, *Der politische Massenstreik* (Berlin: Vorwärts, 1914), 23–24, 27, 68–103, 121–22, 127–28, 137–45, 148–55, 186. In that book he refers to *The Road to Power* as stating that, given the possibility of revolutionary situations, one had to take into account "the possibility, indeed the necessity, of a political mass strike also in Germany, where in normal times the conditions for it are highly unfavorable." Ibid., 212.

37. Kautsky similarly states in his article "Nochmals die amerikanische Statistik," *Die Neue Zeit* 27/2 (1909): 832, that one of the principal tasks of his *Road to Power* had been to emphasize the need for a "common struggle of the Party and the trade unions."

38. Kautsky, "Was nun?," *Die Neue Zeit* 28/2 (1910): 33–40, 68–80, reprinted in Kautsky, *Der politische Massenstreik*, 224–45. The situation in which Kautsky wrote this article is well summarized in Gilcher-Holtey, *Das Mandat*, 234–37, 249.

39. Rosa Luxemburg, "Was weiter?," *Gesammelte Werke,* 2 (East Berlin: Dietz Verlag, 1981), 289–99. Much of Kautsky's debate with Rosa Luxemburg and Anton Pannekoek on the mass strike is reprinted in Antonia Grunenberg, ed., *Die Massenstreikdebatte* (Frankfurt: Europäische Verlagsanstalt, 1970) and in Henri Weber, ed., Kautsky. Luxemburg. Pannekoek, *Socialisme: la voie occidentale,* (Paris: Presses Universitaires de France, 1983).

40. Kautsky, "Was nun?," 77.

41. Kautsky's prediction of an electoral victory proved accurate when, in 1912, the SPD increased its vote by nearly a million to 4,250,000, its share of the vote from 31.7 percent in 1903 and 28.9 percent in 1907 to 34.8 percent, and the number of its seats in the Reichstag from 81 in 1903 and 43 in 1907 to 110. On the other hand, Kautsky's prediction of a coup failed. He offered an explanation in *Der politische Massenstreik,* 247–55. We will never know whether Kautsky's prediction of a confrontation between Social Democracy and the imperial regime would have come true had it not been for the outbreak of World War I two years later (when, much to his chagrin, the majority of the SPD supported the regime) and the collapse of the imperial regime in November 1918.

42. Kautsky, "Was nun?," 80. In 1898, Kautsky had already predicted a coup d'état by the government in response to socialist electoral advances. In the letter to Bernstein of 18 February 1898 cited in note 7 above, he wrote: "Even before we have a hundred deputies, the struggle against us will get started, not about socialism, but about democracy. Coup d'état, abolition of the franchise, emergency legislation will come then if not earlier." Steinberg, *Sozialismus,* 80.

43. Gilcher-Holtey, *Das Mandat,* 248.

44. This is implied when the book is called "by far the most radical of his works," as it is by Fülberth in his introduction to the German edition of 1972 (xvii).

45. Kautsky, "Ein sozialdemokratischer Katechismus," 368, reprinted in *Der Weg zur Macht,* 52; Kautsky, *Der Parlamentarismus, die Volksgesetzgebung und die Sozialdemokratie* (Stuttgart: J. H. W. Dietz, 1893), 155–56.

46. Letter of 8 July 1893 to Franz Mehring, quoted from the Introduction to Rosa Luxemburg, *Gesammelte Werke,* vol. 3: *Gegen den Reformismus* (Berlin, 1925), 23, in Gerhard A. Ritter, *Die Arbeiterbewegung im Wilheminischen Reich* (Berlin: Colloquium Verlag, 1959), 203, n. 170. In 1898, at the SPD Congress in Stuttgart, Kautsky had already argued against Bernstein, just as he did against Ludwig Quessel in 1909 — see note 30, above — that in Germany it was hopeless to wait for "a victory of bourgeois democracy" to precede a Social Democratic victory: "If Bernstein believes that we must first have democracy in order then gradually to lead the proletariat to victory, then I say, here the matter is reversed, here the victory of democracy is dependent on a victory of the proletariat." *Protokoll,* 129.

47. "Sisyphusarbeit oder positive Erfolge?," *Correspondenzblatt der Generalkommiss-ion der Gewerkschaften Deutschlands* 9 (1909): 501–5, 517–19, 529–32, 545–48, 561–64, 577–80, 617–24; republished as *Sisyphusarbeit oder positive Erfolge?*

(Berlin: Verlag der Generalkommission der Gewerkschaften Deutschlands, 1910).

48. Also earlier in Kautsky, "Leichtfertige Statistik," *Die Neue Zeit,* 27/2 (1909): 517–24, and in "Nochmals die amerikanische Statistik," *Die Neue Zeit,* 27/2 (1909): 782–86, 821–32.

49. The growth of trade-union power in the SPD in the 1906–1909 period and the bureaucratization of the Party were well analyzed in Schorske, *German Social Democracy,* 88–145. With respect to trade-union power, he concluded: "The fear that trade-union leaders might withhold electoral support from the party made the executive acutely sensitive to the trade-unionists' demands. The unionists, with their anti-revolutionary attitude, may be presumed to have represented more accurately than the Social Democratic Party the mass of German workers in our period. By organizing these masses where the party could not, the union leaders were able to transmit the subjective attitudes of the politically passive workers into the Social Democratic Party itself, with the party executive as their agent. In this sense the trade-union conquest made the party more representative of German labor than it had been before 1906. Yet herein lay the fatal difficulty: the trade-union bureaucracy was anti-revolutionary in *Permanenz,* by virtue of its corporate interest in the existing order. The working class was not similarly committed, and the party had therefore represented the proletariat's revolutionary potential as well as its reformist actuality. By capitulating before the trade-unions in our period, the party surrendered its political flexibility, and thus prepared the ground for its subsequent dissolution." Ibid., 110. On SPD–trade union relations, see also Guttsman, *The German Social Democratic Party,* 279–87.

As to bureaucratization, Schorske concluded: "The principal positive task of the bureaucracy, to build up the party for electoral victories, necessarily involved a negative attitude toward any pressure for a change in tactic which would either divide the party or alienate the non-socialist voter. What the party functionary wanted above all else was peace and unity in the organization. In the riven condition of the party this made him a natural opponent of both criticism and change. And as the pressure for change came increasingly from the left, the functionary identified himself increasingly with the right." Schorske, *German Social Democracy,* 127. And further, "there is enough evidence to suggest that the defeat of radicalism within the party was aided by the establishment of the regional bureaucracy and regional institutions which based their power on the small-town worker and/or on the non-party trade-union member whose political attitudes toward the social order were not nearly so negative as those of the urban party member." Ibid., 135–136.

50. The fascinating story of the complex ensuing dispute becomes clear from the letters — unfortunately only in German — reprinted in Ursula Ratz, "Briefe zum Erscheinen von Karl Kautskys 'Weg zur Macht,' " *International Review of Social History,* 12/3 (1967): 432–77, and the selected letters reprinted in the appendix to the 1972 edition of *Der Weg zur Macht,* 113–38. Some of it is summarized in Georg Füberth's introduction, ibid., xx–xxiii.

51. A quick survey of the committee's membership suggests that four of its eight members — Ebert, Gerisch, Molkenbuhr, and Pfannkuch — were close to the trade unions, and a fifth, Müller, may also have been chiefly concerned with matters of organization and social policy. Bebel, the Party leader and Kautsky's old supporter, was sick and spent much of his time in Switzerland. Only the two remaining members, Singer and Zietz, were clearly identified with Kautsky's "radical" wing of the Party, but according to Hermann Brill, "Karl Kautsky: 16. Oktober 1854–17. Oktober 1938," *Zeitschrift für Politik* (new series, 1, no. 3) (October 1954): 221, Singer "in particular" opposed the distribution of *The Road to Power*.

52. Letter of 6 March 1909 in Friedrich Adler, ed., Victor Adler, *Briefwechsel,* 495–96; and in *Der Weg zur Macht,* 126–27.

53. Gary P. Steenson, *Karl Kautsky, 1854-1938: Marxism in the Classical Years* (Pittsburgh: University of Pittsburgh Press, 1978; paperback ed., 1991), 166–67.

54. Letter of 9 March 1909 in Friedrich Adler, ed., Victor Adler, *Briefwechsel,* 497, and in *Der Weg zur Macht,* 130.

55. Letter of 25 February 1909, in Friedrich Adler, ed., Victor Adler, *Briefwechsel,* 120–21, and in Ratz, "Briefe," 447.

56. See Zetkin's letter to Kautsky of 24 February 1909, International Institute of Social History, Kautsky Nachlass, D XXIII 378, quoted in Ursula Ratz, "Karl Kautskys Einschätzung von Krieg und Frieden im Zeitalter des Imperialismus," in *Marxismus und Demokratie,* ed. Rojahn et al., 190. See also Karl Kautsky, Jr., ed., *August Bebels Briefwechsel mit Karl Kautsky* (Assen: Van Gorcum, 1971), 203. Massimo Salvadori, *Karl Kautsky and the Socialist Revolution 1880–1938* (London: NLB, 1979), 131, also states that "the revisionists threatened a scission if *Der Weg zur Macht* appeared under the imprint of the party."

57. Steinberg, *Sozialismus,* 82.

58. Letter of 18 March 1909 in Ratz, "Briefe," 477. Haase says in this letter that he cannot understand how the compromise can be seen as a "disgraceful capitulation" on Kautsky's part, thus disagreeing with Clara Zetkin — see her bitter letter to Kautsky of 16 March 1909, ibid., 475–76 and *Der Weg zur Macht,* 137–38 — Kautsky's most fervent defender in the controversy and later a leading member of the USPD, the Spartacus League, and, from its beginnings until her death near Moscow in 1933, of the German Communist Party (KPD).

    Even an East German writer could conclude that "after much back and forth maneuvering, Kautsky succeeded in maintaining his position vis-à-vis the Party Executive Committee" and she quotes a letter of his of 27 March 1909 from the Moscow archives: "My *Road* will appear in the course of next week with a little addition to the preface, in which I alone assume all responsibility for its contents, and with several formal changes, in which not a single thought is being sacrificed." Annelies Laschitza, "Karl Kautsky im Widerstreit," 134.

59. I have compared the first and second editions page by page and have found the following changes of any significance, aside from the addition of more recent

figures or the replacement by them of older ones in the statistics on pages 67, 74, 75, 78, 84, 91, 97, and 99–100 of the second edition: A reference to "revolution" as a real possibility in the foreseeable future is omitted in the final paragraph on page 21, and the word "revolution" is replaced by "decisive struggle" on page 19, by "victory of the proletariat" on page 69, and by the proletariat achieving "political victory" on page 70, where in the same paragraph "such a situation" replaced a "revolutionary situation," "an interest in a revolution" becomes an interest in "gaining political power," and leading the "revolution to victory" becomes leading "the rising class to victory." On page 63, the "overthrow" of a regime hostile to the people has been replaced by it becoming "untenable." In the last sentence on page 70, the phrase "in the foreseeable future" is omitted in the second edition. On page 105 of that edition, "war also means revolution" is replaced by "the experience of the past few decades proves that war means revolution, that its consequence are very great shifts of political power." Also, on page 92, "peacefully" has been replaced by "without a struggle," and on page 69 quotation marks are added to "soldiers of revolution" and the same phrase is omitted in the next paragraph.

Clearly, almost all changes merely eliminated the word "revolution," which would seem to make little difference as that word still appears over and over again throughout the second edition. It is also noteworthy that Kautsky did not change a number of passages, including the final sentence of the book, that had been considered possibly legally objectionable by Joseph Herzfeld, a socialist lawyer consulted by Bebel. See Ratz, "Briefe," 453–55.

60. Gilcher-Holtey, *Das Mandat,* 232. Steenson, who does not analyze Kautsky's controversy with the Party Executive Committee as fully as Gilcher-Holtey, unlike her simply concludes that the committee "gave in." Steenson, *Karl Kautsky,* 168.

61. "Practical politics seeks power, theory seeks knowledge and understanding." Kautsky, "Der Parteitag in Lübeck," *Die Neue Zeit* 20/1 (1901): 19–20. See also Kautsky, "Vorwort," *General-Register des Inhalts der Jahrgänge 1883 bis 1902 der Neuen Zeit* (Stuttgart: Paul Singer, 1905), viii–ix. For Kautsky's view of the role of intellectuals and also of his own role in the party, see my article on Lenin and Kautsky and especially pp. 80–81, above.

62. Gilcher-Holtey, *Das Mandat,* 234. For a beautiful summary statement of the changes in the nature of the SPD and in Kautsky's relation to it, see ibid., 250–51.

63. That consistency is a major theme of Salvadori, *Karl Kautsky,* particularly 11–12.

64. Kautsky, *Das Erfurter Programm* 19th ed. (Bonn: J. H. W. Dietz, 1974), 216–17, The translation of this passage in *The Class Struggle* (New York: W. W. Norton, 1971), 188, is incomplete and inexact.

65. Kautsky, *Der politische Massenstreik,* 213–22.

66. "Centrism" as a new phenomenon has been emphasized particularly by German Communist writers in search of the origins of the "renegadism" that Lenin had attributed to Kautsky, which they place not, like Lenin, in 1914, but at the latest in 1910, when, it is intriguing to note, Lenin evidently tended to side with Kautsky

against Luxemburg (see note 57 to my article on Lenin and Kautsky above). See Hans-Jürgen Mende, *Karl Kautsky — vom Marxisten zum Opportunisten* (East Berlin: Dietz Verlag, 1985), 99–104, 111–28, and the following earlier articles all in *Beiträge zur Geschichte der deutschen Arbeiterbewegung* (East Berlin): Ulla Plener, "Karl Kautskys Opportunismus in Organisationsfragen (1900–1914): Zur Entstehung des Zentrismus in der deutschen Sozialdemokratie," ibid., 3, no. 2 (1961): 349–70; Gerd Irrlitz, "Bemerkungen über die Einheit politischer und theoretischer Wesenszüge des Zentrismus in der deutschen Sozialdemokratie," ibid., 8, no. 1 (1966): 43–59; and Annelies Laschitza, "Karl Kautsky und der Zentrismus," ibid., 10, no. 5 (1968): 798–832; Laschitza says: "The fact that centrism represents bourgeois ideology and bourgeois politics in the labor movement . . . and was therefore a particularly dangerous opportunistic tendency is for the Marxist-Leninist science of history incontrovertible." Ibid. 831–32. See also Laschitza, "Karl Kautsky im Widerstreit," 134. Georg Fülberth, in his introduction to the 1972 German edition of *Der Weg zur Macht,* calls the book Kautsky's "last 'revolutionary' work, shortly before his open shift to 'centrist' positions in 1910." *Der Weg zur Macht,* xvii. Hünlich, who is as critical of Leninist interpretations as he is of Kautsky, entitles his section on *The Road to Power* "a swan song of doctrinaire Marxism?" (*Karl Kautsky,* 153) and sees Kautsky's "shift to the position of centrism" as involving a "deep-going change" (ibid., 170).

67. Kautsky, *The Dictatorship of the Proletariat* (1918) (Ann Arbor: University of Michigan Press, 1964; reprint; Westport, Conn.: Greenwood Press, 1981); Kautsky, *Terrorism and Communism* (1919) (London: National Labour Press, 1920; reprint; Westport, Conn.: Hyperion Press, 1973).

68. Kautsky, *Der Weg zur Macht,* 3d ed., Berlin: Vorwärts, 1920.

69. Ibid., 5.

70. Ibid., 6-7. The final sentence shows that Kautsky could not understand, as we can now, that Lenin could not understand him in 1909.

In his preface to the third edition of *The Road to Power,* Kautsky also explains at some length why, having opposed socialist participation in coalition governments under the Empire, he now favored such participation to preserve the gains of the revolution in the Weimar Republic. Ibid., 14–22.

71. As Hans-Josef Steinberg wrote: "Kautsky believed in principle in a peaceful development to socialism, but as a condition for it democracy or a parliamentary system appeared to him necessary. . . . The difference with Bernstein consisted in Kautsky having doubts as to whether democracy could be achieved in Germany on a road other than that of a political revolution to which a Social Democratic majority would be forced by the resistance to democratization of a reactionary government." Steinberg, *Sozialismus,* 81.

72. In two letters to Franz Mehring written in 1893, when Kautsky was generally regarded as — next to Engels, who was still alive — the prime voice of orthodox Marxism, Kautsky made a statement he could have repeated at any time in the

remaining forty-five years of his life. On 8 July he wrote: "But for the dictatorship of the proletariat I cannot imagine any other form than that of a powerful parliament on the British model with a Social Democratic majority backed by a strong and conscious proletariat." On 15 July he repeated: "Only the parliamentary republic can in my judgment form the basis on which the dictatorship of the proletariat and the socialist society can grow. This republic is the 'state of the future' we must strive for." Quoted ibid., note 233, and in Karl Renner, *Karl Kautsky* (Berlin: J. H. W. Dietz, 1929), 86.

4

J. A. Schumpeter and Karl Kautsky: Parallel Theories of Imperialism

Joseph A. Schumpeter's essay on imperialism[1] is generally and rightly considered one of the most sophisticated theoretical contributions to the subject. Most students also think of it as an attempt to disprove the Marxian theory of imperialism, though they are aware that Schumpeter's own view was avowedly influenced by Marx's economic interpretation of history. Also, in his very effort to settle accounts with the Marxist theory, Schumpeter conceded that it had thrown great light on such phenomena as the role of monopoly, cartels, and protectionism, particularly as elaborated in the work of his contemporary and fellow student at the University of Vienna, Rudolf Hilferding, whose work was later to serve as the basic source of Lenin's ideas.[2] While the relation between Schumpeter's theory and these aspects of the Marxian treatments of imperialism is well known[3] and is, indeed, referred to by Schumpeter himself, it has not been appreciated how close Schumpeter's work came to the work of Karl Kautsky, another Marxist whose writings deserve more attention in this connection.[4]

I

Karl Kautsky, generally regarded as the most authoritative interpreter of Marxism in the generation after Marx and Engels, was one of the first, and indeed probably *the* first, Marxist to attempt to explain

This article is reprinted from the *Midwest Journal of Political Science* 5, no. 2 (May 1961): 101–28, by permission of the University of Texas Press.

131

imperialism. He did so even before the appearance in 1902 of J. A. Hobson's *Imperialism,* which, though not a Marxist work, is usually assumed to have anticipated the main lines of Marxian theory on the subject. Beginning with an article in 1898 and in numerous other writings published in the subsequent forty years, Kautsky developed views of imperialism strikingly similar to those of Schumpeter. The similarities are not confined to a common acceptance of the Marxian scheme of a political and ideological superstructure resting on an economic base or of Hilferding's analysis of capitalism at the turn of the century. They go far beyond these to the very points on which Schumpeter is often considered to score best in his attack on the Marxist theory. Thus, Kautsky agreed with Schumpeter that "pure" industrial capitalism was by nature peaceful and anti-imperialist, that imperialism was not an essential characteristic of mature capitalism, and that it was preindustrial elements in society that were responsible for modern imperialism. Also like Schumpeter, Kautsky emphasized the enduring strength of such preindustrial elements in society and traced their imperialistic tendencies back to prehistoric and ancient times, when warlike nomadic peoples sought unlimited territorial expansion.

At first sight, a relationship that finds the best-known destroyer of the Marxian theory of imperialism and Marxism's most orthodox voice echoing each other is puzzling indeed. It becomes less so once it is realized that there is no single Marxian theory of imperialism. Hilferding's theory, which was taken over and modified by Lenin, is but one of those built on Marxian foundations, Kautsky's is another, and Rosa Luxemburg's is yet another; and Schumpeter himself pointed out that his theory, too, was quite compatible with the economic interpretation of history.[5] The fact remains, however, that the Hilferding-Lenin theory is the one most widely regarded as *the* Marxist theory of imperialism, so that Schumpeter's theory has come to be looked on as a refutation of the Marxist theory. The mere fact that Kautsky shared many of Schumpeter's ideas is enough to cast doubt on the usefulness of the dichotomy. Still, Kautsky's position in the history of the theory of imperialism is an intriguing one, that of a Schumpeterian Marxist.

In view of the similarities between their ideas, it is remarkable that Schumpeter and Kautsky never referred to each other in their work on imperialism, though it is almost impossible to believe they were not familiar with each other's writings on the subject.[6] Kautsky had developed most of the basic ideas just mentioned long before Schumpeter wrote his essay. He also repeated and elaborated them in the postwar period, several years after Schumpeter's treatment had been published. There is no reason to suspect a case of direct influence, much less of conscious unacknowledged borrowing. Theories of imperialism were naturally in the air, especially in Germany, in the first two decades of this century, a period of growing protectionism, colonialism, armaments, and, finally, world war. That Kautsky and Schumpeter would approach the subject similarly was not entirely a coincidence, for they were in the same intellectual tradition of a social science seeking regularities in the broad perspectives of historical development and finding them chiefly in the relationship of social change to the dynamics of the system of production. Both thought it was Marx's chief merit to have been one of the foremost founders of this tradition. Schumpeter, moreover, was under the influence of the Viennese school of Marxism, notably of Hilferding and Otto Bauer, who were themselves disciples of Kautsky. Finally, Schumpeter and Kautsky shared still another attitude that no doubt contributed importantly to shaping their views of imperialism. Both were strong Anglophiles[7] and, during World War I, hoped for a Western victory over their own countries, imperial Austria and Germany. Britain was identified in their minds with pure industrial capitalism, free trade, and bourgeois rule; Germany with finance capitalism, protectionism, and the rule of the militarist Junkers. Their pro-British attitude, then, predisposed them to stress the anti-imperialism of the bourgeoisie and to find the roots of imperialism in preindustrial forces. This provides an important clue to an understanding of Schumpeter's and Kautsky's theories of imperialism, for the wartime writings of both (and, at least in part, Kautsky's prewar writings) on the subject were clearly motivated by their antagonism to the German government.

II

Like Schumpeter, Kautsky traced the beginnings of the tendency of states forcibly to expand their territory back to prehistoric times. To him that tendency was an essential aspect of the nature of the state, and its origins coincided with those of the state — if the state is defined, as it was by Marx, as a tool of the ruling class for the suppression of the ruled. Engels had thought that classes arose gradually within the pre-state community as a result of economic development, especially the division of labor, and that the exploiting classes then erected the state. Classes thus preceded the state.[8] Kautsky, on the other hand, developed a theory similar to those of Gumplowicz and Oppenheimer,[9] according to which classes and the state generally appeared not gradually and within the community but simultaneously, when one tribe, usually a nomadic one, conquered another, usually an agricultural one.

People engaged in agriculture in fertile river valleys become dependent on the land, unable and unwilling to leave it. As a result of this immobility and of their isolation in small villages and of the fact that they lost their warlike skills and habits in the transition from hunting to agriculture, peasants are peaceable and militarily weak. By contrast, nomads raising cattle in less-fertile areas are constantly defending their pasture lands and their cattle from dangerous animals and from other cattle-raising tribes. Cattle-stealing raids sometimes become almost a permanent institution. Thus the nomads are not only highly mobile and skilled in the use of weapons, but they are also accustomed to bloodshed and warfare and are, for all these reasons, militarily strong.

Where nomads come into contact with peasants, they are likely to plunder their villages or they may force them to pay tribute in return for being spared and for being protected against raids from other nomadic tribes. Given the low productivity of primitive agriculture, it is only when a nomadic tribe has succeeded in subjugating a number of peasant communities and in uniting them under its rule that the conquerors can live entirely on such tribute, ceasing to be cattle raisers and yet not becoming peasants, but devoting themselves to the task of government.

In most cases, according to Kautsky, this is the origin of the state and of classes — and of imperialism as well. For, from its very beginnings, the state is distinguished from pre-state, that is, classless, communities by the fact that it can and must expand. While these earlier communities were confined to a relatively small territory by the necessities of their mode of production, whether agricultural or cattle raising, the new ruling warrior aristocracy can travel far and for long periods to engage in warfare. A state's expansion is limited only by geographical conditions and by the power of the conquering tribe to keep the vanquished tribes in subjection and to defend the borders of its state from other would-be conquerors. In time, this military power can increase as the state grows. Thus, the ruling tribe may assign privileges to some of the conquered tribes so as to give them a stake in the existence of the state and to be able to use them to augment its military forces. Nor is there any limit to the will of the rulers to expand their state. A people living by its own labor — free peasants, hunters, shepherds — never wants more land than it can work. For an exploiter, however — given the absence of advanced technology — the most obvious way of increasing his income is to increase the number of those exploited and to add to the amount of land to be cultivated. As long as the state borders on land worth conquering, the urge to expand continues.

Moreover, the ruling aristocracy may be forced to carry on war against neighboring tribes and to annex their lands even if they produce nothing worth taking, merely in order to protect the state against their attacks. Finally, states come to border on each other and, for the reasons mentioned, the stronger proceed to attack and to annex the weaker ones. Each ruling class is suspicious of the other, since each has come to power by war and can only maintain itself by being ready for war, which is regarded as a threat by the others. Thus, preventive wars and wars for prestige are added to those carried on for increased exploitation and for self-protection.

As one empire defeats another, it is sufficient for the new rulers to replace the old ones. The new rulers may eliminate the old ones, or they may merely assume their military functions, leaving the old rulers in the positions of administrators and priests. A succession of conquests can result in several layers of tribes, which may become castes. The life of the bulk of the population, the peasantry, is not altered at all; no attempt is made to change their language, their religion, or the social, political, and economic institutions in their villages, for the new rulers' interest, like that of the old rulers, is only in the peasants' tribute. Once an empire begins in this fashion to conquer other empires rather than isolated peasant communities, it can grow very quickly to a tremendous size, as was the case with the great empires of antiquity.

Thus, like Schumpeter, Kautsky found the origins of expansionism[10] in the desires of warrior aristocracies. Both theorists agreed that these were originally nomads who conquered agricultural territory without becoming peasants themselves or changing substantially the peasants' way of life. Both also emphasized a link between warfare and hunting on the part of the aristocracy, Schumpeter suggesting that both activities served essentially the same function, Kautsky stressing that hunting produced the warlike skills, as well as the love of bloodshed, that made the aristocracy militarily superior to the peasants. Above all, both Schumpeter and Kautsky insisted that expansionism had no limits. Schumpeter spoke of "the tendency of such expansion to transcend all bounds and tangible limits, to the point of utter exhaustion";[11] Kautsky said that "narrowly limited as had been the growth of the tribe, that of the state became unlimited," and he referred to its "ceaseless impulse to expand."[12]

Here, however, we arrive at what appears at first to be an obvious and sharp difference between Schumpeter's and Kautsky's theories of imperialism. According to Kautsky, the continuous need for expansion, "the drive to wars of conquest [has] its deepest root . . . in the drive of every exploiting class to increase the yield of its exploitation, which is most easily achieved by increasing the number of the exploited."[13] To Schumpeter, on the other hand, "imperialism is the objectless disposition on the part of a state to unlimited forcible expansion" — it is never satisfied, exactly because it is "objectless," that is, "it has no adequate object beyond itself" and "cannot be explained by concrete interest," and Schumpeter explicitly rejects "the theory that points to the interest in booty and tribute."[14]

But even here, the difference between the two theories is not as great as it seems. Schumpeter's objectless disposition to expand arose in strata whose position and function in society and whose social organization and interests, habits, and ideologies required war as a justification for their existence and took war for granted as a normal and desirable state of affairs. Such strata — in early times it could also be an entire people (or tribe?) — became a war machine that, once set in motion, kept making war for the sake of war. "Created by wars that required it, the machine now created the wars it required."[15] Attractive as this phrase is, it does not explain what created the wars that created the war machine to begin with. On this point, to which Kautsky devoted so much attention, Schumpeter was virtually silent. The Egyptians are said to have developed a war machine in liberating themselves from the Hyksos, but why had the Hyksos invaded Egypt in the first place? Schumpeter comes closer to an answer — and closer to Kautsky — when he turns to the ancient Persians: "[I]t was geographic factors that made warriors of the Iranian Aryans. For them, war was the only method for keeping alive, the only possible form of life in a given environment."[16] Kautsky, too, had found the origin of warrior tribes in an environment that forced certain tribes into a nomadic and warlike life, and Schumpeter here all but acknowledged that the wars were carried on for booty or tribute, after all, since obviously not war itself but only the results of war could be a "method for keeping alive."

Furthermore, Schumpeter did not deny that conquerors, for example the Assyrians and the Persians, exacted tribute from and thus exploited their subjects; he merely insisted that this was not the goal and hence not the real cause of their wars. Of the Muslim Arabs, he said that they did not kill or convert the infidels: "[N]either course would have paid, for they were dependent on the labor and tribute of subjugated peoples for their livelihood, for their chance to remain a parasitical warrior and master nation. Once the infidel was converted or killed, an object of exploitation was lost"; and with reference to the Franks, Schumpeter stated categorically: "Above all, in order to exhibit a continual trend toward imperialism, a people must not live on — or at least not be absorbed by — its own labor."[17] Exploitation, then, is an essential ingredient of imperialism. This appears to be very close to Kautsky's thought, although a difference still remains. Put very briefly, it is simply that to Schumpeter exploitation was the means that made the end of expansion possible, while to Kautsky expansion was the means to the end of exploitation.

In fact, this is not a sharply defined difference at all, for means and ends have a way of becoming confused in actual practice, especially over a long period of time. I have already noted that Kautsky recognized a number of motives for expansion of a state other than the desire for exploitation that originally led to the state's establishment. We may now add that, just as Schumpeter really approached Kautsky on the matter of exploitation as the original motive for expansion, so Kautsky approached Schumpeter's insight that the expansionist drives of the aristocracy can become so deeply rooted in the attitudes and the social position of that class that they can persist, as Schumpeter put it, "until centuries of peaceful work wear down that war-like disposition and undermine the corresponding social organization."[18] Kautsky knew that the aristocracy in ancient times "achieved its dominant position through war and can maintain it only by constant readiness for war," and he ascribed the imperialistic tendencies of modern aristocracies in part to their desire to maintain themselves and their functions in society by increasing the number of positions in the army and the colonial bureaucracy. Kautsky also stressed that "the mentality of the landed aristocracy, where it has maintained itself, has to this day been the same as the one characterizing the men among nomadic shepherds"; aristocrats looked down with contempt upon productive labor, "only the occupations of the nomads appear to them as proper for their class [*standesgemäss*]: hunting, warfare, pillaging." Kautsky was less inclined than Schumpeter, however, to explain the persistence of "imperialistic" traits in the modern aristocracy as atavistic remnants of attitudes shaped by earlier living conditions and now expressing themselves only in an "objectless" manner:

> If we still discover, as soon as we scratch him, so many traits of the Tartars of yore in the true, status-conscious aristocrat of today, . . . that is due to the fact that the living condition of class are even today in many states still very much in conformity with the living conditions of the nomads. . . . The aristocrat's functions as ruler and exploiter engender always anew in him some of the qualities that gave the nomad greater vigor than the agriculturalist.[19]

III

Kautsky, then, emphasized the continuity of expansionist tendencies from the prehistoric nomads to the modern aristocracy, whose persistent strength in Europe, and particularly in Germany,[20] he, like Schumpeter, recognized. While he did not clearly establish the historical link between the two, which Schumpeter supplied in his brief but brilliant discussion of the Franks and the development of French absolutism, he had, already twenty years before Schumpeter, dealt with the colonialism of absolute monarchies. Perhaps Kautsky tended more to stress the share in monarchical colonialism of the commercial and banking bourgeoisie, whom Schumpeter regarded as mere servants of state policy in this respect; but Kautsky, too, placed most of the blame on the aristocratic elements. Above all, his theme, like Schumpeter's, was the exoneration of "pure" industrial capitalism from responsibility for colonialism in this period as well as in later ones.

The relationship of imperialism to capitalism was, of course, the principal concern both of Schumpeterian and of Marxist thinking about the subject. Chiefly under the influence of Lenin's work on imperialism[21] — in turn a simplification and rigidification of some of Hilferding's doctrines — it has come to be widely assumed that all Marxist theory holds imperialism to be necessarily associated with capitalism and, in fact, to be identical with its last and "highest" stage. It is therefore fascinating to note that, very much like Schumpeter, Kautsky ascribed imperialism to the remnants of precapitalist society, which remained powerful and might even gain renewed strength under capitalism. In this way, Kautsky's theory of what he calls imperialism, that is, expansionism under capitalism, was, just like Schumpeter's, linked with his broader theory of expansionism of states from earliest times.

Already in his first article on imperialism, Kautsky emphasized that industrial capital in its purest form was opposed to imperialism.[22] The colonial expansion of the seventeenth and eighteenth centuries of Spain, Portugal, and, in part, France was originally caused by population pressure and was carried on for the benefit of the monarchy, the aristocracy, and the Church. It produced a decline in the domestic industry and agriculture of these countries. Holland and England, on the other hand, entered on colonial expansion at a time when their feudal absolutism was already beaten, when their colonies were run by merchants and commercial companies, not by bureaucrats and the Church. Thus trade and the bourgeoisie prospered and colonial exploitation became an important element in the original accumulation of industrial capital that preceded capitalist industry. In either case, the colonialism of the seventeenth and eighteenth centuries could not be a result of industrial capitalism.

The colonies England had acquired before the nineteenth century served commercial and banking capital as suppliers of goods sold in Europe at a profit, but hardly as a market for British products. Hence the industrial capitalists had little interest in the colonies, and, as they gained power in Britain, expansionism came to a halt. There was virtually none from the 1840s into the 1870s, since industrial capitalism was interested not in territory but in trade with the natives. Thus, China and Africa were opened up to trade, but they were not conquered even where the process was a warlike one, as in China. Similarly, there was a change in the treatment of the natives of the colonies. Settlers, bureaucrats, soldiers, and even merchants all had interests that might induce them to oppress, enslave, or even kill the natives. Industrial capitalists, however, sought customers in the colonies. Hence while they favored woman and child labor at home, they were philanthropists in the colonies, supported missionaries and prohibited the slave trade. In any case, the colonial market was far too small for rising British industries in the nineteenth century. That industry needed free trade, in which England would be the workshop of the world and the rest of the world would be its agrarian area, and it needed peace. "The more industrial capital, and particularly production for export, advances into the foreground, the greater the capitalist nations' need for peace."[23]

When, in the 1880s and 1890s, the industrial capitalist era of free trade and peace was replaced by one of renewed colonialism,

> it was not the needs of industrial development that brought on the latest phase of colonial policy, but, on the one hand, the needs of classes, whose interests are opposed to the requirements of economic development and, on the other hand, the needs of states, whose interests are opposed to those of advanced civilization. In other words, the most recent phase of colonial policy is, like protectionism, a work of reaction; it is by no means necessary for economic development, often even harmful. It originates, not in England, but in France, Germany, and Russia. Insofar as England is going along with it, it does so only under compulsion rather than of its own free will, defensively, rather than aggressively — speaking in general, of course.[24]

Kautsky sought at some length to show that British expansionism was merely a defensive reaction to save territory for free trade in northwest India, Egypt, and Cyprus against the efforts of Russia and in Africa against the efforts chiefly of France to conquer areas in which Russian and French industry would be given monopoly privileges.[25]

Steps toward democratization in the 1860s in Britain strengthened the proletariat and left industrial capitalists politically predominant. Similar steps at about the same time on the Continent, notably in Germany and France, however, strengthened the petty bourgeoisie and the peasantry, still numerous in these countries. At first allied with liberalism, they placed themselves under the leadership of the big landowners as they were more and more threatened by the growth of big industry. The landowners were also strengthened by militarism, for most officers were drawn from their class. Finally, the bureaucracy, a product of Continental absolutism, also regained power as the declining, despairing classes turned for aid to the government. At the same time, the bourgeoisie, afraid of the proletariat, compromised with reaction and became its ally.

This is the situation from which the new colonial policy originated. . . . That industrial capital, too, wanted to gain from this policy is true, but it does not constitute the driving force of the colonial movement. Militarism yearning for activity and advancement, the bureaucracy wishing for an increase in the number of lucrative posts, the decline of agriculture which drives so many peasants off the land and forces so many younger sons of big landowners to look for positions requiring little knowledge but all the more brutality, the growing greed of the Church, which wants to gain prestige and wealth in uncivilized countries, too, and can do so more easily under governmental protection, and finally the growing power of high finance and its growing need for exotic business—these are the principal driving forces of the latest phase of imperialism.[26]

In his 1898 analysis, it was thus clearly the preindustrial forces of society that Kautsky held responsible for imperialism, that is, for the revival of colonialism in the late nineteenth century; the big landowners and the forces they dominated, the military, the bureaucracy, and the Church; the peasantry and the petty bourgeoisie, which lent their political strength to the landowners; and finally banking capital, which, unlike industrial capital, was historically linked to the landed aristocracy. It was the big banks that handled the export of capital, a business particularly profitable when it was carried on under the protection of the government. Governments had become so dependent on banking capital that they therefore acquired colonies. In turn, governments used colonialism to divert the declining and discontented middle classes with the prospect of markets and places of immigration—though, as Kautsky was quick to point out, colonies were largely unsuitable for both.[27]

IV

After the turn of the century, a certain shift in Kautsky's attitude on the question of what groups were primarily responsible for imperialism became apparent. In 1901 Kautsky wrote a book analyzing the change from a policy of free trade to one of protectionism, particularly in Germany, and the role of various groups and classes in that change. In that book we already find a passage stating that it is "cartel monopolists" who

demand the conquest by violent means of a market in which they would enjoy a privileged position, that is, a policy of colonialism and expansionism. This, in turn, produces conflicts or the danger of conflicts with the competing industrial powers. ... New armaments, which in turn benefit the cartel economy, further colonial adventures, and increased danger of war are the consequence.[28]

Kautsky's characterization in this book of the effects of cartelization on the political outlook of the industrial bourgeoisie is so similar to the views on the subject later expressed by Hilferding in *Finance Capital*[29] as to make it fairly clear that Hilferding owed a significant debt to Kautsky's influence.

On the other hand, there is no doubt that Kautsky was in turn greatly influenced by Hilferding's work on imperialism. In his review of *Finance Capital,* he stated that England was now relatively backward, because individual capitalist ownership predominated in its industry and the dependence on the banks and combination in cartels and trusts of that industry had not advanced as far as in the United States and in Germany.

Not England, but the United States is the country that shows us our social future in capitalism. ... It is to finance capital that the capitalist future belongs. But it is the most brutal and violent form of capital, both in the international competitive struggle and in the domestic class struggle.[30]

Thus Kautsky now implied that imperialism was the product of an advanced form of capitalism rather than of states "opposed to those of advanced civilization," as he held in 1898.

In an important article on imperialism written in 1914, too, Kautsky characterized imperialism as "a product of highly developed industrial capitalism." He defined it as "the drive of every industrial capitalist nation to subject and attach to itself an ever growing *agrarian* territory regardless of what nations inhabit it."[31] This definition rests on Kautsky's theory of the inevitable disproportionality of industrial production and agricultural production.[32] According to it, the expansion of agricultural production cannot keep pace with that of industrial production. Since the latter is nevertheless dependent on the former as a supplier of food and raw materials and as a market, all capitalist industrial nations must expand the agricultural areas with which they exchange products: "One particular form of this drive is imperialism. It was preceded by another form, that of free trade. Half a century ago, that was regarded as the last word of capitalism, just as imperialism is today."[33] To Kautsky, then, imperialism was "only an episode" in the general process of the opening up of agrarian areas by industrial nations, a process of which railroad construction was much more commonly characteristic.[34]

In his 1914 article, Kautsky traced imperialism largely to capitalist rather than precapitalist origins. Western Europe and the United States used protective tariffs against Britain's free trade and divided up the remaining free agrarian areas. "To this England reacted. Thus imperialism began." It advanced further, when capitalists had the governments that they dominated protect their overseas investments in railroads, mines, and so on. Finally, capitalist countries acquired colonies in order to prevent their agrarian regions from developing their own competing industries, as the United States and Russia had been able to do because they had been politically independent. "These are the most important roots of imperialism."[35]

Kautsky's two explanations of imperialism — the earlier one, which, like Schumpeter's, stressed preindustrial forces, and the later one, which, like Hilferding's, focused on industrial capitalism as the chief cause of imperialism — were not quite as inconsistent as they may at first appear. Kautsky could, at one and the same time, consider banking capital, which he regarded as a preindustrial element, as "the principal driving force behind present-day colonial policy" and also hold industrial capital responsible for it, "for the characteristic of the era of imperialism is exactly the growing identification of industrial capital and banking capital. And from this identification arises the increasing interest of industrial capital in colonial policy."[36] With their organization in corporate form,

> the biggest and strongest sections of industrial capital were united with banking capital and simultaneously the way was opened to an understanding between them and big landed property. Trusts and the centralization of the big banks drove this development to its extreme.
>
> The political tendencies of finance capital now became the general tendencies of all the economically ruling classes of the capitalistically advanced states.
>
> That is one characteristic of the present period which is referred to as the imperialist one.[37]

These political tendencies of finance capital are quite different from those of industrial capital before its merger with banking capital. Industrial capital favored international peace, limitations on absolute government, and economy in state expenditures, and opposed tariffs on food and raw materials.

> [T]he class of the big money lenders and bankers, on the other hand, is inclined to favor absolute government and the realization by violent means of its domestic and foreign demands. It has an interest in big governmental expenditures and indebtedness as long as they do not bankrupt the government. It is friendly with the big landowners and does not object to their being favored by agrarian tariffs.[38]

By 1927 Kautsky had explicitly integrated his Hilferdingian theory, which placed the blame for imperialism on finance capital, into his broader theory, which held exploiting classes in general, but not industrial capital, responsible for expansionism. Unlike industrial capital, but "like the landed aristocracy, banking and commercial capital are usually imbued with the urge to expand the sphere of exploitation that is peculiar to the exploiting classes in the state."[39] The development of corporations and trusts and the predominance of borrowed capital in industry brought industrial capital into ever closer association with banking capital, resulting in the new phenomenon that Hilferding called finance capital.

> In this form, industrial capital develops the same spirit of violence toward the exploited and competitors as has hitherto characterized all exploiting classes. To that extent, certainly, finance capital is, then, responsible for imperialism.[40]

As industrial capital and banking capital merge, the ideology of the former is assimilated to that of the latter:

> Beginning in the last decade of the nineteenth century, the industrial capitalist changes from a free trader, a pacifist, and a liberal, from an enemy of the landed aristocracy, of militarism, and bureaucratism into the very opposite of these. Thus his attitude toward colonial policy also changes. Industrial capital now joins other forces favoring such a policy.[41]

Whether Kautsky inclined to the Schumpeterian "preindustrial" or the Hilferdingian "industrial" explanation of imperialism, certain elements of his thought remained constant; it was banking capital rather than industrial capital in its pure form that was a driving force, if not *the* driving force, of imperialism; it was chiefly France, Germany, and Russia that sought imperialist expansion, while Britain merely reacted defensively; and, finally, imperialism was merely one possible form of the general and inevitable phenomenon of industrial expansionism into agrarian areas and hence was not necessary to capitalism.

These three points are also crucial ones in Schumpeter's analysis of imperialism, and his conclusions on them are in many respects strikingly similar to Kautsky's. On the question of British imperialism, so often thought of as the prime example of imperialism, Schumpeter went, if anything, even further than Kautsky. According to Schumpeter, there was no real British imperialism even in the eighteenth century, but only defensive expansionism against France and the "private imperialism" of individual adventurers, which was to be distinguished from conquests by the British state or people. For the nineteenth century, he, like Kautsky, stressed the predominance of the industrial bourgeoisie with its belief in free trade and pacifism. Disraeli's imperialism was only of "verbal character," the Boer War was "merely a chance aberration from the general trend" and, in general, British imperialism in the decades before World War I "did not rise from the true depths" of social evolution.[42]

Second, Schumpeter, like Hilferding and hence like Kautsky, linked modern imperialism to monopoly capitalism[43] and readily acknowledged that under monopoly conditions the industrial bourgeoisie shared an interest in imperialism with the old aristocracy. He differed from Hilferding exactly where Kautsky did so, when he regarded monopoly capitalism as the result of the intrusion into industrial capitalism of a preindustrial element alien to pure industrial capitalism as represented by the Manchester School. To be sure, Schumpeter and Kautsky differed somewhat on the nature of this preindustrial element. For Kautsky it was banking capital, an ally, at least since feudal times, of the landed warrior aristocracy and of the monarchy based on it. For Schumpeter the key element was protectionism, originally a mercantilist method of the absolute monarchy whose needs and interests helped shape the industrial bourgeoisie. Not only are banking capital and protectionism related—Schumpeter himself shows how the latter facilitates the formation of trusts and cartels, which are, in turn, the result of the merger of industrial and banking capital into Hilferding's finance capital — but emphasis on the preindustrial character of both banking capital and protectionism led both Kautsky and Schumpeter to the same conclusion — the third point of similarity between them — "it is a basic fallacy to describe imperialism as a necessary phase of capitalism."[44] To Kautsky's attitude on this last point we must now devote further attention.

V

Kautsky's insistence that, just as imperialism had not necessarily been associated with industrial capitalism in the past, so it was not an inevitable concomitant of capitalism in his own time or in the future and that, therefore, the end of imperialism would not be the end of capitalism, brought him into opposition to both rightist and leftist Marxists. The rightists argued that imperialism was a necessary phase of capitalism that it was foolish to fight,[45] and that to oppose it would be "to oppose world history."[46] Kautsky, in reply, reasoned that imperialism was not a phase but a policy of capitalism. As such, it should be opposed by socialists, just like wage reductions or the extension of working hours,

> not to retard economic progress, but to force the capitalist class to seek the enlargement of its profits, the extension of its area of exploitation, the increase in exports of industrial products and in imports of foods and raw materials, not through the most obvious and simple methods of imperialism, but by the methods of democracy and free intercourse, which, to be sure, require more thought, but which open up the widest opportunities to economic progress and thereby also strengthen the proletariat physically, intellectually, and politically.[47]

Leftist Marxists, quite like the rightists, held that imperialism was a necessary aspect of capitalism and hence could not be fought under capitalism, but, unlike the rightists, they concluded that it could and should therefore be fought only by the socialist revolution.[48] Kautsky's reply, again, was that if imperialism was a tendency of capitalism — even an inevitable one, which he did not concede — it had to be fought under capitalism. The socialist revolution arose precisely out of the conflict between such capitalist tendencies and the proletarian countertendencies they produced, and it did not constitute an alternative to such conflict under capitalism.[49]

In his 1914 article on imperialism Kautsky turned to the question of whether "imperialism is the only form under capitalism under which it is still possible to expand the interchange between industry and agriculture."[50] The drive to expand that exchange was inevitable, but it could assume different forms, of which imperialism was merely one. "Proof that that drive is a vital condition for capitalism by no means demonstrates that any one of these forms constitutes an essential necessity for the capitalist mode of production."[51] In fact, imperialism threatened the capitalist economy. Not only was there growing native opposition to it in more advanced colonies and proletarian resistance at home to higher taxes, but the costs of armaments, expansionism, and war were menacing the rapid accumulation of capital and therefore the export of capital. "Thereby imperialism digs its own grave. From a means of developing capitalism it turns into an obstacle to it. . . . This policy of imperialism cannot be continued much longer."[52]

In what other form, then, could capitalism continue to expand? In answer to this question, Kautsky briefly, and rather cautiously and tentatively, suggested that "from the purely economic point of view, it is . . . not inconceivable that capitalism will live to see yet another phase, a transfer of the policy of cartels to foreign policy, a phase of ultra-imperialism."[53] This, too, would have to be fought by socialists, but it would pose no threat to world peace. Lenin furiously and at some length attacked "Kautsky's silly little fable about 'peaceful' ultra-imperialism,"[54] because it implied that war among the imperialist powers was not inevitable as he had insisted. Lenin thus gave this idea of Kautsky's an importance and definiteness that it does not seem to have held in Kautsky's own mind.

A decade after the first World War, Kautsky noted that imperialism was now receding before an expanding native revolt in Asia and North Africa, but he again emphasized that this "does not at all mean a collapse of capitalism. It will merely foster a new form of capitalism, the Asiatic form."[55] While finance capital tended to be imperialistic, Kautsky counted, for a progressive limitations of imperialism,

> on the growing strength of the industrial proletariat in the countries of decisive importance for capitalism and on the no less growing strength of the national rebellions and independence movements in the colonies themselves. It is, however, also possible that finance capital, taught a lesson by the World War, finds this method of expanding its sphere of exploitation too risky. It might conclude that this way of trying to increase profits

endangers its entire capital and that it would be more profitable to shift to an ultra-imperialism, an international cartelization of the finance capitalists of all countries.[56]

In any case, however, Kautsky continued to insist that "imperialism does not by any means constitute an economically necessary condition of all capitalist accumulation."[57]

When, in 1937, Kautsky discussed prospects for the future in the final chapter of his last work, there was no doubt in his mind that the end of imperialism was at hand.[58] For one thing, since there were virtually no free territories left, the danger of conflicts among colonial powers resulting from further imperialistic expansion had been vastly increased. More important, the growth and ultimate victory of the independence movements in the colonies were as irresistible as those of the proletariat in the advanced countries, for they were produced by the same phenomena that accompanied modern big industry – the development of industrial capital, of communications, of popular education, and of political democracy. To be sure, these conditions developed much more slowly in the colonies, but, on the other hand, the independence movement could unite all classes of a population and it confronted an enemy of different color and culture, religion, and language, thus making it relatively stronger than the proletarian or even the democratic movement in the West. The numerical superiority of the independence movement over its enemy, too, was far greater.

Kautsky expected the process of the liberation of the colonies to be, on the whole, a peaceful one. Wars had become too destructive for any popular movement to use them as the means to its ends. Wars would be the less likely the more democratic the colonial powers were and the more influence in their policy their industrial proletariat could exert. Thus Kautsky was most optimistic in this respect with reference to the British Empire.[59] He pointed out, however, that the liberation of the colonies would not be easy, especially where it would have to overcome the resistance not only of militarists, bureaucrats, and capitalists in the colonial power, but also, as in South Africa, of a substantial population of white settlers, not only of capitalists and farmers but even of proletarians, who had enjoyed a privileged position in relation to the natives.

In any case, though writing at a time of renewed expansionism and military conquests, Kautsky was convinced that imperialism was finished. The conquests by Japan in China and by Italy in Ethiopia were merely "a last echo of a disappearing period, the age of imperialism"; they were "not the beginning of a new imperialist era but . . . mere anachronisms, not necessitated by but only disturbing the laws of social development."[60]

In his conclusion that imperialism was doomed, Kautsky was, once again, in agreement with Schumpeter's conviction that "imperialisms will wither and die,"[61] though Schumpeter, writing during World War I and being probably less optimistic by temperament than Kautsky, implied that imperialism's ultimately inevitable death might yet be some way off. Both also agreed that the forces condemning imperialism to death were industrialization and its accompanying phenomenon, democratization. Neither considered the possibility of industrialization without democratization, and neither offered any clear clue to an understanding of Soviet and Chinese Communist expansionism — though both Schumpeter's "war machine in motion" and Kautsky's expansionism to increase the area of exploitation and the number of exploited may not be entirely irrelevant concepts here.

While Kautsky tended to stress the effects of industrialization also in the colonies, an aspect of the problem with which Schumpeter did not deal, both emphasized that industrialization gave rise to new groups that were opposed to imperialism. In a brilliant passage, again perhaps not without relevance to developments in the Soviet Union, Schumpeter showed how these groups — bourgeoisie, workers, intellectuals and "professionals," and rentiers — were "all inevitably democratized, individualized, and nationalized." "A purely capitalist world therefore can offer no fertile soil to imperialist impulses," for it was hostile to what was merely "instinctual" and traditional. In particular, industrial labor was anti-imperialist; "even less than peasant imperialism is there any such thing as socialist or other working class imperialism."[62] While Kautsky would, of course, have generally agreed with this point, his reference to privileged white proletarians in the colonies and his own conflicts with socialist advocates of imperialism in Germany and in the International lead one to believe that he, the Marxist, might have stated it with more qualifications than the non-Marxist Schumpeter.

VI

What is true of their conclusions on the future of imperialism is generally true of the theories of Kautsky and Schumpeter: They do not contradict each other and, where they do not coincide, they supplement each other. Kautsky is more concerned with and, on the whole, more convincing on the origin of expansionism as rooted in the interests of some social groups. Schumpeter's chief interest is in the element of "objectless" persistence. "Vital needs of situations . . . molded peoples and classes into warriors. . . . Psychological dispositions and social structures acquired in the dim past in such situations, once firmly established, tend to maintain themselves and to continue in effect long after they have lost their meaning and their life-preserving function." "Imperialism thus is atavistic in character. . . . It is an element that stems from the living conditions not of the present, but of the past — or, put in terms of the economic interpretation of history, from past rather than present relations of production."[63]

Kautsky, too, was aware of the fact that much modern territorial expansionism was not directly related to desires for industrial expansion (and was therefore not imperialist, as he used that term). He abhorred the simple view, often associated with Marxism, that all expansionism and all wars involving advanced capitalist countries were necessarily imperialist and therefore similar in nature.

> If we analyze the efforts at expansion of the various capitalist states in recent times in detail, then we find that the imperialist tendencies, characterized by the merger of industrial and finance capital, and the need for capital export, are by no means the only cause of efforts at expansion. Beside them, other more primitive tendencies are effective; the imperialist ones are merely the newest and therefore the most striking.[64]

Very much like Schumpeter, Kautsky emphasized the continuing importance in modern times of the expansionism of eighteenth century absolutism,[65] but he also stressed the continuing importance of the far more ancient desires of aristocratic ruling groups for the acquisition of the products of the labor of others through the collection of tribute, of big landowners for more land, and of the military and the bureaucracy for more lucrative positions.[66]

For Schumpeter, to prove the importance in the present of "surviving features from earlier ages" seems, indeed, to have been the main purpose of his essay. He says himself in its concluding sentence: "The only point at issue here was to demonstrate, by means of an important example, the ancient truth that the dead always rule the living."[67] On this most general and perhaps most important theme we again find Kautsky in agreement with Schumpeter. The latter had, indeed, been at pains to point out that he was offering not a rebuttal but a corrective refinement of the Marxian theory of history:

> I should like to emphasize that I do not doubt in the least that this powerful instrument of analysis will stand up here in the same sense that it has with other similar phenomena — if only it is kept in mind that customary modes of political thought and feeling in a given age can never be mere "reflexes" of, or counterparts to, the production situation of that age. Because of the persistence of such habits, they will always, to a considerable degree, be dominated by the production context of past ages.[68]

Only a discussion of Kautsky's own interpretation of history could fully document his agreement with Schumpeter on this point. Here we can merely quote his statement in defense of the materialist conception of history against Bernstein, written at the turn of the century: "[O]ne cannot explain the history of a period from its own economic history alone, but must take into account the entire preceding economic development and, in addition, its products, beginning with prehistory."[69] And in his chief work on the subject he devoted a special chapter to illustrating that, if the entire body of ideology of a period, and not merely the new elements in it, is to be explained,

> then it becomes necessary to undertake the [following] quite laborious task, which cannot always be carried out completely. One must trace back the various old elements of the dominant ideas to the time of their origin and relate each of them to the economic conditions that newly emerged at that time. And then one must also investigate how the change of these conditions, up to the age whose total ideology is to be studied, modified the ideological element in question.[70]

Schumpeter needed to stress this view chiefly because it called attention to the persistent strong precapitalist elements and the weakness of the bourgeoisie in "capitalist" society on the European continent and, no doubt, particularly in Germany, though he never mentioned that country by name. He pointed out that the bourgeoisie itself was shaped by "needs stemming not from the nature of the capitalist economy as such but from the fact of the coexistence of early capitalism with another and at first overwhelmingly powerful mode of life and business." Thus, established habits of thought long remained strong even where capitalism came into full control, but "actually capitalism did not fully prevail *anywhere* on the Continent." Particularly, capitalism initially

> did not alter the basic outlines of the social structure of the countryside. Even less did it affect the spirit of the people, and least of all their political goals. This explains why the features and trends of autocracy — including imperialism — proved so resistant.

"Whoever seeks to understand Europe must not overlook that even today its life, its ideology, its politics are greatly under the influence of the feudal 'substance,' that while the bourgeoisie can assert its interests everywhere, it 'rules' only in exceptional circumstances, and then only briefly."[71]

Schumpeter was here applying an important corrective to the still widely influential Marxian notion that, regarding social development in England as typical, insists that a bourgeois-capitalist stage must intervene between the feudal and the proletarian-socialist stages of history. Once again we find, however, that Kautsky, too, had become aware of the fallacy of this view, interestingly enough, particularly when he was cast as the defender of orthodox Marxism in the controversy over Revisionism. That controversy can, of course, not be reviewed here, but it must be stated that, contrary to a widespread view, it turned not on the principled question of whether socialism was to be attained by peaceful, democratic or violent revolutionary means (both sides agreed on the first alternative), but on the largely tactical question of how democracy could be attained for labor on the Continent, and particularly in Germany. In the course of acknowledging this quite frankly at the first great Social Democratic Party debate on Revisionism, when he conceded freely that Bernstein's advocacy of gradual "growth into socialism" was quite realistic in Britain but not on the Continent, Kautsky came close to Schumpeter. England, he said, was the classic capitalist country, but it was exceptional politically, "a great state without army, without bureaucracy, without peasantry, with very little agriculture." On the Continent, on the other hand, these precapitalist remnants were still strong; there was "everywhere highly developed militarism, everywhere a bureaucracy that rules absolutely, not only in the monarchic states but also in France. We have further-more on the Continent of Europe the significant influence of the big landowners; the bourgeoisie submits to the rule of the saber."[72]

Schumpeter's charge that "neo-Marxist theory" tries "to reduce im-perialist phenomena to economic class interests of the age in question . . . [and] views imperialism simply as the reflex of the inter-ests of the capitalist upper stratum, at a given stage of capitalist devel-opment," does not really apply to Kautsky's theory, then. "Neo-Marx-ist" theory — which Schumpeter calls "beyond doubt; . . . the most se-rious contribution toward a solution of our problem" — is merely *a* Marxian theory, chiefly Hilferding's, and not the only possible Marxian theory. Schumpeter himself, unlike many commentators, knew this, for he emphasized "that it does not, of logical necessity, follow from the economic interpretation of history. It may be discarded without coming into conflict with that interpretation; indeed, without even departing form its premises."[73] What Schumpeter seems to have re-garded as a mere logical possibility — a theory of imperialism both based on the Marxian interpretation of history and yet also quite com-patible with his own theory — was, in fact, developed, in part before Schumpeter wrote his essay, by Karl Kautsky.

This article was drafted when I was a research fellow in the Russian Research Center, Harvard University. I wish to acknowledge my debt to the Russian Research Center and to the Rockefeller Foundation, whose generous support made my stay there possible. I also deeply appreciate the valuable suggestions and criticism I re-ceived from my colleague, Morris Watnick.

Notes

1. Joseph A. Schumpeter, "The Sociology of Imperialisms," written during World War I and first published in Germany in 1919 as "Zur Soziologie der Imperial-ismen," *Archiv für Sozialwissenschaft und Sozialpolitik* 46 (1919): 1–39, 275–310, published in this country in Joseph A. Schumpeter, *Imperialism and Social Classes* (New York: Augustus M. Kelley, 1951).

2. Ibid., 104, and Rudolf Hilferding, *Financial Capital* (London: Routledge & Kegan Paul, 1981).

3. O. H. Taylor, "Schumpeter and Marx: Imperialism and Social Classes in the Schumpeterian System," *The Quarterly Journal of Economics* 65, no. 4 (Novem-ber 1951): 525–55; Klaus Knorr, "Theories of Imperialism," *World Politics* 4, no. 3 (April 1952): 402–32; and Eduard Heimann, "Schumpeter and the Problem of

Imperialism," *Social Research* 19, no. 2 (June 1952): 177–97. See also E. M. Winslow, "Marxian, Liberal, and Sociological Theories of Imperialism," *The Journal of Political Economy* 39, no. 6 (December 1931): 749–55. Brief relevant statements also appear in E. M. Winslow, *The Pattern of Imperialism* (New York: Columbia University Press, 1948), 234–35; in Paul M. Sweezy's introduction to Schumpeter, *Imperialism,* x; and in J. Hashagen, "Marxismus und Imperialismus," *Jahrbücher für Nationalökonomie und Statistik,* 113 (1919): 206, 210.

4. Winslow, both in his book (151–58) and in his article (719–39), cited above, does deal with Kautsky's theory of imperialism, but his discussion is incomplete and somewhat superficial and hence misleading. His reference (on page 157 of his book) to Kautsky's analysis of modern expansionism as "atavistic" might, however, be taken as a hint at the similarity between Kautsky and Schumpeter, which is the subject of the present article. As Winslow mentions in his article (749–50), Hashagen noted "that Schumpeter's theory was anticipated in 1900 by Franz Mehring [a Marxist writer then close to Kautsky] who held that capitalism at its highest point of development is openly opposed to imperialism" ("Marxismus und Imperialismus," 205, 210), but no one seems to have noted the much more far-reaching similarity between Kautsky and Schumpeter. A recent virulent critic of Schumpeter's theory of imperialism does very briefly compare it with Kautsky's, with which he shows no familiarity, however; Horace B. Davis, "Schumpeter as Sociologist," *Science and Society* 24, no. 1 (Winter 1960): 21.

   [When I wrote the present article, I had not seen Kurt Mandelbaum, *Die Erörterungen innerhalb der deutschen Sozialdemokratie über das Problem des Imperialismus* (Ph.D. dissertation, University of Frankfurt, 1926 [Frankfurt: Peuvag, n.d.]), who, in several notes on pages 36–41, briefly points to similarities between Kautsky's and Schumpeter's theories and finds that "it is particularly interesting that in most important points Kautsky anticipated what Schumpeter later developed." Ibid., 36, n. 9.]

5. Schumpeter, *Imperialism,* 7, also 84, 96.

6. The two were also in personal contact with each other, at least in December 1918 and January 1919, the very period when Schumpeter's essay was first published, when he served on the German socialization commission under Kautsky's chairmanship. In one of his few references to the Marxist theory of imperialism in a later work, Schumpeter almost seems to go so far as to imply that Kautsky made no contribution to its development: In *Capitalism, Socialism, and Democracy* (New York: Harper & Brothers, 1942), 49, he stated that "the" Marxist theory of imperialism was "developed by the Neo-Marxist school which flourished in the first two decades of this century and, without renouncing communion with the old defenders of the faith, such as Karl Kautsky, did much to overhaul the system [of Marxism]. Vienna was its center, Otto Bauer, Rudolf Hilferding, Max Adler were its leaders." See also Schumpeter, *History of Economic Analysis* (New York: Oxford University Press, 1954), 880.

7. Both spent periods of their early lives, which were clearly happy ones and important in their intellectual development, in England. Schumpeter was there for a few months in 1906–1907, at the age of twenty-three; Kautsky visited Marx and Engels in 1881 at the age of twenty-six and lived in London, working closely with Engels, for four years (1885–88 and 1898–90).

8. Frederick Engels, *Herr Eugen Dühring's Revolution in Science (Anti-Dühring)* (New York: International Publishers, n.d.), 203–7, 316; Frederick Engels, *The Origin of the Family, Private Property, and the State* (New York: International Publishers, 1942), 93–97. For Kautsky's criticism of Engels' theory, see Kautsky, *The Materialist Conception of History,* abridged ed. (New Haven, Conn.: Yale University Press, 1988), 267–74.

9. Ludwig Gumplowicz, *Der Rassenkampf,* first published 1883; republished as vol. 3 of *Ausgewählte Werke* (Innsbruck: Wagner, 1928); reprint, Aalen: Scientia, 1973. Franz Oppenheimer, *Der Staat,* first published 1907; translated as *The State* (New York: Huebsch, 1922). Kautsky first formulated his theory at the age of twenty-two, in 1876, before either of these or Engels's work on the subject had appeared, "Entwurf einer Entwicklungsgeschichte der Menschheit," first published half a century later in *Die materialistische Geschichtsauffassung* (Berlin: J. H. W. Dietz, 1927), 1:155–65. Later versions, partly modified under Engels' influence, appeared in *Der Parlamentarismus, die Volksgesetzgebung und die Sozialdemokratie* (Stuttgart: J. H. W. Dietz, 1893; later editions appeared under the title *Parlamentarismus und Demokratie*) and in "Sklaverei und Kapitalismus," *Die Neue Zeit* 29/2 (1911): 713–25. Kautsky finally returned to something close to his original theory of the beginning of the state and of classes, developing it in its most complete and mature form, in part under the influence of Max Weber's work, in *The Materialist Conception of History,* 274–91. The following paragraphs briefly summarize these pages.

10. As a Marxist, Kautsky tended to apply the term "imperialism" only to expansionism under capitalism, but, like Schumpeter, he regarded such expansionism not as a unique phenomenon, but as merely a modern manifestation of an ancient tendency.

11. Schumpeter, *Imperialism,* 7.

12. Kautsky, *Die materialistische Geschichtsauffassung,* 2:135. Shortly before Schumpeter's essay was published, Kautsky had similarly written: "The new state [*Herrschaftsorganisation*] can be expanded without limit, it produces a drive for continuous expansionism." *Die Befreiung der Nationen,* 4th ed. (Stuttgart: J. H. W. Dietz, 1918), 14. The same theme was developed in *Nationalstaat, imperialistischer Staat und Staatenbund* (Nuremberg: Fränkische Verlagsanstalt, 1915), 7.

13. Kautsky, *The Materialist Conception of History,* 293.

14. Schumpeter, *Imperialism,* 7, 38.

15. Ibid., 33.

16. Ibid. 35.

17. Ibid., 54, 60.

18. Ibid., 36.

19. Kautsky, *The Materialist Conception of History,* 291, 285, 286.

20. "In no modern civilized country did the landed aristocracy have as decisive a voice as in the new German Empire." *Die materialistische Geschtsauffassung,* 2:120.

21. Lenin, *Imperialism, the Highest Stage of Capitalism,* in *Collected Works,* 45 vols. (Moscow: Progress Publishers, 1960–70), 22:185–304. For an excellent discussion of Lenin's doctrine of imperialism, its implications, and its place in the general system of Leninism, see Alfred G. Meyer, *Leninism* (New York: Praeger, 1962), 235–73.

22. Kautsky, "Aeltere und neuere Kolonialpolitik," *Die Neue Zeit* 16/1 (1898): 769–81, 801–16.

23. Ibid., 804–5. See also Kautsky, "Der imperialistische Krieg," *Die Neue Zeit* 35/1 (1917): 475–76, and *The Materialist Conception of History,* 292. In his last completed major work, written almost forty years later, Kautsky repeated his analysis of 1898, holding "dynastic, feudal, militarist, bureaucratic interests" and commercial and banking capital responsible for colonialism in the period from the fifteenth to the early nineteenth centuries and considering industrial capital as opposed to it. Kautsky, *Sozialisten und Krieg* (Prague: Orbis, 1937), 289–90.

24. "Aeltere und neuere Kolonialpolitik," 806.

25. Ibid., 806–9, 814–15.

26. Ibid., 811–12.

27. Ibid., 812–14.

28. Kautsky, *Handelspolitik und Sozialdemokratie* (Berlin: Vorwärts, 1901), 41.

29. Hilferding, *Finance Capital,* 334–36.

30. Kautsky, "Finanzkapital and Krisen," *Die Neue Zeit* 29/1 (1911): 769.

31. Kautsky, "Der Imperialismus," *Die Neue Zeit* 32/2 (1914): 909; emphasis in the original.

32. Kautsky, "Finanzkapital und Krisen," 838–46; "Der Imperialismus," 909–16; and *The Materialist Conception of History,* 421–22.

33. Kautsky, "Der Imperialismus," 917.

34. Kautsky, *The Materialist Conception of History,* 423.

35. Kautsky, "Der Imperialismus," 918, 919. It is interesting to note that Lenin, evidently because he considered Kautsky the leading orthodox Marxist at the turn of the century but a renegade in 1914, concentrated his attack on Kautsky's theory of imperialism (to which large sections of Lenin's *Imperialism, the Highest Stage of Capitalism* are devoted) on this 1914 article, where Kautsky came relatively close to Lenin's own view, and completely ignored the 1898 article which was actually much more anti-Leninist in its implications. It is unfortunate that, due to Lenin's lengthy references to it, this 1914 article has often come to be regarded as Kautsky's principal and most typical work on imperialism, when, in fact, in its emphasis on advanced industrial capitalism as the chief cause of imperialism, it is rather atypical of his general thinking on the subject. See also my Introduction, pp. 10–11, above.

36. Kautsky, "Nochmals unsere Illusionen," *Die Neue Zeit* 33/2 (1915): 232. Also, capitalists in mining and heavy industry, fields that were becoming predominant in industry, shared their interests in monopolistic gains and in the policy of imperialism with the big landowners, clearly a precapitalist element. Kautsky, "Imperialismus und reaktionäre Masse," *Die Neue Zeit* 35/2 (1917): 113.

37. Kautsky, *Nationalstaat,* 23.

38. Ibid. In analyzing American foreign policy, Kautsky, in *Die Wurzeln der Politik Wilsons* (Berlin: Neues Vaterland, 1919), ascribed the acquisition of the Louisiana Purchase territory and Florida, the expansion into Texas, and the war with Mexico to the precapitalist expansionism of the big landowners of the South intent on enlarging the area of their exploitation. On the other hand, after the Civil War, favored by the rapid expansion of privately owned railroads, by the importance of mining, and by protective tariffs, finance capital developed first in the United States, and the first imperialist war produced by it was fought by the United States against Spain. But Americans "were also the first ones to show that imperialism is not an inescapable necessity, not even under capitalism." Ibid., 24. There was rising resistance to armaments and the threat of war, and, on the other hand, with peace and disarmament, U.S. capital could thrive and secure a dominant position in China and Latin America. Hence the policy of conquest was replaced by that of the Open Door and of Pan-Americanism.

39. Kautsky, *The Materialist Conception of History,* 292.

40. Ibid.

41. Kautsky, *Sozialisten und Krieg,* 291. See also Kautsky's much earlier similar statement on this theme in *Handelspolitik,* 404–41, referred to above.

42. Schumpeter, *Imperialism,* 23–24, 17, 18, 29.

43. Schumpeter did not use Hilferding's term "finance capital" but referred to the same thing with his term "monopoly capitalism": "everywhere except, significantly, in England, . . . monopoly capitalism, has virtually fused the big banks and cartels into one." Ibid., 106–7.

44. Ibid., 118.

45. Heinrich Cunow, *Parteizusammenbruch? Ein offenes Wort zum inneren Parteistreit* (Berlin: Vorwärts, 1915), 14–16. Kautsky's reply to Cunow is to be found in "Zwei Schriften zum Umlernen," *Die Neue Zeit* 33/2 (1915): 107–16.

46. Karl Renner, *Marxismus, Krieg und Internationale* (Stuttgart: J. H. W. Dietz, 1916), 112–13. Kautsky's reply to Renner was his book *Kriegsmarxismus* (Vienna: Wiener Volksbuchhandlung, 1918); see 42–45 on imperialism. Cf. also the earlier important debate on colonialism at the 1907 Congress of the Second International, where Kautsky vigorously and successfully attacked a proposed rightist resolution envisaging a possible socialist colonial policy. Secretariat du Bureau Socialiste International, *VIIe Congrès Socialiste International tenu à Stuttgart du 16 au 24 août 1907* (Brussels: Désiré Brismée, 1908), 313–16. See also Kautsky, *Sozialismus und Kolonialpolitik* (Berlin: Vorwärts, 1907), and "Methoden der Kolonial-

verwaltung," *Die Neue Zeit* 26/1 (1908): 614–21. For a well-documented summary of the debate at the Stuttgart Congress and of the opposing points of view expressed during the preceding decade, see Brynjolf J. Hovde, "Socialistic Theories of Imperialism Prior to the Great War," *The Journal of Political Economy* 36 (October 1928): 569–91.

47. Kautsky, *Nationalstaat*, 80.

48. Paul Lensch, "Eine Improvisation," *Die Neue Zeit* 30/2 (1912): 308–13, 359–68; Karl Radek, "Zu unserem Kampfe gegen den Imperialismus," *Die Neue Zeit* 30/2 (1912): 194–99, 223–41.

49. Kautsky, "Der improvisierte Bruch," *Die Neue Zeit* 30/2 (1912): 519–22.

50. Kautsky, "Der Imperialismus," 919–20. He made it clear here that he rejected the use of the term "imperialism" to characterize all phenomena of modern capitalism, not only colonialism, but also cartels, protectionism, and the domination of finance capital. Such broad use of the term would necessarily reduce the answer to the question of whether imperialism was inevitable under capitalism to a mere tautology. Ibid., 908.

51. Ibid., 917.

52. Ibid., 921.

53. Ibid., 921–22. For similar statements, see "Zwei Schriften," 144, and "Der imperialistische Krieg," 483. Kautsky's "ultra-imperialism" is evidently Hilferding's concept of the "general cartel" transferred to the international arena. See Hilferding, *Finance Capital*, 234–35, 296–97.

54. Lenin, *Imperialism, Collected Works*, 22:273. See also *Collected Works*, 22:103–7, for Lenin's introduction of December 1915, antedating his more famous pamphlet, to Nikolai Bukharin, *Imperialism and World Economy* (New York: Howard Fertig, 1966), and Bukharin's own ch. 12. For another Leninist critique of what is there described as Kautsky's theory of imperialism, see Michel Pavlovitch, *The Foundations of Imperialist Policy* (London: Labour Publishing Co., 1922), 46–53, 69–85. See also my Introduction, pp. 11–12, above.

55. Kautsky, *The Materialist Conception of History*, 423.

56. Ibid., 292–93.

57. Ibid., 423.

58. Kautsky, *Sozialisten und Krieg*, 653–63.

59. Already twenty years earlier, Kautsky had emphasized that in some imperialist states, evidently notably in Britain, in the last twenty years before World War I, an increasingly powerful opposition to imperialism had developed among the bourgeoisie as well as the proletariat. He predicted that after the War the supporters of imperialism would be confined to those who immediately profited from it. The notion that imperialism advanced the welfare of society would no longer be widespread in other strata, as it had been, even among labor, before the War. Kautsky, "Imperialismus und reaktionäre Masse," 113–15.

60. Kautsky, *Sozialisten und Krieg*, 656, 652.

61. Schumpeter, *Imperialism*, 130.

62. Ibid., 88–89, 90, 94.

63. Ibid., 83–84.

64. Kautsky, *Nationalstaat*, 24–25.

65. Kautsky, "Der imperialistische Krieg," 478–81.

66. Kautsky, *Nationalstaat,* 25–36. As was mentioned earlier, however, to Kautsky these tendencies continued to be important not so much as atavistic remnants of the past persisting in an "objectless" manner, but because the conditions that had given rise to them in the past still existed in the present.

67. Schumpeter, *Imperialism*, 130.

68. Ibid., 7–8. See also his statement in a note on page 84: "The application of the economic interpretation of history holds out no hope of reducing the cultural data of a given period to the relations of production of that same period. This always serves to support objections to the basic economic approach, . . . but this does not actually refute the economic interpretation."

69. Kautsky, "Bernstein und die materialistische Geschichtsauffassung," *Die Neue Zeit* 17/2 (1899): 10.

70. Kautsky, *The Materialist Conception of History*, 233.

71. Schumpeter, *Imperialism*, 121, 122.

72. *Protokoll über die Verhandlungen des Parteitages der Sozialdemokratischen Partei Deutschlands, abgehalten zu Stuttgart vom 3. bis 8. Oktober 1898* (Berlin: Vorwärts, 1898), 128, 129. [As I point out in my article on *The Road to Power,* above, Kautsky therefore expected the democratization of the German Empire to be brought about not by the bourgeoisie, but only through the victory of the proletariat.]

73. Schumpeter, *Imperialism*, 8.

5

Karl Kautsky and Eurocommunism

Kautsky versus Lenin versus Eurocommunism

A juxtaposition of some statements by leading Eurocommunists of the 1970s with the words of Karl Kautsky, on the one hand, and of Lenin, on the other, taken from their famous polemic of 1918, can set the stage for a consideration of the intriguing relationship between Kautsky and Eurocommunism.[1]

Karl Kautsky wrote in *The Dictatorship of the Proletariat* in August 1918:

> For us . . . Socialism without democracy is unthinkable. We understand by modern Socialism not merely social organisation of production, but democratic organisation of society as well. Accordingly, Socialism is for us inseparably connected with democracy. No Socialism without democracy.[2]

Lenin responded three months later in *The Proletarian Revolution and the Renegade Kautsky*:

> That is the sort of twaddle Kautsky uses to befog and confuse the issue,

This article was presented as a paper at the annual meeting of the American Historical Association in Washington, D.C., on 29 December 1980, and so does not take into account subsequent political changes. Statements in the present tense refer to the 1980 period; to change them to the past tense would often have been misleading. The article is reprinted here, by permission, from *Studies in Comparative Communism* 14, no. 1 (Spring 1981): 3–44.

for he talks like the liberals, speaking of democracy in general, and not of *bourgeois* democracy. . . . Bourgeois democracy . . . always remains, and under capitalism is bound to remain, restricted, truncated, false and hypocritical, a paradise for the rich and a snare and a deception for the exploited, for the poor.[3]

Sixty years later, Enrico Berlinguer, the general secretary of the Italian Communist Party (PCI), wrote:

[E]ssential features common to some Western European Parties have emerged, and it is to this phenomenon that the term "Euro-Communism" refers. The first such feature lies in seeing democracy and socialism as inseparable (the inseparability, that is, of political democracy, which we want to make real and expand to the fullest, and the transformation of the economic structures of society in the socialist direction).[4]

Gian Carlo Pajetta, another member of the PCI Executive Committee and, in 1975, of the Secretariat, wrote of the history of Western European democracy "that in the course of this history certain principles and institutions have established themselves to which we can and must attribute a universal value: principles and institutions that have represented, on the one hand, the highest point of the bourgeois revolutions and, on the other, the goal of the great working-class and popular struggles."[5] Very similarly, Georges Marchais, the general secretary of the French Communist Party (PCF), wrote:

The working class has everything to gain with democracy. Our position in this matter is fundamental, is one of principle. . . . [W]e think there will be no socialism in France without political democracy. . . . We consider that the principles which we enunciate concerning socialist democracy are of universal value. It is clear that we have a disagreement with the Communist Party of the Soviet Union about this problem.[6]

And Jean Elleinstein, the leading Eurocommunist in the PCF, said simply: "We want democracy more than we want Socialism."[7]

In his attack on the Bolsheviks, Karl Kautsky also wrote: "The dictatorship of the proletariat was for [Marx] a condition which necessarily arose in a real democracy, because of the overwhelming numbers of the proletariat" and "by the dictatorship of the proletariat we are unable to understand anything else than its rule on the basis of democracy."[8] To this Lenin replied:

> To transform Kautsky's liberal and false assertion into a Marxist and true
> one, one must say: dictatorship does not necessarily mean the abolition of
> democracy for the class that exercises the dictatorship over the other classes;
> but it does mean the abolition (or very material restriction, which is also a
> form of abolition) of democracy for the class over which, or against which,
> the dictatorship is exercised. . . . Dictatorship is rule based directly upon
> force and unrestricted by any laws. The revolutionary dictatorship of the
> proletariat is rule won and maintained by the use of violence by the prole-
> tariat against the bourgeoisie, rule that is unrestricted by any laws.[9]

Pajetta had this to say on the same subject:

> [T]he marxist concept of the "dictatorship of the proletariat" can be achieved
> in the new society in democratic constitutional forms, just as occurred for
> what Marx called the "dictatorship of the bourgeoisie" without, that is, any
> confusion with dictatorial, tyrannical forms of State administration and
> government. In other words, bourgeois democracy is not suppressed, it is
> completed, thus achieving a democracy that rejects privilege.[10]

Do the Eurocommunist leaders seem like followers of Lenin or of
Kautsky? The passages I have quoted appear to provide a clear answer,[11] but the PCI and PCF leaders certainly do not openly profess to
be Kautskyists. Still, there is a real question about their Leninism. The
PCI's Giorgio Napolitano stated quite bluntly: "We are fully aware of
the fact that our conception of the relation between democracy and
socialism does not correspond with that elaborated by Lenin."[12] Similarly, the PCF's Jean Elleinstein wrote that Lenin had "not elaborated
a theory of the transition to socialism valid in all circumstances" and
that therefore the expression "Marxism-Leninism" should not be used.[13]
On the grounds that "the formula 'Marxism-Leninism' fails to express
all the wealth of our theoretical patrimony and thinking,"[14] the PCI at
its Fifteenth Congress in March 1979 did remove explicit references to
Leninism from the Party statutes.[15] However, it is not only in their words
but in their policies of peaceful participation in electoral, parliamentary, and coalition politics in the pursuit of reformist and gradualist
goals that the Eurocommunist parties of Western Europe have in recent years been far more Kautskyist than Leninist.

Why the Parallels between Kautskyism and Eurocommunism?

At a time when German and Austrian socialists and the Socialist International, in whose past Kautsky played such a major role, have largely forgotten him, it seems like an irony of history that certain Communist parties, of all people, should be the ones who, by their policies and their theories, are now reviving his memory. It was, after all, Communists who, for the last twenty years of his life, bitterly hated and denounced Kautsky as a traitor, and whom he detested for what he saw as their abandonment of both socialism and democracy. While this new affinity on the part of Communists for the "renegade Kautsky," the man Lenin regarded as his worst enemy in the days of the Russian Revolution, may be treated as a mere curiosity, it may also be seen as a logical — even though curious — development. An attempt to explain it as such in terms of parallels between the situation faced by Kautsky in Germany and by the Communists in France and Italy may throw some light both on Eurocommunism and on Kautsky's thought.[16]

Briefly, I shall argue that in some significant ways the French and Italian Communist parties have repeated the history of German Social Democracy and particularly the policies advocated by Kautsky, always lagging about forty years behind that model. The first four decades of Communist history, from about 1920 to about 1960, marked mostly by a policy of working-class separatism, correspond to the four decades from the beginning of Kautsky's links to the SPD in imperial Germany about 1880 to the German Revolution in 1918–19, a period when he advocated a similar policy of separatism. Eurocommunism of the 1960s and 1970s, then, corresponds to Weimar-period Kautskyism, which stood for full participation by socialists in parliamentary and coalition politics. Since Kautsky died in 1938, any parallels beyond the Weimar Republic and beyond the Eurocommunism of the 1970s will not concern us here.

Two factors, above all, have concealed the parallelism between Kautskyism and French and Italian Communism from almost everyone, including Kautsky himself and the Communists themselves. One factor is the striking and much publicized difference between Kautsky's attitude toward democracy[17] and the attitude of the PCF and PCI toward democracy during their respective first four decades. The other is the fact that in their first four decades the French and Italian Communists regarded themselves as Leninists and looked to the Soviet Union as their guide and model. Given the bitter enmity between Lenin and the Soviet regime, on the one hand, and Kautsky (in his last two decades) on the other, any claim of parallelism between Kautskyism and Communism — however limited to a few Communist parties and to only some of their policies — would have seemed quite farfetched at the time and probably still seems so both to anti-Communist Social Democrats and to Leninist Communists. In their Eurocommunist period, however, when the PCF and PCI changed their attitudes toward democracy and the Soviet Union, the similarities between their policies and Kautsky's became more visible. How can one explain the more or less visible but always intriguing parallelism between professed enemies?

Unlike small sects, major political parties, like the SPD, the PCF, and the PCI, with their huge electoral constituencies and their links to the biggest trade-union federations of their countries, are not free to adopt any policy arbitrarily chosen by their leaders or ideologues. To be sure, they can persuade their followers to some degree, but they cannot control either the numbers of those who are available as their followers or even their interests and attitudes as these are shaped by the changing positions they occupy in society. Party policies, then, can be understood as appeals to their constituencies, and so can the views of party theoreticians, like Kautsky, which were influential because and as long as they conformed to the needs of their parties. Where these appeals have obviously been successful in attracting and maintaining a large constituency for decades, as is true of the SPD, the PCF, and the PCI, party policies must be explained as meeting the needs of that constituency, and policy changes must be due to changing needs.[18]

Seen in this light, the parallels between SPD history from the 1880s to 1933 and PCF and PCI history from the 1920s through the 1970s, particularly the similarities between the Weimar Kautskyism of the 1920s and 1930s and Eurocommunism of the 1960s and 1970s, become quite understandable. I will note below similarities between the three parties' constituencies and their changing needs in different periods, but I want to stress here the basic fact underlying my attempt at explanation of the parallelism between Kautskyism and Eurocommunism: France and Italy are in important ways several decades behind Germany in their economic development.[19] Both with respect to industrialization and to working-class political mobilization, Germany was from about 1910 to 1933 where France and Italy have been only since World War II. It was this period of advanced industrialization and high mobilization that produced Weimar Kautskyism and Eurocommunism.

My emphasis in the following pages on similarities between Kautskyism and Eurocommunism is not meant to deny or even to minimize the differences between them. Both inherited and acquired characteristics keep the Communist parties of France and Italy from being purely Kautskyist or exactly like the pre–World War II German Social Democrats. Some of the patterns of thinking they inherited from their Leninist and Moscow-oriented Comintern and Cominform periods are difficult to shed for party intellectuals, and, similarly, party bureaucrats have a stake in maintaining old patterns of organization. Furthermore, the environment of France and Italy in the last decade or two, from which the Eurocommunist parties have acquired their new characteristics, is obviously in many ways very different from that of Weimar Germany.

Clearly, there are both similarities and differences between Eurocommunism and Kautskyism, and one can choose to emphasize either of them. Similarities have been noted both by scholars and by those who criticize the Eurocommunists for their lack of radicalism (a few to be cited below), who charge that Eurocommunists have become "mere" Social Democrats and Kautskyists and have hence betrayed the revolutionary Communist tradition. Differences are stressed, on the one hand, by the Eurocommunists themselves and their defenders against these charges and, on the other hand, by implication, by all those to the right of the Eurocommunists in their own countries and in the advanced industrialized countries (like Henry Kissinger in the United States),[20] who question whether these Communists have become "genuinely" democratic and who often assume that "basically" Communists never change and that any apparent change can only be a deceptive trick or a tactical maneuver.[21]

It is not my purpose here to argue that Eurocommunists are somehow more similar to than they are different from Kautskyist Social Democrats — or vice versa. I therefore need not at all systematically review or compare the histories of Social Democracy and Eurocommunism. Rather, taking both similarities and differences for granted, I pursue the much more limited objective of explaining why similarities of Eurocommunism to Kautskyism have developed, referring both to the similarities themselves and to the differences only as far as is necessary.

In the next section I shall call attention to similarities between Eurocommunism and Kautskyism as they have been noted by scholars and leftist critics of Eurocommunism and as they emerge from some Eurocommunist writings. Turning then to an explanation of the parallels between Kautskyism and Eurocommunism, I shall, in the following section, deal with Kautsky's "centrist" position within the SPD and account for its appeal in terms of the peculiar, ambiguous position of the working class in the Wilheminian Empire; I will also comment on Kautsky's attitude toward the Weimar Republic and toward Communism. This will be followed by two sections discussing the PCF and PCI in their forty-year "separatist" phase, which corresponds to Kautsky's in imperial Germany, and in their Eurocommunist phase, which corresponds to Kautskyism in the Weimar Republic. I conclude by locating Kautskyist Social Democracy and French and Italian Communism and Eurocommunism in similar positions within a conception of the history of Western European labor movements in terms of three phases.

Eurocommunism and Kautskyism Linked in the Literature

Before I turn to my principal aim of explanation, I should note some of the ways in which, explicitly or implicitly, Eurocommunism has been linked to Kautskyism by various writers.

Massimo Salvadori, the careful Italian student of Kautsky's work, states that his

awareness of the complex problems posed to the workers' movement by the social evolution of the developed capitalist countries, beyond the perspectives of Marx and Engels, and opposite in direction to that of the revolutionary heirs of Marx and Engels (Rosa Luxemburg, Lenin and Trotsky, to mention the major names) . . . has . . . made its way, after many vicissitudes, into the Western Communist movement itself, after the crisis of Leninism as a model of theory and practice and of the Soviet state as a model of organized power. Indeed, the approach of the Western Communist Parties to these problems today has assumed a shape which in my view can be defined, without the slightest polemical provocation, as essentially 'Kautskyist'.[22]

Carl Boggs, having referred to Marx, Lenin, Kautsky, and Luxemburg, writes:

> As for Kautsky, his strategy of democratic transformation (which guided
> the Second International) is perhaps closest to the Eurocommunist model —
> in its emphasis, for example, on utilizing elections and extending parliamentary institutions, civil liberties, freedom of political opposition, and
> ideological diversity, and creating a favorable balance of forces as the
> precondition for conquering state power.[23]

And the Italian senator and journalist Enzo Bettiza states: "In 1977 it
is apparent that the Eurocommunists are tied more cautiously than
ever to the Kautsky-type, democratic, parliamentary, and electoral
strategy."[24]

Similarly, Eric Shaw says

> [t]here can be little doubt — if such historical analogies are at all meaningful — that PCI leaders would find Kautsky's outlook far more to their taste
> than Lenin's. Indeed one can go further. Eduard Bernstein, the first "revisionist", could yet well be claimed as a precursor of the PCI's present
> conception of an evolutionary transition to socialism. Classical Marxist
> Social-democracy [that is, Kautskyism], by the turn of the century, believed
> that power could be obtained by electoral means. But it did, nevertheless,
> assume that, as Socialist parties gathered in strength, bourgeois resistance
> would stiffen and social and political antagonisms would grow more acute.
> The strategy of the Historical Compromise, in contrast, rejects the notion
> of any rupture with capitalist society in the transition to socialism.[25]

This author thus rightly suggests that recent PCI strategy is not the one
advanced by Kautsky in imperial Germany when, because of the lack
of democracy, he strongly disagreed with Bernstein's faith in the possibility of an imperceptible, gradual growth into socialism. However,
it is Weimar Kautskyism that I think is similar to Eurocommunism
for, with the establishment of Weimar democracy, this difference between Kautsky and Bernstein had disappeared, and the Historical
Compromise is hence as Kautskyist as it is Bernsteinian.

A convenient way to demonstrate the far-reaching Kautskyist character of Eurocommunist views is to quote some passages from a summary of these views by a leftist critic of Eurocommunism. Were it not
for the references to "bourgeois" democracy and the convoluted lan-

guage and the quotation marks in the first paragraph, these passages could well have come from Kautsky's pen:

> Between "democracy" and socialism there is a relationship not of discontinuity but of inherence and consubstantiality. So-called bourgeois democracy and its valued "formal liberties" . . . are . . . in a proportion that varies with the relationship of forces . . . an instrument of bourgeois domination and a machine with which the proletariat wages war against such domination.
>
> . . . [T]he transition to socialism does not necessarily run up against the institutions of the bourgeois-democratic State. It may perfectly well be achieved inside the framework of these institutions. . . .
>
> . . . [S]ocialist democracy does not imply a radically new institutional system, qualitatively distinct from bourgeois parliamentary democracy, but can blossom fully within the framework of the latter's (rejuvenated) institutions. . . . [W]hile the structures of rank-and-file power or direct democracy can and should be useful correctives to parliamentary democracy, they can in no way serve as a substitute for it. . . . [I]t is necessary to allocate the role of centralization and synthesis to a parliament elected by a secret, universal and territorially-based vote. . . .
>
> The transition to socialism is a decades-long process of socialization of economic and political power. The conquest of power is not effected through a paroxysmal crisis.[26]

In spite of striking parallels, Eurocommunists themselves still do not explicitly link their theories to Kautsky's. As Ernest Mandel acidly remarks: "For people who still call themselves communists, it is obviously more comfortable to claim allegiance to Gramsci than to Kautsky,"[27] to which one may add that Rosa Luxemburg, too, is popular with Eurocommunists as a Marxist ancestor with an appropriately ambivalent attitude toward Lenin. To be sure, according to Henri Weber, "Luciano Gruppi is expressing a growing recognition . . . by PCI theoreticians" of the parallels between Eurocommunism and Kautskyism and "he urges the Eurocommunists to accept this 'compromising' lineage without embarrassment. After all, so much water has flowed under the bridge since 1920!"[28]

Though only with embarrassment, another Eurocommunist, the Spaniard Fernando Claudín, accepts the Kautskyan lineage of Eurocommunism and speaks of "the covert turn of the European Communist Parties to Kautskyism."[29] He is a "left" Eurocommunist, a leader of the PCE until expelled from that Party in 1964, who, like all Communists, still uses the term Kautskyism as one of opprobrium and condemnation to criticize what he does not like about Eurocommunism.

> Schematically, we can say that the great majority of the European proletariat, and in particular the German, followed the tactic of Kautsky and not of Lenin: strict subordination of the workers' movement to the frameworks and mechanisms of bourgeois democracy, gradual progress through social and political reforms, and so on. In short, it followed the road which, forty years later, was to be called the democratic, parliamentary and peaceful road to socialism. Thus the international communist movement which succeeded the Communist International turned to Kautsky without admitting it, and without the vast majority of communist militants noticing, since knowledge of Kautsky's thought was rare except through 'The Renegade Kautsky'.[30]

It is critics of the Eurocommunists on their left, like the Trotskyists Weber and Mandel, who are most likely to link Eurocommunism openly to Kautskyism in order to condemn the former. Mandel scathingly refers to "the Eurocommunist disciples of Kautsky" who remain, in some ways, even "well below the level of Kautsky."[31] Comparing the Eurocommunist concern "that any 'catastrophic' crisis of the 'democratic state' would endanger the 'gains of the working class'" with that of the Social Democrats of 1910–30, he says that it is incontestable "that Eurocommunism today is repeating the reasoning of Social Democracy yesterday word for word," and he refers to the so-called attrition strategy of Karl Kautsky as a "historic root of Eurocommunism."[32] Mandel thus rightly suggests that a similar perception of the gains of their respective working-class constituencies by Kautsky and the Eurocommunists led them to similar policies. In particular, Mandel attacks Santiago Carrillo, the general secretary of the Spanish Communist Party, whose book *Eurocommunism and the State* represents to him "the clearest reflection to date of all the contradictions of Eurocommunism." Having quoted him, Mandel says: "Let us note that Carrillo does not say *overthrow* capitalism, but *transform* it, which implies progressive, gradual transformation. Now this is the very definition that pre-1914 Social Democratic reformist revisionists gave to their strategy, which Kautsky took up again after 1921."[33]

Carrillo does indeed go so far as cautiously to "take the liberty of considering that the conception of democracy which Lenin expresses . . . is a restrictive conception of democracy which arose in the heat of arguments against the defenders of the 'democracy' of the bourgeois state."[34] He even says that "defending the revolutionary reality . . . led Lenin to underestimate and belittle the generic concept of democracy" and stresses that the generations of Marxists who experienced fascism and Stalinism " . . . appraise the concept of democracy in a different way, and not in opposition to socialism and communism, but as a road towards them and *as a main component of them.*"[35]

This last passage in particular sounds Kautskyist indeed, but even Carrillo nowhere cites Kautsky in support of his positions. He grudgingly concedes that "[f]rom the *formal* Marxist point of view Kautsky was right in affirming that in Russia the conditions did not exist for achieving socialism in 1917," but he adds immediately that "the *formal* Marxism of Kautsky could not be applied to the revolutionary crisis of Russia in 1917."[36] Referring to Kautsky's 1918 attack on the Bolsheviks in his *Dictatorship of the Proletariat,* Carrillo also says: "It cannot be denied that in Kautsky's work there are certain abstract, general arguments which, if considered apart from the context in which this work was written, might seem reasonable; they relate to the value of democracy for the proletariat and to the importance of capitalist development for the creation of a socialist economy." However, this sentence appears between the following two passages: "Today, when we read the polemics between Lenin and Kautsky — *The Dictatorship of the Proletariat* and *The Proletarian Revolution and the Renegade Kautsky* — our approval goes without hesitation to Lenin's positions. . . . Kautsky's *The Dictatorship of the Proletariat* turns out to be, above all, a skillful attempt to justify the betrayal by social democracy. . . . With good and sufficient reason Lenin regarded him as a renegade!"[37]

Having thus explicitly sided with Lenin against Kautsky as of 1918 and as far as Russia is concerned, Carrillo implicitly sides with Kautsky against Lenin when he says that he is convinced that "in the democratic countries of developed capitalism . . . socialism is not only the decisive broadening and development of democracy, the negation of any totalitarian conception of society, but . . . the way to reach it is along the democratic road, with all the consequences which this entails."[38] Though Carrillo cannot acknowledge it, that was the burden of Kautsky's argument in *The Dictatorship of the Proletariat,* not of

Lenin's in *The Proletarian Revolution and the Renegade Kautsky.*

Fernando Claudín also feels the need to review the Kautsky-Lenin debate about democracy,[39] and, like Carrillo, he comes down heavily on Lenin's side. Indeed, he blames "the Kautskyan road" for the failure of the German Revolution, which in turn was responsible for the rise of Stalinism in the Soviet Union and of fascism in Germany, and hence of the Second World War. Kautskyism also led to the Spanish Civil War and the French Popular Front and hence to Munich. Finally, Claudín points to "the most recent result . . . of this fetishistic respect for the channels and mechanisms of bourgeois democracy which Kautsky recommended fifty-six years ago as the safest and least tragic road to socialism: the Chilean tragedy."[40] While Kautskyism is, without a doubt in the author's mind, held responsible for the worst political disasters of the century, Lenin is treated far more delicately and criticized more hesitantly: "[I]t is at least possible that the leader of the Russian Revolution did not grasp the full significance of . . . the profound roots of the Western workers' movement in . . . democracy, which, though bourgeois, is no less a conquest of the working-class movement."[41]

Intriguingly, though, Claudín's strongly pro-Leninist and anti-Kautskyist piece concludes on a remarkably neutral note:

> The Kautskyan road to socialism — parliamentary, democratic and peaceful — has led to defeats and catastrophe for the workers' movement, disarming it against fascism and war. . . . [T]he régime which Lenin defended against Kautsky's attacks . . . has evolved in the direction of a new class society. It seems, then, that history is playing one of its tricks. It justifies Lenin against Kautsky and Kautsky against Lenin. . . . One will not win with democracy alone, one will not become the dominant class and advance towards the classless society. But without democracy, one will lose even when one thinks one is winning; for from one's own ranks a new ruling and exploiting class will tend to emerge.[42]

That last sentence is pure Kautsky, and so is the statement that "[w]ithout general elections, without unrestricted freedom of press and assembly, without a free struggle of opinion [there results] . . . a dictatorship, to be sure, not the dictatorship of the proletariat, however, but only the dictatorship of a handful of politicians." The words are not Kautsky's — Claudín would not be comfortable quoting him with approval — but Luxemburg's; however, as Claudín himself adds, "the revolutionary Luxemburg essentially agrees with the 'renegade' Kautsky in foreseeing the dangers which lay in wait for the evolution of the régime, if it persisted in the suppression of political freedom."[43]

Reading Eurocommunists like Carrillo and Claudín, one is reminded of Marx's insightful remark on the first page of his *Eighteenth Brumaire of Louis Bonaparte*:

> The tradition of all the dead generations weighs like a nightmare on the brain of the living. And just when they seem engaged in revolutionising themselves and things, in creating something entirely new, precisely in such epochs of revolutionary crisis they anxiously conjure up the spirits of the past to their service and borrow from them names, battle slogans and costumes in order to present the new scene of world history in this time-honoured disguise and this borrowed language. . . . In like manner the beginner who has learnt a new language always translates it back into his mother tongue, but he has assimilated the spirit of the new language and can produce freely in it only when he moves in it without remembering the old and forgets in it his ancestral tongue.[44]

The Eurocommunists "seem engaged in revolutionising themselves," and while I am arguing here that they are *not* "creating something entirely new," it is new to them and, to the degree that they are still uncomfortable with it, "they anxiously conjure up the spirits of the past" — which is their own past, too — and frequently borrow Lenin's name and the slogans of his battles against the Social Democrats.[45] They are still learning their new language and feel the need to translate it back into their Leninist mother tongue, and they are still in the process of assimilating the spirit of the new language and of forgetting their ancestral one. It must be added, however, that by the 1970s particularly some of the Italian (and also the Spanish) Eurocommunist leaders had learned their new language quite well.

Kautsky's Centrist Position in the SPD

As I now seek to explain the parallels between Kautskyism and Eurocommunism, I must begin by locating Karl Kautsky in the spectrum of the German and international Marxist politics of his day. Just as in the 1970s Eurocommunists were blamed by some for being Communists and by others for abandoning Communism, so Kautsky was described in his own lifetime and still is in much of the literature down to the present both as an overly rigid orthodox Marxist, an inflexible and dogmatic ideologue,[46] and as a traitor to and renegade from Marxism.[47] The latter charge, best known thanks to the title of Lenin's famous book, is, of course, important in a discussion of the relation of Eurocommunism to Kautskyism, both because it involves the standard Communist view of Kautsky and because it is on the very issues on which Communists accused him of becoming a renegade that the Eurocommunists have followed in his footsteps.

How can one person be seen in such different lights, as an advocate both of proletarian revolution and of petty bourgeois reform and "vulgar" liberalism? It was his position in the Marxist Center that made Kautsky subject to attack from both right and left. Eventually, both these sides won out against his middle and developed into the two major ideological branches that grew out of Marxian roots — modern Social Democracy and Communism. Kautsky's own "orthodox" Marxism is not well represented by either of them[48] — which has not helped to enhance his reputation. However, it must be remembered that Kautsky's was the classical Marxist position in the third of a century between Marx's death and the Bolshevik Revolution, a position that was dominant among Marxists in the Second International and in Germany, which had by far the largest professedly Marxist party then.

Kautsky's "centrist" position and its appeal can be explained by the similarly central position that imperial Germany occupied, not only geographically but also politically between autocratic, tsarist Russia and the democratic West. On the one hand, Germany was a country governed by an emperor and a powerful bureaucracy and a military dominated by a reactionary landed aristocracy. The new industrial and banking bourgeoisie was both subordinate to this aristocracy and allied with it. Democracy was suspected in the eyes of the ruling classes of being only a little less dangerous than socialism, and no democratic, let alone a socialist, opposition movement had any realistic hope of coming to power peacefully and constitutionally. The labor movement was regarded — and regarded itself — as excluded from society and as vaguely disloyal and subversive. Thus, trade-union members and SPD members and voters could not be civil servants, teachers, or professional military men. Wilhelm II himself, in a famous remark, referred to the Social Democrats as *"vaterlandslose Gesellen,"* that is, roughly, bums or vagabonds without a fatherland, a serious slur among people to whom the term *"Vaterland"* was sacrosanct.

On the other hand, the German Second Empire became an advanced industrialized and urbanized country with a rapidly growing labor movement. Well-established trade unions benefited from economic growth, from social insurance legislation, and, until the turn of the century, from rising real wages. A highly organized Social Democratic Party could register success after success in free elections with universal suffrage, and, except from 1878 to 1890, it enjoyed quite far-reaching freedom of speech, of the press, and of assembly.

Corresponding to this ambiguous situation,[49] Kautsky, on the one hand, in contradistinction to the Revisionists, insisted, as long as the Empire lasted, on a policy of no compromises and no alliances with the regime and its supporters.[50] He advocated this policy of Social Democratic separatism in order to maintain and strengthen the unity and class consciousness of the labor movement in preparation for what he regarded as labor's eventually inevitable assumption of power. And he described and justified this policy by employing the Marxian terms "class struggle" and "revolution," terms that had considerable appeal to a still alienated working-class constituency. On the other hand, Kautsky demanded no revolutionary action, welcomed reforms as strengthening labor, and considered labor's existing rights to the suffrage and civil liberties as significant aids in its rise to power. An advocate of reforms who, unlike Bernstein, never believed that the reforms that could realistically be expected from the ruling classes could bring labor to power in the German Empire, Kautsky was, in a sense, truly both a reformist and a revolutionary. He was hence subject to attack both by radical revolutionaries, who had no use for reforms, and by moderate reformists, who objected to Kautsky's expectation of an eventual "revolution."[51]

Steenson, with great insight, explains the role and the appeal of Kautsky's centrist theory within the SPD of the Second Empire:

> The theory of the SPD was far less important as an objective analysis of the inevitable course of human history than as a rationalization of the socioeconomic and political realities of the Wilhelmine state. Kautsky's orthodoxy repeatedly prevailed over Bernstein's revisionism and Luxemburg's radicalism because Bernstein failed to perceive the sense of isolation and exclusiveness prevalent among party members and Luxemburg overrated the willingness of the workers to act aggressively. Kautsky

captured in theory many of the ambiguities of the Second Reich. He may have insisted on an exclusively working-class party because Marx's theory demanded it, but the SPD was receptive to this concept because most of its members felt themselves to be isolated in, and excluded from, the rest of society.[52]

Above all, Kautsky sought a thorough democratization of the German political system, which really involved the establishment of a parliamentary republic. In the Wilhelminian Empire, this was a far-reaching demand, indeed, and was what his call for a political revolution in fact amounted to.[53] Even his *Road to Power* (1909),[54] where he places most emphasis on revolution, culminated in a demand for parliamentary democracy. Under the prevailing circumstances, Kautsky could never quite define the form of the democratic revolution he expected. He hoped it would be peaceful, yet he realized that the imperial regime was not at all likely to yield peacefully. He understood well the facts his radical opponents did not want to see, that German workers were not willing to confront the regime by means of violence and that they could not have hoped to do so successfully given the strength of the military and the bureaucracy and the regime's considerable popular support. This added up to no prospect for revolution or for democratization, something that Kautsky could never admit, given his nineteenth-century belief in progress and his Marxist conviction that labor must inevitably rise to power. In the final decade of the Empire, for example in his *Road to Power,* Kautsky suggested that a defeat in war might cause the fall of the imperial regime and thus bring the political revolution he hoped for, if under exceptionally difficult circumstances. This, of course, did in fact happen in 1918–19.

Once the Weimar Republic had been established, Kautsky thought that democratization had been attained and that no further political revolution was needed or possible. He assumed, as he always had, that with continuing industrialization the working class must continue to increase in numbers and that, since more and more workers would inevitably become socialists, it would grow in organizational strength and class consciousness as well. Now that Germany had a democratic government, the SPD need and could no longer confine itself to the role of an opposition party, but would come to play a growing part in shaping government policy. At first, during a transition period, it would do so by participating in coalition governments with bourgeois parties, and eventually it would become strong enough to win a parliamentary majority and hence to form a government by itself. Step by step, in a period possibly extending over decades, socialist measures would be introduced, and thus the inevitable socialist revolution would gradually occur. Socialism, then, would be achieved peacefully by electoral and parliamentary means, as Kautsky had always considered both probable and desirable in democratic countries, and the democratic, parliamentary system introduced in Germany in 1919 would continue to function under socialism.[55]

Here we must add a word about Kautsky's hostility towards Communism. It was directed at the Communism of the Bolshevik Revolution in Russia and of the parties in Europe that followed Soviet leadership. Kautsky held this Communism responsible for the split in the Western European labor movement and hence, in part, for the failure of the German Revolution to bring labor to power and subsequently for the rise of fascism. And he attacked the Bolsheviks for perverting Marxism because they sought to introduce socialism in an industrially backward society not ready for it and because they made this attempt by means of dictatorship and terror, while it seemed obvious to Kautsky that both the achievement of the socialist society and the future under it were unthinkable without democracy.

Salvadori sums up Kautsky's position very well: "To Kautsky — veteran theorist of the organizational unity of the proletariat, of the need for a parliamentary majority as the precondition for the assumption of power, of the technical indispensability of parliament and representative democracy in all great modern states, of civil and political liberties as the common patrimony of all society — Bolshevism appeared as a demon of scission in the ranks of the working class, a merciless and barbaric force destroying the political freedoms won by popular struggles over the course of decades, the champion of an implacable bureaucratic, police, and militarist dictatorship."[56] It is striking how all the views Salvadori lists as reasons for Kautsky's opposition to Communism are now held by the Eurocommunists.

The PCF and PCI in their "Separatist" Phase

Communism traveled from Russia to other underdeveloped countries, but, for the most part even earlier, it also came to the West. There it had little appeal to workers in advanced industrialized countries, except temporarily in Germany first as an immediate consequence of World War I and then as a reaction to the rise of Nazism. However, in industrially more backward France and Italy, Communism proved attractive to workers and intellectuals as a successor not to socialist parties but, rather, to the socialist parties' anarcho-syndicalist rivals, and as an expression of working-class alienation, isolation, and separatism.

The French Communists, from their beginnings in 1920 until the 1960s, pursued policies in some ways similar to those advocated by Kautsky in imperial Germany, save only during the relatively brief Popular Front interlude from 1934 to 1938[57] and the period from 1941–47 when they collaborated in the Resistance and then in the postwar tripartite coalition of the Left. As a party *pur et dur* (pure and hard), they avoided entanglements with all other parties, maintaining a position of rigid opposition to all of them, and sought to keep their working-class constituency unified by keeping it isolated and uncontaminated. Like Kautsky, they described and justified this policy of separatism with the Marxian terms of "class struggle" and "revolution." And they participated in elections and sat in parliament and wanted workers to benefit from pro-labor reforms and freedoms of speech, press, and assembly — all in order to prepare them for an ill-defined revolution in the more or less distant future.

The PCF, most of the time from the early 1920s to the early 1960s, pursued policies somewhat similar to those advocated by Kautsky in Germany about four decades earlier, because they appealed to and responded to the need of a somewhat similar constituency. As then in Germany so now in France, workers were already too strong and successful to want to risk their gains in violent revolutionary attempts or even in the violent strikes advocated by revolutionary syndicalists in the quarter-century before World War I. On the other hand, due to the relatively low level of French industrial development, workers were confronted by powerful antilabor majorities in the society and in parliament. They were and they thought of themselves as excluded and disadvantaged, and the Communist Party's attempt to form for them a friendly society within a hostile one was attractive to them. So was the Marxian vocabulary of class struggle, which seemed to correspond to their reality, and of revolution, which vaguely promised a better future.[58]

Obviously there were also differences between the situations Kautsky and the PCF confronted and hence between their responses. For one thing, there was the relationship of the PCF to the Soviet Union, to be mentioned below, which has, of course, no parallel in SPD history. For another thing, the parties the SPD opposed in the German Empire were all "bourgeois," that is, nonlabor, parties. The PCF, on the other hand, opposed the Socialist Party as well and hence could never represent the French labor movement as successfully as the SPD represented the German one. Finally, Kautsky's policies—his separatism, his reformism, his revolutionism—were all directed in the first place toward the achievement of parliamentary democracy in Germany. But France, under the Third and Fourth Republics, and to a lesser degree under de Gaulle's Fifth Republic, was already a parliamentary democracy, a form of government that had from its beginnings in France tended to strengthen the enemies of labor more than the workers because the former were much more numerous. Therefore, though the PCF took advantage of elections and parliamentarism, it had not much more love for democracy than did the antiparliamentary syndicalists it had succeeded.

The French Communists' policy of separatism, corresponding to the exclusion of workers from French society, and also their disdain for parliamentarism, were linked to their view of the Soviet Union as their model and guide. Workers who feel like aliens in their own society can imagine that they would feel at home in an alien country that they can view as representing the future they hope for. In the eyes of such workers, the PCF's links with Moscow could be a source of strength, and the Party could therefore maintain these links closely and openly.[59] In the Soviet Union, however, Lenin had been deified, and, if his words were eternal truths, Kautsky had to remain damned. It was therefore impossible for the PCF, which thought of itself as following Soviet guidance, to see, let alone to say, that it was pursuing policies similar to those once advocated by Kautsky in imperial Germany.

On the other hand, since the French Communists were enemies of working-class unity and of what they called "bourgeois" parliamentary democracy, both so dear to Kautsky, and since they were attached to the Soviet Union, Kautsky never saw them as following policies for which he had once stood. He opposed them as he opposed the Soviet Communists and counseled the socialists against united fronts and Popular Fronts with the Communists, who, of course, reciprocated his aversion.

While, unlike the French Communists, the Italian Communists could function only illegally and in exile during about two of the first four decades of their history, their policies roughly paralleled those of the PCF in the other two decades. Like the French Communists, they played a prominent role in the antifascist resistance of World War II and in the postwar coalition government until 1947, and they pursued a policy comparable to the PCF's (and Kautsky's earlier one) of proletarian separatism most of the rest of the time. This was true in the early 1920s in the brief period before their suppression by Mussolini; and even afterwards Gramsci, writing in a fascist prison in the 1930s, advocated a policy of a "war of position."[60] From 1948 till 1956, during a period of international cold war and domestic confrontation with the Christian Democratic government, the PCI's policy was one of "a vigorous return to orthodoxy which enabled the party to capitalize fully on the deepest instincts of its cadres and members—faith in Stalin and the Soviet Union, hostility to political, class, and religious enemies at home, solidarity with the party and the working class."[61]

Although in this last phase of separatism the PCI tended to turn inward and devoted much of its members' energies to strengthening the organization of the Party and its affiliated groups, unlike the PCF it maintained, at least nominally, its alliance with the Socialist Party and, perhaps more importantly, clung to some hope of entering broader alliances, especially with Catholic elements, in the future. The Italian Communists had seemed reluctant to depart from their alliance strategy in 1947–48 and were eager to return to it in 1956 when Khrushchev loosened their bonds with the Soviet Union by his revelations about Stalin and his talk of different roads to socialism.[62] The French Communists' attitude had been and, to some degree, even after Khrushchev's revelations, remained a rather different one, in part perhaps because their experience with fascist suppression had been briefer than that of their Italian comrades; in part because they tended to identify clericalism with reaction rather than seeing part of the working class associated with it, as did the PCI; and in part because, unlike the PCI, they could not collaborate with the Socialist Party between 1948 and 1962.[63] The policy of separatism and isolation, even though it was externally imposed on the French Communists in 1947 just as it had been on the PCI, seemed more congenial to the French, and they departed from it and weakened their links to the Soviet Union much less eagerly and more slowly than did the PCI.[64] The fact that, despite these different previous positions, the PCF and the PCI nonetheless eventually arrived

at similar policies of Eurocommunism shows that these policies constituted a response to similarly changing conditions in their two countries.
It is to these similar conditions we turn next.

Why the PCF and PCI Turned to Eurocommunism
and Kautskyism

In the decades after World War II, both France and Italy made rapid
and far-reaching industrial advances.[65] As a result, industrial labor grew
in strength, both in absolute numbers and organization, and relative to
the rest of the population, where a good part of the antilabor petty
bourgeoisie and peasantry was replaced by a white-collar new middle
class. The latter is less sharply distinct from and shares many interests
with the working class, and hence the possibility of collaboration and
coalitions arose.[66] Having won substantial benefits and representation,
French and Italian workers began to feel more a part of their societies,
and the policies of their principal political representatives, the PCF
and the PCI, necessarily reflected this change from alienation to integration.

That Communist parties respond to the new character of their working-class constituency is nicely shown by a remark by Palmiro Togliatti,
the then leader of the PCI, in a conversation with the American Marxist economist Paul Baran in 1962. The editors of the *Monthly Review*
report in a note:

> Baran asked questions which indicated skepticism about the compatibility
> of the Italian CP's electoral and parliamentary tactics with the Marxist-
> Leninist theory of state and revolution. Togliatti answered with another
> question. It's all well and good, Togliatti said, for you, living in the United
> States where there is no significant working-class party, to talk about
> revolution. But what would you do if you were in my place, responsible
> for a mass party which the workers expect to represent their interests in
> the here and now? Baran admitted that he had no satisfactory answer.[67]

One of the most prominent exponents of Eurocommunism, the PCI's
Executive Committee member Giorgio Amendola, speaking in an interview, responded similarly:

> [P]eople want to know: what does a party like ours have to propose? Not
> so as to construct socialism tomorrow on the ruins of the present system,

but to prevent the latter's ruin from destroying the living conditions of the workers. . . . Woe betide us if we advocate a solution to the crisis whose purpose is to destroy the present system. The far left, which does advocate such remedies, does not have much of an audience; Democrazia Proletaria got 1.5% of the votes and six deputies.

[W]hat does being revolutionary mean? It means acting to establish a new system. Well, we think that in order to establish a new system, we must start from the present situation: a working class which has improved its standard of living, and above all extensive petty-bourgeois layers whose existence we cannot ignore. . . . [T]here is a great store of energy in the European working class. . . . This energy goes into the defence and improvement of living standards won after many struggles — a defence which will eventually lead to the socialist reorganization of society.[68]

As cautious an observer of French Communism as Ronald Tiersky wrote in 1976:

The PCF itself, understood as a "counter-community" (or, as Annie Kriegel calls it, a "counter-society"), is in a process of vast transformation. The national strategy of broad political alliance and peaceful-legal tactics, like détente at the international level, implies a mutual if selective interpenetration between the Communist and non-Communist worlds. In a large sense, this only repeats the Popular Front and Liberation experiences. Yet institutions and organizations usually do not remain unchanged over long periods, partly for the simple reason that people within them change. And the PCF, after half a century, is in many ways "new."[69]

When workers feel at home in their own country, they no longer need a mythical "workers' fatherland" abroad; when they believe that their future at home is promising, they no longer look abroad for models of an imaginary future. In this situation, the Western Communist parties less and less need to or can afford to associate themselves with the Soviet Union (whose government, in turn, long ago lost interest in the Western European working class — though not in Western European Communist parties). This becomes both another symptom and a cause of the better integration of the Communist parties into the national political systems that corresponds to the better integration of their working-class constituencies into their societies. However, it also means that Lenin's and Soviet hostility to Kautsky is no longer a barrier to a recognition by Western Communists of the relevance of

Kautsky to their policy concerns, even if that recognition was not or not yet made explicit by them.

Just like Kautsky, the Eurocommunists now recognize as genuinely valuable to the working class the democracy and the liberties associated with it that were formerly denigrated by Communists, beginning with Lenin, as merely "bourgeois" or "formal." As Gian Carlo Pajetta, member of the PCI Executive Committee, wrote:

> Essential for us today is the development of democracy. This involves the necessity of guaranteeing and defending rights and institutions that represent historical acquisitions. . . . For those who have reflected, as we have, on the history of past centuries in the vast majority of the Western European countries and who have paid dearly, as we have, [in] the periods of tyranny when these rights were denied, the free dialectics of parties in the elective assemblies, universal suffrage, direct proportional voting, the secret ballot, and civil liberties are more than just inalienable rights of man and of the citizen. We say that these rights can become, and indeed (in our situation) are, the only instruments suited to achieving socialist transformation and guaranteeing a solid base for a new form of society.[70]

Just as it did for Kautsky, this commitment to democracy also involved a commitment to a policy of gradualism. Giorgio Napolitano stated quite bluntly that "whether we accept or do not accept the concept of gradualism" did not distinguish the PCI "from the traditional theory and practice of social-democratic parties."[71] He said that

> it is certainly necessary to change profoundly the direction of society and of the state. We do not, however, conceive of this in terms of a working-class "conquest of power" and a rapid transition to socialism but in terms of an effective accession of the laboring classes into social and political leadership in terms of the introduction of certain elements proper to socialism in the functioning of the economy and of society. The most important of these elements is precisely programming or planning the economy, and the participation of the working class, occupying a determining position, in planning decisions at all levels from below and from above. In this context, we do not deny private initiative.[72]

Not only will the working class not conquer power by a frontal assault, but it will not assume power as a result of the breakdown of capitalism either. Napolitano said that "the policy of our party is based on the profound conviction that we must not expect a socialist-oriented change to derive from the collapse of a capitalist economy."[73] This is precisely a point repeatedly made by Kautsky, both against the Revisionists, who accused him of adhering to a supposedly Marxist "breakdown theory," and against the Communists, who did adhere to such a theory in his time.

Just as Kautsky did until his death, the Eurocommunists couch their defense of democracy in the Marxian terms of class struggle and, especially, of revolution. After all, like the German and Austrian workers of the interwar period, to whom Kautsky sought to address his appeals, French and Italian workers now do not yet feel as integrated into their societies as do present-day American, British, or German workers. To these latter, the Marxian vocabulary would seem irrelevant to their situation, but to the Eurocommunist working-class constituency only now emerging from its isolation and alienation, it may well still be appealing and ease its ideological transition from alienation to integration. To be sure, it is also possible that the party intellectuals' willingness to abandon a conceptual vocabulary with which they have grown up lags behind their constituents' readiness for such a change.

So far, only one major Marxist concept has been officially abandoned by Eurocommunists, that of the dictatorship of the proletariat.[74] It is precisely the one Marxian concept that Kautsky, too, in the period of his polemics with the Bolsheviks, thought should be given up; he felt it was subject to too many misunderstandings. Indeed, he went so far as to propose that one of Marx's most famous, if quite vague, predictions now had to be reformulated on the basis of recent experience. Where Marx, in his *Critique of the Gotha Programme,* had said that during the transition from capitalism to communism the state would have to be a "revolutionary dictatorship of the proletariat," Kautsky argued that between the time when the democratic state was under a purely bourgeois government and the time when it was under a purely proletarian government, there would be a period of political transition whose government "will as a rule take the form of a coalition government."[75]

When in the 1960s and, especially, the 1970s the Eurocommunist parties entered their own "Weimar period" as potential coalition partners of "bourgeois" parties, this line of thought must indeed have been more attractive to them than Kautsky's opposition in the days of the German Empire to coalitions and alliances with "bourgeois" parties (except for electoral agreements). What Kautsky wrote in 1923 could well have been written, word for word, by the Eurocommunist parties half a century later:

> [T]he socialist movement of the most developed countries . . . [is] now at the stage in which the necessity for propaganda gives way to the need to take part in the life of the state, no longer merely from the critical standpoint of an opposition but primarily from the positive vantage point of government — if not yet as the sole government party — either by participating in a coalition or by preparing itself to assume governmental power in the foreseeable future. Thanks to the irresistible rise of the strength of the proletariat, this stage must sooner or later become a reality in every country with a capitalist industry.[76]

Indeed, in 1975 Giorgio Napolitano said virtually the same thing, and after the 1976 elections the PCI effectively maintained a Christian-Democratic government in power and influenced its policies:

> There is no doubt that in the last five or six years Italy has seen a growth in the political influence of the working class and of its capacity to intervene in the economic, social and political life of the country. . . . Today the problem of a change of the governing class is on the agenda, at least and above all in the sense of acknowledging an adequate place in the government for the working class, for the working masses. We can thus imagine a more or less long period of transition, during which forces representing in the broadest manner the working class and forces representing other classes would coexist in the government of the country.[77]

And in startling contradiction to the Leninist insistence on the vanguard role of the Communist party, Napolitano also stated that: "ideas which assign to the Communist Party an exclusive leadership role in the process of transforming the society in a socialist direction must be completely and definitively overcome."[78]

What of the PCI's and the PCF's future policies, beyond their "Weimar period" of the 1960s and 1970s with which we have been concerned? In the case of the PCI, one might well expect the Party to follow the path of German Social Democracy and eventually, uninterrupted by anything like the Nazi period, to develop into the equivalent of the post-1945 SPD. Indeed, the Party quite officially looks toward convergence with Social Democracy. "On the national and international level, the P.C.I. has worked and works to promote discussion

and convergence with the Socialist and Social Democratic Parties
... towards an overcoming of the historical divergencies and a new
unity of the Western European workers' movement."[79] After a three-
year period of collaboration with the Christian-Democratic government, the PCI suffered serious losses in the 1979 parliamentary elections and had to return to the role of an opposition party. Yet even
when Berlinguer's lieutenant Gerardo Chiaromonte called for a reevaluation of past and future party policies, he concluded: "We remain
convinced of the validity of our line of democratic solidarity. . . . [W]e
consider ever more pressing the need to work for collaboration, . . . for
convergence and for unity between communists and socialists in Italy
and in Western Europe."[80]

In the case of the PCF, which, unlike the PCI, has been unsuccessfully competing with a socialist party, there has been some doubt since
its break with the Socialists in 1977–78 about its continuing commitment to a Eurocommunist course leading to governmental office.[81]
Indeed, since no other course to power is imaginable, one could doubt
the PCF's serious interest in gaining national office at all, as distinguished from maintaining its strength within the French working class.
Still, it does not seem probable that the PCF will never return to
Eurocommunist policies unless it is resigned to face internal factionalism and to see the Socialist Party continue to gain on it. It is, to be
sure, not impossible that party bureaucrats may, after all, prefer the
security of living in the proletarian ghetto they have helped create and
of confining the PCF to its traditional — but now shrinking — working-
class base to the risks involved in broadening that base, in the give and
take of coalition politics, and in assuming the responsibilities of national office.[82] Not surprisingly, Italian Communists expressed their
disapproval of any such policy.[83]

Kautsky and Communism in Western European Labor History

Many Eurocommunists had a long way to go to shed the remnants
of Leninist thinking and to become Kautskyists. On the other hand,
some may already have gone beyond Kautsky in their de-emphasis on
class conflict. As I stressed at the outset, I have not here been interested
in emphasizing the differences between Eurocommunism and
Kautskyism but only in explaining the similarities. These similarities
can, in conclusion, be well explained if the foregoing is placed in the

framework of the following schematic conception of the history of the Continental Western European labor movements.

In the course of industrialization, these movements have typically, though obviously with local variations, passed through three phases:

1. Revolutionary anarcho-syndicalism
2. "Revolutionary reformism"
3. Reformist social democracy

Each phase corresponds to and is defined by a certain level of labor strength relative to the rest of society and by certain characteristic political attitudes on the part of labor.

Put simply, in the first phase, labor is very weak numerically and organizationally and hence politically. Pro-labor reforms are unobtainable, and workers therefore express their alienation by acts and dreams of violence and by hopes for a mythical revolution. In the second phase, labor is strong enough to obtain substantial reforms and thus acquires a stake in existing society, and violent tactics are abandoned. However, workers continue to be and to feel excluded and discriminated against; they cannot conceive of sharing governmental power short of some drastic change. The myth of revolution and of the wholly different and better future it will bring hence remains powerfully attractive. In the third phase, labor is sufficiently strong and — which is the same thing — its opponents are sufficiently weak that its political representatives can enter the government, at first in coalition with other parties not wholly out of sympathy with labor, and perhaps eventually alone. There is no longer any need to hope for revolution, for part of what this word stood for, chiefly governmental power, has been obtained or seems obtainable in the foreseeable future and the rest, that is, a wholly different society, is no longer what workers dream of.

In historical reality, the three phases are not sharply distinct, for both the strength of a movement and, especially, its attitudes change gradually, not abruptly. Also, different sections of a labor movement can pass from one phase to the next at somewhat different times. Indeed, we have here been particularly interested in a transitional period: While SPD Kautskyism and PCF and PCI Communism in their respective first four decades, that is, in Germany from the 1880s to 1918 and in France and Italy from the early 1920s to the early 1960s, constitute the second phase, which I labeled revolutionary reformism,

Weimar Kautskyism and Eurocommunism constitute a transition to or the beginnings of the third phase. Labor had now become strong enough to be purely reformist, but some revolutionary attitudes and symbols characteristic of the second phase still survived, blurring the distinction between the second and third phases.

Now, if one regards the entire second phase as a transitional one in which labor moves from the weakness, isolation, and alienation of the first phase to the strength and integration of the third phase, Kautskyism can be seen as an ideology appealing to labor in this process of transition. As it was expressed by Kautsky himself throughout his active six decades, but as it was adopted by the PCF and PCI only in their last two, Eurocommunist, decades, Kautskyism is characterized by its peculiar dual emphasis on both parliamentary democracy and revolution. It is therefore an ideology relevant neither in underdeveloped countries, where revolution cannot be parliamentary or democratic, nor in advanced industrialized (or "postindustrial") countries, where parliamentary democracy is not revolutionary and does not even operate with revolutionary symbols. In the former, the Marxian vocabulary is taken over by Leninism and often by other modernizing movements; in the latter, "classical" Marxism has been succeeded by non-Marxist Social Democracy (and, among some intellectuals, by the New Left).

It is for this reason that Kautskyist Marxism, unlike the Leninist variety, has had no appeal in underdeveloped countries and is now merely a dead part of the history of Social Democracy in the advanced industrialized countries. Similarly, the Eurocommunist parties have become isolated from the modernizing movements in underdeveloped countries, including even the Communist ones, with whom they barely still share a common vocabulary inherited from their Leninist past. And, as was the case with Kautskyism in the SPD, Eurocommunism will be transmuted into reformist Social Democracy, a process requiring chiefly the disappearance of the vocabulary and mythology of revolution. That process was already well advanced in the PCI and should eventually be repeated in the PCF, too, if it is not to become an increasingly out-of-date, isolated, and impotent sect.

One can, then, see the German and the French and Italian labor movements develop through their three phases in parallel fashion, with the German one about forty years ahead of the other two. What has tended to obscure this parallelism is the fact that the German labor movement passed through the second and into its present third phase politically organized in the Social Democratic Party and firmly committed to the attainment and then the maintenance of parliamentary democracy. French and Italian labor, on the other hand, have followed the corresponding course politically divided between socialists and Communists, and in the second phase its Communist wing, in which we have been interested here, was by no means firmly committed to parliamentary democracy. Why this difference between German and Franco-Italian labor history?

In Germany industrialization proceeded rapidly, and the Social Democratic Party, dedicated both to effective pro-labor reforms and to the prospect of revolution, that is, drastic change, quickly overcame the early anarchist competition for labor support. Since the Bismarckian and then the Wilheminian regime it opposed was an antidemocratic and antiparliamentary one, the SPD consistently stood for democratization and parliamentarism, and the revolution it looked forward to was, ambiguously, both a political revolution to bring about democracy and a parliamentary republic and a social revolution to bring about socialism. As we have seen, Kautskyism stood for this combination of reform and such a revolution.

In contrast to industrialization in Germany, industrialization in France and Italy proceeded slowly. In small, scattered enterprises, workers became organized, if at all, in small, decentralized syndicalist unions rather than in the centralized mass unions of Social Democracy, and, since the governments opposing labor were parliamentary ones, the antiparliamentarism of syndicalism appealed to workers. Anarcho-syndicalist currents thus remained strong in the French and Italian labor movements in the quarter century before World War I, and in this period the socialist parties never managed to overcome their competition for the workers' support.

The war gravely weakened syndicalism as an organized movement, but by the postwar period its followers could flock to the colors of the Russian Revolution. That revolution can in retrospect best be interpreted as a revolution of modernizing intellectuals in an underdeveloped country, but at the time it was seen by the revolutionaries themselves and by both their sympathizers and most of their adversaries abroad as the first anticapitalist proletarian revolution, which would spread to the West. It hence had great appeal to revolutionary syndicalists, and so did the Bolsheviks' attacks on "bourgeois" parliamentarism, which seemed to coincide with the syndicalists' traditional rejection of electoral and parliamentary participation.

So it happened that while the German labor movement entered its revolutionary-reformist phase organized in a Social Democratic Party dedicated to democracy, the French and Italian labor movements entered this phase four decades later, organized, in part, in Communist parties opposed to parliamentary democracy. In fact, as we have seen, the PCF and PCI pursued, broadly speaking, the same policies of proletarian separatism as had the SPD, combining advocacy of pro-labor reforms with the hope for a future revolution. However, since France and, in the periods when the PCI was legal, Italy were already parliamentary democracies, the word "revolution" did not stand largely for democratization, as it did in imperial Germany. On the other hand, with the French and Italian labor movements having moved from their first, revolutionary anarcho-syndicalist phase to their second, revolutionary-reformist one, the PCF and PCI did participate in electoral and parliamentary politics.

While the SPD pursued its revolutionary-reformist course in the name of Marxism as interpreted by Kautsky,[84] the PCF and PCI, having grown out of native support for the Russian Revolution, pursued their similar policies in the name of Marxism as interpreted by Lenin. In fact, the PCF and the PCI, try as they might, were never Leninist or Stalinist; the interests they represented were quite different from those represented by Lenin and Stalin. The PCF and PCI were labor parties (though not the sole ones) in capitalist industrial countries, not movements of modernizers in underdeveloped countries. The societies in which they functioned and the problems they faced were utterly different from Lenin's and Stalin's. Obviously, they could not copy Russian society; what they could and did copy, however, was the language, the concepts, the thought patterns, and the attitudes of Leninism and Stalinism. These in turn affected the behavior of French and Italian Communists and the forms of their organizations and thus modified, to some degree, the political environment in which they functioned. Consequently, while pursuing similar policies of proletarian separatism, the PCF and PCI were very different from the SPD in their respective revolutionary-reformist phases.

When the German labor movement entered its third phase, and the SPD could contemplate participating in government coalitions and achieving its pro-labor reforms through parliamentary politics and legislation, Kautsky did not have to change his position or his interpretation of Marxism to support such policies. The change from Wilheminian autocracy to Weimar democracy made the shift from separatism to coalition politics easy and consistent with his past statements.

When the French and Italian labor movements entered their third phase of reformist Social Democracy forty years later, the PCF and PCI, as had been true of the SPD, now had to think in terms of participation in coalition governments and in reformist parliamentary politics, but they had to make a far more drastic change ideologically than had Kautsky or the SPD. Not only had there been no equivalent to the German Revolution of 1918–19 in the France and Italy of the late 1950s to ease the change, but the two Communist parties had hitherto been speaking and thinking in Leninist rather than in Kautskyist terms. The policy of proletarian separatism in labor's second phase could be pursued in the name of Leninism in France and Italy as it had been in the name of Kautsky's "classical" Marxism in Germany. But the coalition and parliamentary reformist policies of labor's third phase, while in their beginnings quite compatible with Kautskyism, are from the start incompatible with Leninism. As the PCF and PCI have moved into their third phase, they have had to shift from Leninism to Kautskyism — and thus to Eurocommunism.[85]

Both Communists and anti-Communists long did their best to suggest that Communists could and would remain ever faithful to Leninist precepts. Obviously, however, Communists are in fact not exempt from change in a changing world. Just as, in wholly different ways, the Communist parties of the Soviet Union and China have changed as they have industrialized their countries, so the history of the Western Communist parties that have been genuine labor parties was bound to be conditioned by the changes industrialization brought to their working-class constituencies from weakness to strength, from alienation to integration. That these Communist parties should more and more openly, if still without using his name, adopt theories and policies of Lenin's greatest Marxist adversary is a symptom of the magnitude of the change they have been undergoing.

I am grateful to my colleagues Barry Ames, Lawrence Joseph, Barbara Salert, Egon Schwarz, and John Sprague for their helpful critical comments on earlier drafts of this article, and to Juan Linz and Sidney Tarrow for encouraging expressions of interest in the present version.

Notes

1. Throughout, I shall ignore the question of whether Eurocommunist statements are sincere (which has been doubted by many) as well as the question of whether Kautsky or Lenin were sincere (which is evidently never doubted) because it is irrelevant to my concerns. For one thing, the change in what Western European Communists have been saying over the past few decades is real, whether they are saying it sincerely or not, and that change is worth explaining. Second, statements repeatedly made by authoritative political leaders, whether sincere or not, evoke responses from their followers and from their actual and potential allies and opponents; they thus have policy consequences whether originally intended or not. In the case of the Eurocommunists, such consequences have already been obvious. Finally, political ideas and theories, whether sincerely held or not, may be worthy of consideration. No one cares whether Burke or Bentham was sincere.

2. Karl Kautsky, *The Dictatorship of the Proletariat* (Ann Arbor: University of Michigan Press, 1964; reprint, Westport, Conn.: Greenwood Press, 1981), 6–7.

3. Lenin, *The Proletarian Revolution and the Renegade Kautsky,* in *Collected Works,* 45 vols. (Moscow: Progress Publishers, 1960–70), 28:232, 243.

4. Enrico Berlinguer, "An Emergency Government to Tackle a Crisis of Exceptional Gravity," Report to the Central Committee, 6 January 1978, *The Italian Communists. Foreign Bulletin of the PCI* no. 1 (January–March 1978): 73–74.

5. Gian Carlo Pajetta, "For Socialism in Europe," *The Italian Communists: Foreign Bulletin of PCI* no. 5–6 (September-December 1975): 60. Giorgio Napolitano, a third member of the PCI Secretariat, is more explicit with respect to this "universal value" of democracy, which Lenin had denied, when he specifically refers to Communist-ruled and underdeveloped countries: "I believe that in any country the process of socialist transformation as well as socialist regimes have to be founded on a broad basis of consensus and democratic participation, whatever the specific forms of expression these might have. In this regard, neither the socialist countries nor the third-world nations can be exempted from scrutiny and discussion." Eric Hobsbawm, *The Italian Road to Socialism: An Interview with Giorgio Napolitano* (Westport, Conn.: Lawrence Hill & Co., 1977), 78.

6. Quoted from *L'Humanité* of 15 January 1976, in Ronald Tiersky, "French Communism in 1976," *Problems of Communism* 25, no. 1 (January–February 1976): 42. Marchais also told an interviewer that "Socialism is synonymous with liberty. . . . This idea is valid in all countries, under all circumstances. There is a divergence between us and the CPSU with regard to socialist democracy." Quoted from *Le Monde* of 9 January 1976, in Kevin Devlin, "The Challenge of Eurocommunism," *Problems of Communism* 26, no. 1 (January–February 1977): 10.

7. Jean Elleinstein, "The Skein of History Unrolled Backwards," in *Eurocommunism,* ed. G. R. Urban (New York: Universe Books, 1978), 92. Elleinstein, to be sure, is a "liberal" dissident intellectual in the PCF who "wrote a series of articles in *Le*

Monde after the 1978 elections attacking the party leadership for, among other things, not sufficiently criticising Soviet society." Peter Morris, "The French Communist Party and Eurocommunism," in *The Changing Face of Western Communism*, ed. David Childs (New York: St. Martin's Press, 1980), 171, n. 31.

8. Kautsky, *The Dictatorship of the Proletariat*, 45, 58.

9. Lenin, *The Protelarian Revolution*, 235, 236.

10. Pajetta, "For Socialism in Europe," 61–62.

11. Other Eurocommunist statements are, of course, far less reminiscent of Kautsky. Thus, French and Italian Communists have declared that socialism and democracy are inseparable and are universal values, and some have denounced the Soviet Union for the absence of democracy there, but they have been reluctant to draw the logical conclusion that the Soviet Union is not socialist. See the article reviewing a dozen studies of Soviet history by French and Italian Communists, Michael J. Sodaro, "Eurocommunist Views of Soviet History," *Problems of Communism* 29 , no. 3 (May–June 1980) 65–71. Spanish Communists have been more outspoken on this point. Thus, Manuel Azcárate, a leading spokesman for the Spanish Communist Party (PCE), refers to the USSR as "a State which is neither Socialist nor democratic" and sneers at its elections where candidates poll over 99.9 percent of the votes. "What is Eurocommunism?", in *Eurocommunism*, ed. Urban, 23.

12. Hobsbawm, *The Italian Road to Socialism*, 99.

13. Jean Elleinstein, *Lettre ouverte aux Français sur la République du Programme commun* (Paris: Albin Michel, 1977), 89–90.

14. Draft Thesis No. 15, "Draft Theses for the 15th National Congress of the PCI," *The Italian Communists* (Special Issue, 1978): 18.

15. Sharon Wolchik comments that "this action represented the culmination of a process which has been occurring over a period of years, rather than an abrupt break with the PCI's past. To some extent a formalization of what had already occurred in practice, this step is nonetheless significant, for it illustrates how far the PCI has departed from its former reliance on the Leninist tradition. It also is a natural outcome of the party's judgment concerning the limited value of Leninism as a guide to action or source of legitimacy in a democratic environment." Sharon L. Wolchik, "The PCI, Leninism, and Democratic Politics in Italy," in *Marxism in the Contemporary West*, ed. Charles F. Elliott and Carl A. Linden (Boulder, Colo.: Westview Press, 1980), 67. The PCE, after prolonged and complex intraparty debates, voted 968 to 240 at its Ninth Congress in 1978 to drop the word "Leninism" from its description. Eusebio Mujal-León, "The PCE in Spanish Politics," *Problems of Communism* 27, no. 4 (July–August 1978): 32–35.

16. Such an analysis is facilitated by the publication of two excellent scholarly books on Karl Kautsky: Gary P. Steenson, *Karl Kautsky, 1854- 1938: Marxism in the Classical Years* (Pittsburgh: University of Pittsburgh Press, 1978), and Massimo Salvadori, *Karl Kautsky and the Socialist Revolution 1880–1938* (London: NLB, 1979). (For my review of these two works, see *The American Political Science Re-*

view 75, no. 3 (September 1981): 752–54.) Neither of them deals with Kautsky's relation to Eurocommunism, but both throw a great deal of light on it by setting forth his position in his major controversies with other Marxists. Moreover, Salvadori tends to focus on the issues of interest to Eurocommunism, like democracy and dictatorship and, more particularly, elections and parliamentarism, bureaucracy and coalitions with "bourgeois" parties. Both authors seek to explain Kautsky's views in the context of SPD politics, contrasting them to alternative ones held by other tendencies within the Party. Precisely because they do not deal with Kautsky's thought as abstract political theory unaffected by the politics of his time or judge it from present-day perspectives, as is so often done to political ideas and especially to Marxist ones, they permit us to understand his thought as a response to particular situations in a particular political environment. This invites us to explore whether similar theories and policies of Eurocommunism can be explained in terms of a similar political environment.

17. That Kautsky's advocacy of democracy as the best road to socialism remained consistent and substantially unchanged throughout his six active decades is a major theme of Salvadori, *Karl Kautsky.*

18. In the following, I shall effectively confine my analysis to the working-class constituency of the three parties. In fact, the social makeup of the membership, let alone the electorate, of these parties has by no means been homogeneous, but the industrial workers have provided their most stable and most highly organized core of supporters and, especially, of activists throughout their history. It is hence not unreasonable to assume that changing party policies reflect, above all, changing working-class attitudes and needs, though this is obviously not the whole story.

19. Graphs plotting various measures of the industrialization of the three countries show more or less parallel ascending lines, with Germany fairly consistently twenty to forty years ahead of France and thirty to fifty years ahead of Italy. See, for example, the following figures taken from B. R. Mitchell, *European Historical Statistics* (New York: Columbia University Press, 1975), 801, 802, 808, and 811, indicating the percentage of the national product drawn from industry and construction in selected years:

	1882	1892	1898	1909	1925	1933	1938	1946	1949	1951	1960	1969
Germany	32	37	39	43	56	45						
France	30	32	34	36			36	32	40	49	48	48
Italy	20	19	17	24	34	28	31	33	38	43	44	45

Similarly, a graph showing the combined votes of the working-class (socialist and Communist) parties of the three countries as a percentage of total votes cast in parliamentary elections, from the beginnings of socialist parties in the late nineteenth century, presents a striking picture of three parallel ascending lines, with the one representing the German parties about twenty-five years ahead of the other two (and the Italian ones more often than not slightly ahead of the French). Here are the relevant percentages for elections held in selected periods:

	1884–87	1893–95	1898–00	1902–04	1906–09	1910–14	1919	1921–24	1928	1932	1936
Germany	10	23	27	32	29	35	46	35	40	37	
France		9	11	10	12	17	23		31	30	35
Italy		7	13	21	19	23	34	30			

	1946	1951–53	1958	1962–63	1968	1972–73	1976–78
France	48	41	36	37		43	47
Italy	40	40	41	45	46	45	49

20. See, for example, Henry A. Kissinger, "Communist Parties in Western Europe: Challenge to the West," *Atlantic Community Quarterly* 15, no. 3 (Fall 1977): 261–74. The same speech by Kissinger appears in *Eurocommunism: The Italian Case,* ed. Austin Ranney and Giovanni Sartori (Washington: American Enterprise Institute, 1978), 183–96.

21. For an excellent brief survey of a great deal of literature on Eurocommunism representing different views of it, see Philip Elliott and Philip Schlesinger, "Eurocommunism: Their Word or Ours?," in *The Changing Face,* ed. Childs, 37–57. For a summary of "The Debate over Eurocommunism in the West," with quotations ranging from those regarding it as a deceptive maneuver through those — mostly Social Democrats — who view it with more or less benevolent skepticism to those who welcome it, see Wolfgang Leonhard, *Eurocommunism: Challenge for East and West* (New York: Holt, Rinehart, and Winston, 1979), 18–27.

22. Salvadori, *Karl Kautsky,* 12–13. Sidney Tarrow had already noted some time ago that "Togliatti's formula of the Via Italiana al Socialismo recalls Lenin's great enemy Kautsky. For example, Togliatti's insistence upon the need for a multiparty system in Italian politics, as well as the need for internal democracy in the Soviet Union, recall these words of Kautsky's written long ago in polemic against Lenin: 'Socialism and democracy are therefore not distinguished by the one being the means and the other the end. Both are means to the same end.'" Sidney G. Tarrow, *Peasant Communism in Southern Italy* (New Haven, Conn.: Yale University Press, 1967), 124. The quotation from Kautsky is from his *Dictatorship of the Proletariat,* 5.

23. Carl Boggs, "The Democratic Road: New Departures and Old Problems," in *The Politics of Eurocommunism,* ed. Carl Boggs and David Plotke (Boston: South End Press, 1980), 431–32.

24. Enzo Bettiza, "Eurocommunism in Limbo," in *Eurocommunism,* ed. Ranney and Sartori, 123.

25. Eric Shaw, "The Italian Historical Compromise: A New Pathway to Power?," *Political Quarterly* 49, no. 4 (October–December 1978): 418–19. Carl Boggs, too, in a recent unpublished paper on "Gramsci and Eurocommunism," concludes that "Bernstein emerges as the first creative theoretical genius behind the Eurocommunist

dream of a democratic road." See also Boggs, "The Democratic Road," 432. Kevin Devlin had already in 1967 opened a lecture by saying "there is a specter haunting West European Communism; it is the specter of Eduard Bernstein." Kevin Devlin, "Prospects for Communism in Western Europe," in *The Future of Communism in Europe,* ed. R. V. Burks (Detroit: Wayne State University Press, 1968), 21.

26. Henri Weber, "Eurocommunism, Socialism, and Democracy," *New Left Review,* no. 110 (July–August 1978): 3–5. Kautsky could also have subscribed to what Pierre Hassner, a French commentator who stresses differences among the Eurocommunist parties, says they all share, that is, "the affirmation that in developed societies socialism is inseparable from democracy and freedom and that respect for the rules of parliamentary democracy and social and cultural pluralism must not be regarded as valid only during a transition phase." Pierre Hassner, "Eurocommunism and Western Europe," *Atlantic Community Quarterly,* 16, no. 3 (Fall 1978): 266.

27. Ernest Mandel, *From Stalinism to Eurocommunism* (London: NLB, 1978), 201.

28. Weber, "Eurocommunism", 7. The reference is to PCI Central Committee member Luciano Gruppi, "Sur le rapport democratie-socialisme," *Dialectiques,* no. 17/41. "[T]he PCI leadership at present holds a positive view of international social democracy and its historical achievements — including those of the Social Democratic Party of Germany, so strongly condemned by the PCF." Heinz Timmermann, "The Eurocommunists and the West," *Problems of Communism* 28, no. 3 (May–June 1979): 52. In 1978 PCI "commentaries on Bauer . . . argued that his writings and views should be seen as part of the communist as well as social-democratic tradition." Wolchik, "The PCI, Leninism," 69. Otto Bauer, the Austro-Marxist theoretician and leader of the interwar Austrian Social Democratic Party, though differing sharply with Kautsky in his hope for an eventual reunification of the Socialist and Communist Internationals and parties, agreed with Kautsky's condemnation of the Bolshevik dictatorship. In the 1920s, he also shared Kautsky's view of the impossibility of creating socialism in backward Russia, but in the 1930s he came to believe that the Five-Year Plan might, through industrialization, gradually bring both democracy and socialism, a possibility denied by Kautsky. For an excellent summary presentation and explanation of Bauer's views on these issues, see Melvin Croan, "Prospects for the Soviet Dictatorship: Otto Bauer," in *Revisionism: Essays in the History of Marxist Ideas,* ed. Leopold Labedz (New York: Praeger, 1962), 281–96. Given Bauer's views, it is understandable that the PCI, not yet ready to look to Kautsky for inspiration, can turn to Otto Bauer.

29. Fernando Claudín, "Democracy and Dictatorship in Lenin and Kautsky," *New Left Review,* no. 106 (November–December 1977): 65. The editor of this journal says in his introductory note that "currents in the Western Communist Parties become increasingly willing to invoke the ideas of Kautsky with some benevolence." Ibid., 2.

30. *New Left Review,* no. 106 (November–December 1977): 64.

31. Mandel, *From Stalinism to Eurocommunism,* 206, 208.

32. Ibid., 34; see also 190–91, where Mandel blames this Kautskyist strategy for "the collapse of the German workers' movement" through the stages of 1914, 1918, 1923, and 1933; the failures of the French and Spanish Communists 1935–38 and of the French and Italian ones 1944–47; and the overthrow of the Chilean Unidad Popular in 1973.

33. Ibid., 79, 80; italics in the original.

34. Santiago Carrillo, *Eurocommunism and the State* (Westport, Conn.: Lawrence Hill & Co., 1978), 88. While I do not deal with Spanish Communism here, Claudín and Carrillo must be cited as among the most outspoken representatives of Eurocommunism.

35. Ibid., 90; italics in the original.

36. Ibid.,18; italics in the original. The implication appears to be that there is a distinction between formal and informal Marxism, and Lenin's informal one was better than Kautsky's formal one for Russia in 1917.

37. Ibid., 151.

38. Ibid., 154.

39. Introduction to a volume published in Mexico containing both Kautsky's *Dictatorship of the Proletariat* and Lenin's *Proletarian Revolution and the Renegade Kautsky,* translated in Claudín, "Democracy and Dictatorship," 59–76.

40. Ibid., 64–65.

41. Ibid., 68.

42. Ibid., 75.

43. Ibid., 74.

44. Karl Marx, "The Eighteenth Brumaire of Louis Bonaparte," in *The Marx-Engels Reader,* 2d ed., ed. Robert C. Tucker, (New York: W. W. Norton, 1978), 595.

45. Kevin Devlin once remarked that it was tempting to refer to Western European Communist positions as " 'Bernstein redivivus.' But this would be to underestimate the Communist capacity for ideological rationalization of ideological change. If Bernstein rides again he does so disguised as Lenin, so to speak." Devlin, "Prospects for Communism," 29.

46. Steenson, *Karl Kautsky* 5, 159–60, shows Kautsky to have been quite flexible and capable of compromise. See also Salvadori, Karl Kautsky, 18.

47. One of Salvadori's central concerns is to demonstrate that Kautsky was no renegade. See the passage I quote from his book on Kautsky in note 44 of chapter 2, above, which concludes: "My answer to the question of whether Lenin was 'correct' to call Kautsky a 'renegade' because of his conception of the state and democracy is therefore clear: by the end of the 19th century, Kautsky held a view of them that would inevitably clash with Soviet theory and the practice of the government of the Bolsheviks." Salvadori, *Karl Kautsky,* 11–12; see also 251–55. "There was never any real 'apostasy' or 'betrayal'. Rather two antithetical conceptions of

socialism had taken the field against each other." Ibid., 255.

48. This is true, too, of a third branch, critical theory, which is also foreshadowed by attacks levied at Kautsky, in this case for abandoning the Hegelian dialectic and the subjective element in Marxism and for his emphasis on objective laws of historical development at the expense of voluntarism. Interestingly, all three lines of attack object to Kautsky's determinism or what is often referred to as his evolutionism, which goes back to his early interest in Darwin and natural science as well as in the social scientific aspects of Marx's and Engels's thought that attracted him to Marxism from the beginning. On Kautsky's relation to Darwinism, see Steenson, *Karl Kautsky,* 24–30, 62–66, and Hans-Josef Steinberg, *Sozialismus und deutsche Sozialdemokratie,* (5th ed., (Bonn: J. H. W. Dietz, 1979), 48-53, and also Walter Holzheuer, *Karl Kautsky's Werk als Weltanschauung* (Munich: C. H. Beck, 1972), 14–25.

49. For an interpretation of post–1890 Social Democratic policy as a response to this situation, see Guenther Roth, *The Social Democrats in Imperial Germany: A Study in Working-Class Isolation and National Integration* (Totowa, N.J.: Bedminster Press, 1963), especially 165–71, 184–92. Roth concludes "that both the deterministic character of the radical ideology and the moderate practices of the labor movement were largely shaped by the peculiar combination of repressive and permissive policies in Imperial Germany." Ibid., 170. See also Dick Geary, "The German Labour Movement, 1848–1919," *European Studies Review* 6, no. 3 (July 1976): 308. Erich Matthias says: "Kautskyism succeeded as the ideological expression of an attitude which originated from the tradition of persecution and was kept alive and conserved by the situation of the Party in Wilheminian Germany." Erich Matthias, "Kautsky und der Kautskyanismus: Die Funktion der Ideologie in der deutschen Sozialdemokratie vor dem ersten Weltkriege," in *Marxismusstudien,* 2d series, ed. Iring Fetscher (Tübingen: J. C. B. Mohr, 1957), 177–78.

50. "For the state, the churches, and bourgeois society of imperial Germany, Social Democracy stood, in fact, outside the official nation so that an attitude of irreconcilable protest was a matter of 'party honor' for the mass of Social Democratic adherents." Matthias, "Kautsky und der Kautskyanismus," 173. Referring to these adherents' "genuine need to distance themselves" (176) from the other political parties, especially the Liberals, Matthias writes: "When the Social Democratic leadership regarded it as its principal task to improve the material position of the workers within the bourgeois state, it was in full accord with the interests and expectations of the bulk of its following. But the same following, which never thought of revolution, would have regarded it as intolerable if the workers' party had appeared as one party among the others." Ibid., 175. The SPD policy of irreconcilable "non-participating opposition" and "official self-differentiation" is the central theme of Peter Nettl, who refers to Kautsky as "the champion of social isolation." Peter Nettl, "The German Social Democratic Party 1890–1914 as a Political Model," *Past and Present,* no. 30 (April 1965): 66–67, 82.

51. For a massive study focusing on the policies of the Marxist Center, see Dieter Groh, *Negative Integration und revolutionärer Attentismus: Die deutsche Sozialdemokratie am Vorabend des Ersten Weltkrieges* (Frankfurt a.M.: Ullstein-Propyläen, 1973), especially 36–39, 158–59, 185–92, and 491. He argues that the process of negative integration of Social Democratic workers "is characterized, on the one hand, by growing economic improvement and tendencies toward the legal and factual enjoyment of equal rights, coupled, on the other hand, with the simultaneous principled denial of equal rights in state and society and persistence of exploitation and of repressive measures. . . . The labor leaders' tactic of diverting feelings of aggression [aroused among the workers by their situation] toward the strengthening of their organizations additionally decisively increased the effects of the integrating elements. . . . To the process of negative integration corresponded the behavioral model of revolutionary expectancy [*Attentismus*], which became ever more hardened by confrontation with daily reality. Karl Kautsky, the leading theoretician of prewar Social Democracy, reduced this conglomerate of a political attitude of patient waiting [*Abwartehaltung*], of revolutionary hopes aiming at the overthrow of existing conditions, and of verbal radicalism to the classical formula that German Social Democracy was a revolutionary but not a revolution-making party." Ibid., 36. For my brief discussion of Kautsky's "classical formula," see p. 71 and also pp. 107–108 above. See also Matthias, "Kautsky und der Kautskyanismus," 183. Groh says of Kautsky that "the Darwino-Marxism propagated by him for decades—which was tantamount to revolutionary 'attentism'—was both the ideological reflex of the situation of the Party and had also helped create this situation." Groh, *Negative Integration,* 468.

52. Steenson, *Karl Kautsky,* 248.

53. Steinberg says: "Kautsky's concept of revolution . . . referred quite concretely to the overthrow by force of the existing constitutional order. Its goal was the erection of a parliamentary democratic system on the basis of which socialism could be peacefully realized. . . . [T]o him, the victory of the proletariat was identical with the victory of democracy. He differed with Bernstein in that he doubted that democracy could be achieved in Germany by some route other than that of a political revolution, which a Social Democratic majority would finally be forced to take by the resistance to democratization of the reactionary government." Steinberg, *Sozialismus,* 81–82.

54. *Der Weg zur Macht* (Frankfurt: Europäische Verlagsanstalt. 1972). See my article on this book above.

55. Obviously, the Weimar Republic developed differently. While Kautsky understood better than many other Marxists before and during World War I that capitalism could survive a war, he did not appreciate the power of institutional and ideological elements of Wilhelminian society that survived in Weimar Germany or the full significance of Nazism, which rose when he was in his seventies and ruled when he was in his eighties. I deal with his analyses of fascism in my Introduction on

pp. 19–22, above, but they are irrelevant for our comparison of Kautsky's ideas with the policies of Western Communist parties in what may be seen as their "Weimar period."

56. Salvadori, *Karl Kautsky,* 227. I discuss Kautsky's views of the Soviet Union somewhat more fully in my Introduction on pp. 31–38, above.

57. Even the antifascist Popular Front policy finds parallels in Kautsky's support of electoral agreements with bourgeois left parties against the supporters of the imperial regime and in his rejection of the concept of "one reactionary mass." See my long note 32 in chapter 3, above; Steenson, *Karl Kautsky,* 112–14 and 173–74; and especially Steinberg, *Sozialismus,* 79–80; and also Salvadori, *Karl Kautsky,* 46–47, 150–52.

58. Just as Dieter Groh, cited above, thought that the SPD "negatively integrated" the working class in Wilhelminian Germany by channeling its aggressions into organizational and electoral activities, so Georges Lavau says "that the political system can derive a certain degree of security from this dual activity of the PCF, which consists on the one hand of posing as the great defender of the underdog, and on the other hand of channeling all these protest movements into organized and orderly mass demonstrations and into an opposition vote at election time." Georges Lavau, "The PCF, the State, and the Revolution: An Analysis of Party Policies, Communications, and Popular Culture," in *Communism in Italy and France,* ed. Donald L. M. Blackmer and Sidney Tarrow (Princeton, N.J.: Princeton University Press, 1975), 90.

59. Traditionally, explanations of the links between the Soviet government and Communist parties have one-sidedly emphasized controls exercised by and benefits accruing to Moscow but have tended to ignore the needs of the parties — and, indeed, of their adherents — that these links served.

60. Perry Anderson argues at length that there are striking parallels, both formal and substantive, between that policy and the "strategy of attrition" advocated by Kautsky in 1910 in opposition to Luxemburg's call for mass strikes. Perry Anderson, "The Antinomies of Antonio Gramsci," *New Left Review,* no. 100 (November 1976–January 1977): 55–72. He also stresses, however, that "the parliamentarist conclusions of Kautsky's strategic theory were absolutely foreign" to Gramsci. Ibid., 72.

61. Donald L. M. Blackmer, "Continuity and Change in Postwar Italian Communism," in *Communism in Italy and France,* ed. Blackmer and Tarrow, 53.

62. "[W]hen the Twentieth Congress of the CPSU presented us with the opportunity to vigorously resume the interrupted search . . . [t]he leadership of the Italian party . . . confronted quite fundamental questions: the question of a socialist regime based on a multiparty system, based on the recognition of the autonomy of the various forces of civil society. . . . At the same time, we clarified our relationship to democratic institutions and liberties. We talked about liberties which could not correctly be called bourgeois because of the role which the working class in countries like ours had in the conquest and consolidation of these liberties. . . . We

spoke of the need to 'correct' certain things in the way in which Lenin had presented the problem of the destruction of the bourgeois state apparatus, the problem of the dictatorship of the proletariat." Giorgio Napolitano in Hobsbawm, *The Italian Road to Socialism*, 27–28.

63. For an excellent summary of "the influences of the past" accounting for differences between the PCF and PCI, see Sidney Tarrow, "Communism in Italy and France: Adaptation and Change," in *Communism in Italy and France*, ed. Blackmer and Tarrow, 577–86. On the different Communist-Socialist relations in the two countries, see also Norman Kogan, "The French Communists — and Their Italian Comrades," *Studies in Comparative Communism* 6, no. 1–2 (Spring–Summer 1973): 192–93. Thomas Greene explains "a large part of the differences between the PCF and the PCI . . . by differences between the levels of political competition characterizing their respective environments" (Ibid., 353). He shows that for the PCF, it was only "the advent of Gaullism [that] provided the critical mass of adaptive challenges that tilted the balance of forces in favor of change" while "the PCI's political environment has become increasingly competitive since World War II." Thomas H. Greene, "Non-Ruling Communist Parties and Political Adaptation," *Studies in Comparative Communism* 6, no. 4 (Winter 1973): 352, 356–57.

64. For a summary history of "the hesitant and fitful consolidation of a Socialist-Communist alliance" beginning in 1959 and culminating in the Common Program of 1972, see Ronald Tiersky, "Alliance Politics and Revolutionary Pretensions," in *Communism in Italy and France*, ed. Blackmer and Tarrow, 441–50.

65. For a brief summary of relevant social changes in Italy, see Joseph LaPalombara, "The Italian Communist Party and Changing Italian Society," in *Eurocommunism*, ed. Ranney and Sartori, 111–14, which notes that "[a]t the end of World War II almost half of the Italian labor force was in agriculture; today that sector accounts for only one-sixth of the labor force. The modern industrial sector advanced so rapidly in Italy . . . that in less than two decades the country moved from near destitution to seventh place among the world's most productive and prosperous nations." Ibid., 111.

66. This is explicitly recognized by Giorgio Napolitano: "[W]e have to take into account that the problem of working-class alliances in Italy today has to be posed in very different terms even from the way it was posed in our own country thirty years ago, because there have been wholly new developments in social stratification. . . . [T]he fundamental question has become that of alliances with the non-proletarian strata in the cities which have grown formidably over the last decades in Italy. I am speaking of the alliance with the strata of small and medium-size producers and with those strata of the urban middle class engaged in tertiary activities; above all, I am thinking in terms of the precipitous growth of the ranks of white-collar workers and intellectuals in our country. The masses of intellectuals are themselves extremely composite in character as a result of their diverse relations to the production process, their disparate social functions and

their varying levels of income." Hobsbawm, *The Italian Road to Socialism,* 73–74. For a very similar analysis and a list of groups to be appealed to, presented to the French Party's 1974 Congress by PCF General Secretary Marchais, see Georges Marchais, "Rapport du Comité Central au XXIᵉ Congrès Extraordinaire," *Cahiers du Communisme* 50, no. 11 (November 1974): 47–48.

67. The Editors, "The New Reformism," *Monthly Review* 28, no. 2 (June 1976): 8.

68. Giorgio Amendola, "The Italian Road to Socialism," *New Left Review,* no. 106 (November–December 1977): 42, 50.

69. Tiersky, "French Communism in 1976," 46.

70. Pajetta, "For Socialism in Europe," 59. A joint statement issued by PCI General Secretary Enrico Berlinguer and PCF General Secretary Georges Marchais on 15 November 1975 stated: "[A]ll the freedoms — which are a product both of the great democratic-bourgeois revolutions and of the great popular struggles of this century, headed by the working class — will have to be guaranteed and developed. This holds true for freedom of thought and expression, for freedom of the press, of assembly, of association and demonstration, for free movement of persons inside and outside their country, for the inviolability of private life, for religious freedom and total freedom of expression for currents of thought and every philosophical, cultural and artistic opinion. The French and Italian Communists declare themselves for the plurality of political parties, for the right to existence and activity of opposition parties, for the free formation of majorities and minorities and the possibility of their alternating democratically. . . . A socialist transformation . . . requires the existence, guarantee and development of democratic institutions fully representative of popular sovereignty and the free exercise of direct, proportional universal suffrage." "Joint Declaration by the Italian Communist Party and the French Communist Party," *The Italian Communists,* no. 5–6 (September–December 1975): 75–76. Another translation appeared as "Declaration of the French and Italian Communist Parties," *Socialist Revolution* 6, no. 3 (July–September 1976), 71-72. For similar statements by Berlinguer addressed directly to the Soviet Communists, see his "Our Socialism: Greetings to the 25th Congress of the C.P.S.U. February 27, 1976," *The Italian Communists* no. 1 (January–March 1976): 43; and his "For New Roads towards Socialism in Italy and Europe: Speech to the Conference of the Communist and Workers' Parties of Europe — Berlin, June 29–30, 1976," *The Italian Communists* no. 2–3 (April–July 1976): 60.

71. Hobsbawm, *The Italian Road to Socialism,* 29.

72. Ibid., 52.

73. Ibid., 46.

74. Marchais said: "At present the word 'dictatorship' does not correspond with what we seek in any way. It contains a significance which is completely contrary to our hopes, and to our plans." Quoted from *Le Monde* of 9 January 1976 in Neill Nugent and David Lowe, "The French Communist Party: The Road to Democratic Government?," *Political Quarterly* 48, no. 3 (July–September 1977): 278. See also

Victor Leduc, "The French Communist Party: Between Stalinism and Eurocommunism," *Political Quarterly* 49, no. 4 (October–December 1978): 406.

75. Karl Kautsky, *The Labour Revolution* (New York: Dial Press, 1925), 54, quoted in Salvadori, *Karl Kautsky,* 327.

76. Quoted in Salvadori, *Karl Kautsky,* 327–28, from Karl Kautsky, *Die Marxsche Staatsauffassung* (Jena: Thüringer Verlagsanstalt, 1923), 5.

77. Hobsbawm, *The Italian Road to Socialism,* 30.

78. Ibid., 78.

79. Draft Thesis No. 44, "Draft Theses for the 15th National Congress of the P.C.I.," 49. On contacts and points of convergence between the Social Democratic parties of northern and central Europe and the Eurocommunist parties, especially the PCI, and their background, see Heinz Timmermann, "Democratic Socialists, Eurocommunists, and the West," in *The European Left: Italy, France, and Spain,* ed. William E. Griffith (Lexington, Mass.: D. C. Heath, 1979), 167–98. On SPD-PCI contacts, see Angela Stent Yergin, "West Germany's Südpolitik: Social Democrats and Eurocommunism," *Orbis,* 23, no. 1 (Spring 1979): 51–71. Representatives of the British and Dutch Labour parties and of the French, Belgian, Portuguese, and Swiss Socialist parties attended the Fourteenth or Fifteenth PCI Congresses, or both, and an SPD observer was present at the former. *The Italian Communists* no. 2–3 (March–May 1975): 146–47; and no. 1–2 (January–June 1979): 140–42. In March 1980 Berlinguer held talks with the SPD chairman and president of the Socialist International Willy Brandt and with the French Socialist leader François Mitterrand, by then more a rival than an ally of the PCF. Joan Barth Urban, "Moscow and the PCI in the 1970s: Kto Kovo?," *Studies in Comparative Communism,* 13, no. 2–3 (Summer/Autumn 1980): 166.

80. Quoted from *Rinascita,* 8 June 1979, in Sidney Tarrow, "Historic Compromise or Bourgeois Majority? Eurocommunism in Italy, 1976–1979," in *National Communism in Western Europe: A Third Way to Socialism?,* ed. Howard Machin (London: Methuen, 1983), 138–39. This article, an excellent discussion of the period of PCI cooperation with the Christian-Democratic government and of its costs to the PCI, concludes that, though going into opposition, the Party would not return to oppositionism, for the precepts of the Historic Compromise were too deeply rooted in PCI strategy to be easily reversed. Tarrow quotes Berlinguer (in *Rinascita,* 24 August 1979) calling on his comrades after the 1979 election defeat "to return to and to make explicit and deeper the terms of the compromise that is necessary today." Ibid., 146.

81. Frank L. Wilson, "The French CP's Dilemma," *Problems of Communism* 27, no. 4 (July–August 1978): 1–14. On conflicts between the French Communists and Socialists after the adoption of their Common Program of 1972, see Tiersky, "French Communism in 1976," 35–38, and William J. Davidshofer, "France: The Evolution of the PCF," in *Communism and Political Systems in Western Europe,* ed. David E. Albright (Boulder, Colo.: Westview Press, 1979), 104–07, 115–28.

For good brief explanations of the rift between the French Communists and Socialists and some of its consequences, see Morris, "The French Communist Party," 166–70, and Ronald Tiersky, "Ambivalence Yet Again Unresolved: The French Left, 1972–1978," in *The European Left,* ed. Griffith, 64–67.

82. Ronald Tiersky says of the PCF: "The Communist party, to the extent it remains within its old appeals and old limitations, is fated to wither as its historic social bases are transformed by macrosocial and economic processes." Tiersky, "Ambivalence Yet Again Unresolved," 52; he elaborates on this point on 65–66, 72. For a comparison of the Italian and French Communists at the time, it is noteworthy that, after Berlinguer had sharply condemned the Soviet invasion of Afghanistan and Marchais had justified it as a "totally legitimate intervention," a PCI spokesman is quoted in *Time* magazine of 4 February 1980, p. 37, as saying "we are closer to the Social Democrats of Germany and Benelux than to the [Communist] party in France." See also Joan Barth Urban, ''Moscow and the PCI," *Studies in Comparative Communism* 13, no. 2–3 (Summer–Autumn 1980): 163–164, and more generally on PCI-PCF relations, Alex MacLeod, "The PCI's Relations with the PCF in the Age of Eurocommunism, May 1973–June 1979," *Studies in Comparative Communism* 13, no. 2–3 (Summer–Autumn 1980): 168–96, and also Michael J. Sodaro, "The Italian Communists and the Politics of Austerity," *Studies in Comparative Communism* 13, no. 2–3 (Summer–Autumn 1980): 236–38.

83. MacLeod, "The PCI's Relations with the PCF," 181–83.

84. After the turn of the century, this was no longer wholly true of much of the SPD leadership.

85. I have sought to show here that major shifts in Communist party policy can, in good part, be explained as responses to changes in the parties' socioeconomic environment. I have thus avoided the approach, still pervasive in the literature, that deals with Communist policy in terms of "strategy" and "tactics" and implies that Communists, unlike other politicians, can choose their policies at will. But I do not contend that all Communist policy changes can be wholly accounted for in terms of changing levels of industrialization and of working-class mobilization. Thus, my scheme of three phases, taken literally and by itself, clearly cannot explain such phenomena — none of them dealt with here — as the strength of Eurocommunism in Spain, working-class support in the Weimar Republic for the antireformist German Communists, or the reformist policies of the French socialists in the late Third and the Fourth Republics. (I added this note in response to a penetrating critique of this article by Frank Lee Wilson.)

6

The Dictatorship of the Proletariat

Karl Kautsky's *Dictatorship of the Proletariat* is a well-reasoned and strong plea to socialists to be faithful to democracy both before and after their expected advent to governmental power. Democracy was a more clearly defined concept to Kautsky than it is today, when all kinds of regimes, parties and ideologies claim to be democratic. When he wrote his book, democracy meant to Kautsky, what it still vaguely means to most of us in the West, a system in which great masses of people participate in the political process, particularly through universal suffrage, and are enabled to do so through civil liberties such as freedom of speech, press, and organization.

Those of us who are attached to this kind of system as most likely to assure a maximum of individual freedom can easily sympathize with Kautsky's values and associate ourselves with his side in his conflict with the Bolsheviks. However, as a plea for democracy and freedom, Kautsky's book speaks for itself and there is little need for me to call attention to its message. Any reader will find much in it of relevance to recent and present-day ideological conflicts and will shape his own attitude toward it accordingly.

Rather than engage in ideological conflict here, I propose to indicate briefly the place of Kautsky's pamphlet in the politics of the period and the function it served. I shall also critically examine some aspects of his work as a contribution to empirical social science apart from its value orientation. It seems both interesting and fair to do so, since like most Marxist writings, Kautsky's book contains both normative discussion and empirical analysis. As is typically true of Marxian works, the two are often difficult to disentangle, but the empirical and analytical elements loom large in Kautsky's writings, for he was one of those Marxists who regarded himself above all as a social scientist rather than as a politician and had, in fact, ample justification for doing so.[1]

The social scientific emphasis of this essay is chosen on the assumption that most of the readers of a new edition of Kautsky's book will be quite different from those who read the original. There are few left who still want to refight the ideological battles of the period of the Russian Revolution. And those who fight ideological battles today are not likely to turn to Karl Kautsky's arguments for ammunition. To the Communists, he remains a renegade and—in spite of his role as the chief defender of Marxism against Bernstein's Revisionism—has even become a Revisionist.[2] To most of those who choose to fight Communism on ideological grounds, Kautsky will not appeal simply because he was a Marxist. The heirs of Kautsky's political tradition, the present-day socialist and social democratic parties, have lost their attachment to Marxism and their interest in the kind of "theory" it stood for, as the groups they represent have become integrated into existing social and political systems.

The serious Marxist students of Marxism, as represented by such thinkers as Kautsky and Rudolf Hilferding, Max Adler, and Otto Bauer, have left the scene. The brilliant polemics of the first half-century after Marx's death, as carried on by Bernstein and Kautsky, Luxemburg, Lenin, and Trotsky, degenerated into Stalin's heavy-handed attacks on his enemies. They now find only a faint echo in the dull disputations of the theoreticians of Peking and Moscow. At last the field of Marxism has been left to the social scientists. There has been a remarkable growth of excellent scholarly literature on Marxism in recent years. It is both as an object of social science study and as a contribution to social science that I want to look at Kautsky's pamphlet here.

A dozen years after the publication of *The Dictatorship of the Proletariat* Kautsky described the attitude he had held when writing the pamphlet as follows:

If [the Bolsheviks] succeeded in making their expectations and promises come true, it would be a tremendous accomplishment for them and for the Russian people and, indeed, for the entire international proletariat. The teachings of Marxism, however, could then no longer be maintained. They would be proved false, but, on the other hand, socialism would gain a splendid triumph, the road to the immediate removal of all misery and ignorance of the masses would be entered in Russia and pointed out to the rest of the world.

How gladly I would have believed that it was possible! How gladly I would have been persuaded! The most powerful, best-founded theory must yield when it is contradicted by the facts. However, they must be facts, not mere projects and promises.

Though still in doubt, I watched the Bolsheviks' first steps with benevolent expectation. I considered it impossible that they could immediately attain socialism, as they thought. Still, they were intelligent and knowledgeable people and they had acquired great power. Perhaps they would succeed in discovering new ways to raise the working masses from which the nations of the West, too, could learn.

However, my expectant benevolence did not last long. To my chagrin, I saw ever more clearly that the Bolsheviks totally misunderstood their situation, that they thoughtlessly tackled problems for the solution of which all conditions were lacking. In their attempts to accomplish the impossible by brute force, they chose paths by which the working masses were not raised economically, intellectually, or morally, but on the contrary, were depressed even deeper than they had been by tsarism and the World War.

Under these circumstances, I considered it incumbent on me to warn the Bolsheviks urgently against the road they had taken. I did this while the war was still in progress, in the summer of 1918, in my pamphlet *The Dictatorship of the Proletariat* (Vienna). I felt called upon to raise my warning voice all the more as, next to the German and Austrian Social Democrats, I stood — and still stand — in closer relations with the Russian ones than with any others.

In the most active contact with the Russian socialist emigrés since 1880, I had the good fortune to gain as my friends the founders of Russian Social Democracy, above all Axelrod, but also Plekhanov, Vera Sassulich, and Leo Deutsch. The members of the younger generation of the Russian Social Democrats have done me the honor and given me the pleasure of counting me, along with Plekhanov and Axelrod, among their teachers.

Most of them also became my personal friends, on the one side Martov, Dan, Abramovich, etc., as much as on the other side Lenin, Trotsky,

Rakovsky, and so on, with whom Parvus and Rosa Luxemburg were at times closely connected. In the closest and most active contact with my Russian friends and disciples, which has now lasted for half a century, we have mutually provided each other with intellectual stimulation. It is to this circumstance, above all, that I owe my insight into Russian conditions.

Now the moment had come to render thanks to my Russian friends for what I had learned from them and to participate in their intensive discussions of the road to be taken. I did so to salve my conscience, not because I expected any practical success. How could a single German pamphlet in the midst of war, published in Vienna, be effective in Petrograd and Moscow! Most Bolsheviks did not even hear of its existence. But even if they had read my pamphlet, it was bound to remain ineffective. They could no longer turn back without abandoning themselves. The logic of facts has always been stronger than the logic of ideas.[3]

The Dictatorship of the Proletariat was the opening gun in what became the greatest debate between social democratic and Communist interpreters of Marxism. Lenin replied to it in his famous *The Proletarian Revolution and the Renegade Kautsky.* Kautsky returned to his attack on the Bolsheviks in *Terrorism and Communism.* Trotsky counterattacked in a pamphlet of the same name, to which Kautsky responded in his *Von der Demokratie zur Staatssklaverei.*[4] To explain Kautsky's leading role in this debate, I can do no better than to quote from Max Shachtman's foreword to the new University of Michigan Press edition of Trotsky's contribution to the debate:

The choice of main target for the Bolshevik barrage was not accidental. The leaders of the Russian socialist opposition to the Bolsheviks — the Mensheviks and the Social Revolutionists — were very little known to the mass of the socialist movement outside of Russia; their writings were even less well known. The position of Kautsky was altogether different.

Karl Kautsky had known both Karl Marx and Friedrich Engels in his youth. After their death, he became the principal literary executor of the two founders of modern socialism. His writings on a wide variety of subjects were regarded everywhere as classical statements of the socialist view. He virtually founded and for thirty-five years edited the theoretical organ of the German Social Democracy, *Die Neue Zeit,* and it is no exaggeration to say that no other periodical had so profound an influence upon the whole generation of Marxists before World War I, not in Germany alone but throughout the world. In his own party and in the Socialist (the

Second) International for most of its quarter of a century before the war-brought about its collapse, he was unique in the prestige and authority in the sphere of Marxian theory that he enjoyed among socialists of all schools. His renown was scarcely diminished, at least up to the outbreak of the war, by occasional questioning of his Marxian orthodoxy by the small but more radical wing of socialism or by the fact that the actual political leadership of his party shifted steadily away from him. It is worth noting, too, that except for the Poles and of course the Russians, no one in the international socialist movement showed a greater interest, knowledge, and understanding of Russian problems under tsarism and of the Russian socialist movement than Kautsky. The Russian Marxists of all tendencies held Kautsky in almost awesome esteem. Up to August 1914, the writings of Lenin in particular are studded with the most respectful and even laudatory references to Kautsky, with whose views he sought to associate himself as much as possible and whose approval he, Lenin, adduced whenever he could as a most authoritative contribution to Russian socialist controversies.

. . . When the Bolsheviks took power in Russia . . . and Kautsky, not unexpectedly, promptly came forward as their opponent on an international scale, so to say, the breach between them became wide and deep and irreparable.

From the very beginning of the revolution, the Bolsheviks sought the active support of socialists outside of Russia, not only as sympathizers of the revolution they had already carried out but for the world revolution which was to be led by the Communist (the Third) International which they proposed to establish as quickly as possible. The opposition of a socialist of Kautsky's standing was therefore a matter of exceptional concern. Hence the vehemence, the intensity, and extensiveness, of Lenin's and Trotsky's polemics.[5]

However, it was not only the Bolsheviks who opposed Kautsky. As he himself wrote:

Many of my political friends in Germany and Austria also disapproved of my stand against Bolshevism. They considered it possible that it would push through its program and demanded that it not be disturbed and discouraged in its efforts. Measures which I regarded as utterly wrong and as fatal mistakes appeared to them as mere blemishes, either the transient consequences of the war or the price that must be paid for every new experience — as infantile disorders of early youth.[6]

Under these circumstances, it took courage in socialist circles to attack Lenin when Kautsky did so. Having cut himself off from the German Majority Socialists during World War I because he refused to support the imperial government's war effort, he now isolated himself from many in his own Independent Social Democratic Party. He was then one of the relatively few socialists, certainly among the Independents, who was not carried away by the general enthusiasm for the Bolsheviks, which has long been forgotten as a result of the subsequent sharp anti-Communism of most Social Democrats. Even the editor of the English translation of *The Dictatorship of the Proletariat,* as published in 1919 by the National Labour Press for the Independent Labour Party Library, found it appropriate to write in his preface that the Bolsheviks had "accomplished wonderful achievements" and that "Lenin himself is the first to admit that they have made mistakes." He considered it necessary to say that he made "no apology" for the publication of the book, but, far from approving of it, merely pleaded the need for "impartiality and tolerance" as his reasons for the publication.

Kautsky's pamphlet was written in early August 1918, less than a year after the Bolshevik seizure of power in St. Petersburg and Moscow, after the conclusion of the Treaty of Brest-Litovsk, but before the end of World War I and before the revolutions in Germany and Austria. Kautsky expected these revolutions and wanted to prevent them from coming under Communist influence. This was, indeed, one of the main purposes of his book and particularly of its final chapter, which is directed against "The New Theory" of dictatorship on the Soviet pattern as an inevitable part of proletarian revolutions everywhere.

Immediately after the outbreak of the German revolution in November 1918, a revised edition of Kautsky's pamphlet appeared in Berlin under the title *Demokretie oder Diktatur,* which omits the sections directly concerned with Russia (chapters 1, 6, 7, 9, and 10) and substitutes a new first chapter. In it, Kautsky states that the Bolsheviks' call for dictatorship would not be taken seriously in the Western democracies, but that it had some appeal in Germany which, like Russia, had lived under a militarist and police autocracy.

Therefore it has become necessary to examine once again the problem of democracy in relation to the proletariat and to socialism, a problem that had appeared to us as well settled for decades. For this purpose I published a few weeks before the [German] Revolution a pamphlet entitled *The Dictatorship of the Proleteriet* (Vienna: Volksbuchhandlung, I. Brand).

Its major part was concerned with Russian conditions. Everything I said on that subject has unfortunately been confirmed by the facts.

Today we have a revolution ourselves. Today we confront, not for Russia but for Germany, the question: dictatorship or democracy?[7]

To understand *The Dictatorship of the Proletariat,* one must not confuse the dictatorship Kautsky attacks with modern totalitarianism. In 1918 rival parties had been outlawed, the suffrage had been restricted, and open organized opposition had been suppressed by the Bolsheviks, but there was as yet not effective terror or propaganda or regimentation affecting the bulk of the population. At that time, modern totalitarianism, Communist or fascist, which has since shaped our concept of "dictatorship" was still unknown. Kautsky's image of dictatorship was hence quite different from ours. To him dictatorship was distinguished from democracy chiefly because it lacked universal suffrage and popular participation in politics, while we have come to know universal suffrage and mass participation as characteristics of modern totalitarianism. Similarly, Kautsky thought that dictatorship with its reliance on military suppression would lead to civil war unless there was total political apathy. He did not—and could not yet— understand that totalitarian methods can avoid both apathy and civil war.

In opposition to dictatorship, Kautsky (especially in chapter 4) makes his case for a strong parliament as the only way to control the bureaucracy and the military, for universal equal suffrage, and for the protection of minorities and groups opposing the government. To appreciate Kautsky's emphasis on these, one needs to remember not only that his book was directed against Bolsheviks and at their followers and potential followers in Central Europe but also that it was written in Berlin when the Prussian three-class suffrage and the German Empire with its bureaucracy and military unchecked by any effective parliament were still intact.

Kautsky suggested (in chapters 6 and 7) that the Bolsheviks should have followed democratic procedures. Thus, he felt that they should have accepted the constituent assembly elected by universal suffrage; that the soviets, as representatives of only part of the population, should not serve as governmental organizations; that the suffrage should be universal rather than limited to ill-defined categories of citizens, as it was in the early Soviet Republic; that opposition groups, including proletarian ones, should not be excluded from the soviets. In retrospect, all this may well appear to us as irrelevant. At the time, however, these statements served some functions. For one thing, they expressed Kautsky's bitterness and disappointment that a faction that had grown out of the Marxist movement—which to Kautsky was, above all, a democratic movement—should have abandoned the very goals for which he had by then fought for some forty years. Second, his words were to be a warning to other socialists, who were also attached to democratic values, not to follow Lenin. And, third, they served as a sharp polemical weapon to which Lenin was particularly vulnerable, because having used Marxian, that is, Western democratic, symbols all along, he could now be accused of having betrayed his own past.

In our own time, the Communists, whom Kautsky here accuses of betraying Marxism, have so successfully assumed its mantle that Marxism and Communism are widely held to be identical and most democratic socialists no longer lay claim to the Marxian heritage. Kautsky's book now serves as a useful reminder that, until about 1918, it was generally taken for granted that Marxism stood for democracy. Only under these circumstances could the Marxist Kautsky, addressing himself chiefly to other Marxists, make the Bolsheviks' abandonment of democracy his principal charge against them.

One of the main bases of Lenin's claim that the Bolshevik regime was Marxian in character lay in his reference to the until then rarely used Marxian term "the dictatorship of the proletariat." Since the Bolshevik claim has since been widely accepted, it is not without interest to note that Kautsky (in chapter 5) could advance some good arguments for his interpretation of the dictatorship of the proletariat not as a form of government, but as a condition that must necessarily arise where the proletariat, being preponderant in numbers, has conquered power and established democratic government.[8]

While any attempt to establish "what Marx really meant" may seem to us both futile and, except from the point of view of the historian of ideas, rather unimportant, it must not be forgotten that Kautsky and Lenin were not engaged in a mere scholarly dispute (though Kautsky, at any rate, was sufficiently scholarly in temperament to regard even this aspect of the conflict as important). The stakes were not merely historical accuracy but political power. The authority of Marx was then still tremendous among the European socialist parties and particularly their intellectual elites. Whoever could claim that authority to support his position gained a political advantage. Until then, Kautsky had been widely regarded as the most authoritative interpreter of Marx's thought. He now sought to use that position to influence the European, and especially the German, socialist parties in favor of democracy and to minimize the Bolsheviks' appeal among them.

Lenin, on the other hand, insisted on his Marxian orthodoxy in the hope of winning over the European socialist parties (and again especially the German socialists) to support his revolution. In order to do so he had to destroy Kautsky's prestige as a Marxist. It was undoubtedly for this purpose, as well as to express his personal bitterness, that he employed an extremely abusive tone in his polemics with Kautsky.[9]

In chapter 3 Kautsky lists the prerequisites of socialism: an interest on the part of the proletariat in socialism, superior proletarian numerical strength, and large-scale industry. All these are created only by advanced capitalism. Here Kautsky lays the groundwork for his orthodox Marxist attack on the Bolsheviks: that Russia was not "ripe" for socialist revolution. There is no question that on this central point Kautsky's interpretation of Marx's materialist conception of history was right and Lenin's was wrong. Social classes and certainly the ideological superstructure cannot arise before the mode of production that gives rise to them; the gravediggers of capitalism cannot bury it before capitalism has created them.

But Kautsky did more than to repeat the elementary Marxian point that the socialist revolution and socialism can only be the product of, and hence must be preceded by, advanced capitalism. Far more than Marx and Engels, he stressed as prerequisites of socialism not merely those created by the growth of capitalism, but the "maturity" of the working class, which it acquires in the course of its conflicts with capitalism. By this he meant chiefly the organizational and intellectual advance of the workers. It results from the growth of mass labor organizations and a large-scale daily socialist press which are possible only under conditions of democracy; secret organizations and a few handbills are no substitute for them. Hence democracy emerges in Kautsky's thought as an essential prerequisite of one of socialism's essential prerequisites, the maturity of the proletariat: "the more democratic a state is, the better organized and trained is its proletariat.

Democracy may sometimes inhibit its revolutionary thought, but it is the indispensable means for the proletariat to attain that maturity which it needs to gain political power and carry through the social revolution."[10]

Before we criticize this conception in the light of historical evidence, it should be admitted that Kautsky does here usefully point to the link between the rise of democracy and that of the labor movement, each strengthening the other, for which there is much evidence in the history of some of the most industrialized countries. Marx and Engels were by no means unaware of it, but died too soon to see it as clearly as Kautsky could, and Lenin, confronting the situation he did in Russia, had to deny it.

It is worth noting that Kautsky's insistence that the proletariat could rise to power only through the use of democratic procedures did not, as has often been asserted, make him a Revisionist. The question whether socialism was to be attained by democracy or revolution was not an issue in Kautsky's famous controversy with Bernstein. Both stood for the achievement of socialism through democracy. The issue on which they differed was how to attain democracy, especially in imperial Germany. In *The Road To Power*,[11] generally — and even by Lenin — regarded as his most "revolutionary" anti-Revisionist work, Kautsky demanded only the democratization of the German government and implied that it could not be attained peacefully in view of the resistance of the German ruling classes.

What Kautsky wrote in 1918, then, is quite consistent with what he had been saying even before and during his controversy with Revisionism. His anti-Bolshevism was consistent with his anti-Revisionism, and both flowed from his conception of orthodox Marxism. It is significant that in *The Dictatorship of the Proletariat* some of his discussion of the role of democracy in the proletariat's rise to power takes the form of a long quotation from an article of his of 1893 — when Kautsky was generally regarded as the leading theoretician of orthodox Marxism — an article that had been previously reprinted in his *Road to Power* of 1909. On the other hand, it is also significant that in his anti-Bolshevik work under discussion here, Kautsky does not hesitate to reprint his earlier view that as valuable as democracy is to the proletariat, it cannot remove the class conflicts of capitalist society or prevent the eventual inevitable overthrow of capitalism. Even in a democracy, the proletariat will not forego the social and political revolution—that is, the attainment of governmental power and the institution of socialist measures—but these are seen as peaceful processes. As Kautsky wrote in 1893: "This so-called peaceful method of the class struggle, which is confined to nonmilitary methods, parliamentarism, strikes, demonstrations, the press, and similar means of pressure, has the more chance of being retained in a country the more effective its democratic institutions are, the higher the state of political and economic understanding, and the self-control of the people."[12]

Kautsky's work rests on the Marxian conviction that the proletariat must conquer political power. He is certain (particularly in chapter 2) that it will do so through democracy. All this is based on assumptions that have since proved wrong, assumptions of growing numbers and of growing alienation and exploitation of the workers and of their consequently growing class consciousness. We now know, as Kautsky did not and probably could not know, that the trend is the other way. For one thing, with mechanization increasing beyond a certain point, and especially with automation, the number of workers engaged in production declines. Second, growing industrialization and, in part, the very democracy Kautsky extolled as the road to power lead not to the "maturity" of labor that prepares it to take power and introduce socialism, but to less alienation, exploitation, and class consciousness, and hence workers become integrated into society instead of "conquering" it. To be sure, in this process, workers acquire more education, a higher standard of living, and, in many cases, also stronger organizations—all aspects of Kautsky's proletarian maturity. However, fewer and fewer of them—rather than more and more as Kautsky still took for granted—think of themselves as workers. Hence socialist parties in advanced industrial countries—the formerly Marxian German and Austrian ones no less than the British Labour Party—have recently felt the need to broaden their appeal to go beyond the working class. It is fruitless to argue whether this development constitutes the victory of the proletariat or of the bourgeoisie. It is neither, because such Marxian categories are simply inadequate in an analysis of the history of the past half-century in the most advanced countries.

Kautsky was by no means wholly unaware of the decline of class conflicts and of ideology in advanced democratic countries. In his 1893 article, which he quotes here, he spoke of "the democratic-proletarian method of struggle" being "duller" and "less dramatic" than the upheavals of the bourgeois revolutions, and he noted with irony, but not incorrectly, that some of the literary intelligentsia but not the workers would regret this. Kautsky also stated (in chapter 4) that what he calls an interest in theory, a concern with the broad aspects of society, is a reaction to despotic regimes, to a situation in which only a small elite can be active in oppositional politics. Under democracy, greater masses are drawn into politics, more workers are involved in the administrative details of mass organizations, they become concerned with petty matters and momentary successes and develop opportunism and contempt of "theory." Today one may or may not share Kautsky's value judgment, but there is little doubt that he diagnosed the trend correctly. However, given his ideological position (which could be squared with reality much more easily half a century ago), Kautsky would only admit that it was a short-run trend, though it could last for years or even decades. Since even democracy could not remove the "contradictions" and conflicts of capitalist society, the workers — and now not merely the elite but the masses themselves (especially if labor time was reduced and free time increased) — would sooner or later necessarily face situations that would raise their minds beyond everyday problems and would kindle what he calls revolutionary thought and aspirations, that is, those directed at a large-scale reorganization of society. Here ideology, as is so often true in Marxist thought, has, almost imperceptibly, taken over from social science.

According to Kautsky the proletariat needs democracy not only before its conquest of power but also afterward. He therefore attacks the concept of a dictatorship of the proletariat (especially in chapter 5). There can, he points out, be no dictatorship of a class, but only of a party. If there are several proletarian parties, it will be a dictatorship of one over the others. If the one came to power as a result of an alliance with peasants, then the dictatorship is one of proletarians and peasants over proletarians.

To Kautsky, there is no reason why the proletariat should resort to dictatorship at all. It will ordinarily come to power only when it is in the great majority, and it would then be suicidal for it to give up democracy, for universal suffrage is its greatest source of moral authority. If a proletarian party did come to power without majority support — which Kautsky considered very unlikely in an advanced country — it could not maintain itself in power and realize its goals. It could not maintain itself through intellectual superiority, for as long as the majority of the population is opposed to socialism, most intellectuals will be, too. The alternative is the use of centralized organization and military power. It, however, is likely to produce civil war as a reaction, and it is impossible to reorganize society along socialist lines in the midst of war and especially under conditions of chronic civil war. If the proletarian revolution does involve civil war, socialists have an interest in keeping that war as brief as possible and having it serve only to establish democracy. The social revolution should then be carried out under democracy, for it must not at any time go farther than the majority will accept if it is to be permanently successful.

All this, of course, is based on Kautsky's conception of socialism:

> [It is] the organization of production by society. It requires economic self-government by the entire people. State organization of production by a bureaucracy or by dictatorship of a single stratum of the population does not constitute socialism. It requires organizational experience of broad masses of the people, presupposes numerous free organizations, both economic and political, and needs the most complete freedom of organization. The socialist organization of labor must not be an organization along military lines.[13]

And, as Kautsky states categorically at the beginning of his pamphlet:

> For us, therefore, socialism without democracy is unthinkable. We understand by modern socialism not merely social organization of production, but democratic organization of society as well. Accordingly, socialism is for us inseparably linked with democracy. No socialism without democracy.[14]

Once this conception of socialism is accepted, Kautsky's opposition to dictatorship follows naturally, and he wins his argument with Lenin hands down. As long as the socialist movement was largely a Western phenomenon and socialist parties in Eastern Europe were merely groups of intellectuals who had adopted the Western socialist doctrines, Kautsky's view was, in fact, very generally held, and he was perhaps justified in stating categorically what "socialism" was and what it was not.

With the Russian Revolution, the term "socialism" (much as has been true of the word "democracy") ceased to have a single meaning. The problem Lenin confronted was, in fact, not the one that Marx had in mind: that of workers coming to power in an advanced capitalist country in order to transfer the means of production from private to public hands. It was an utterly different one we have since become familiar with in many underdeveloped countries, that of intellectuals coming to power in a largely agrarian country in order to industrialize it. But though the substance changed, the words did not, deceiving an entire generation. Once this is recognized, the argument about what constitutes socialism loses much of its interest, for it has become an argument about a word that no longer corresponds to any one thing.

Neither Kautsky nor Lenin could be aware of this. Hence each argues that what he advocates is socialism and what the other stands for is not "true" socialism. Today, when not only Western European labor parties, but Mao and Castro, Nkrumah and Touré, Nasser and Nehru all stand for something they choose to call "socialism," it should be obvious that the term has become devoid of substantive meaning and might as well be discarded for analytical purposes. Not only was this not as clear in 1918 as it ought to be today, but the contestants in the dispute were engaged not only in analytical pursuits but in a struggle for power. They used the term "socialism" not merely as an analytical concept but as a symbol. Since it was then in the European labor movement as it is today among nationalist intellectuals in underdeveloped countries a powerful positive symbol, it became important for each side to lay claim to "true" socialism and to expose the opponents' socialism as " false."

Lenin could not afford to admit even to himself that Marxism, as a product of Western conditions, was largely irrelevant to his problems in Russia, for Marxism was widely popular in his circles as holding out the promise of a revolution whose success was scientifically guaranteed. Kautsky, on the other hand, like Marx himself a Western-oriented thinker who looked to the history of England and France as the model of social development, also saw the Russian Revolution in terms of Marxian, that is, Western, categories. Marx provides two categories for revolutions, the bourgeois revolution and the proletarian revolution. Since Kautsky saw clearly enough that the Bolshevik revolution was not proletarian in character, he argued that it must be bourgeois (see especially chapters 8 and 9). It does not occur to Kautsky that both categories are inapplicable in an underdeveloped country like Russia, with a small proletariat and hardly any bourgeoisie.

Industrialization comes to underdeveloped countries by a very different process from that which produced it in the West, on the initiative of intellectuals operating through government ownership or control of industry and agriculture,[15] intellectuals who are therefore neither private capitalists nor proletarians who expropriated such capitalists. Not once does Kautsky suggest that the Western pattern might not fit Russia; all his comparisons, even those regarding the peasantry, are with Western countries. Here his thought, like Marxian thought generally, and, indeed, almost all Western thought of the period, reveals its parochialism. It is only in the past few decades that we have begun to recognize that the political development of the West with its peculiar institutions of capitalism and of democracy and its class structure and ideologies, far from being a model that the rest of the world will follow, is quite exceptional.

That Kautsky was unable to offer an adequate interpretation of the Russian Revolution and the Communist regime is borne out by the fact that his predictions regarding its future course failed to be fulfilled. Yet, to write off *The Dictatorship of the Proletariat* simply as a failure even as an attempt at social scientific analysis—quite apart from the political impact the pamphlet may have had—would be grossly unfair.

In the post-World-War-II decades, traditional aristocratic regimes all over the underdeveloped world were yielding to movements led by Western-educated intellectuals committed to rapid modernization of their backward societies by means of some government control of industry and agriculture and more or less totalitarian political methods. It then became relatively easy to place the Russian Revolution in the same category with these upheavals, and, indeed, some went so far as to regard Soviet development as a relevant model for other underdeveloped countries.

In the first half of our century, any such comparison was virtually impossible. What became a worldwide process dominating the daily headlines in the second half had hardly begun as yet. Only the Chinese and Mexican revolutions preceded the Russian one in their outbreak, but their character as modernizing movements evolved slowly and was by no means clear in 1918. Besides, China and Mexico, like the underdeveloped world generally, were given very little attention in European political thinking.

Russia, on the other hand, was a European country, and its revolutionaries, being Western-influenced, had always used Western symbols to describe their movements. No wonder Kautsky was misled by these symbols to draw irrelevant parallels with the West, just as all too many have been similarly misled in recent years by the appearance of "socialism," "democracy," "nationalism," and so on all over Asia, Africa, and Latin America. Far from being alone in this respect, Kautsky shared his "Western" view of the Russian Revolution with virtually all of its interpreters of all political tendencies. To this day, we tend to think of the Russian Revolution as akin more to the English and especially the French Revolutions than to the revolutions in Mexico and Turkey, Guinea and Indonesia.[16]

Limited as Kautsky was by his own Western-Marxist categories, however, he at least never accepted the very common interpretation of the Russian Revolution, shared by the Communists and many anti-Communists, that it was a proletarian revolution and hence part of an international anticapitalist movement. He thus did his best to stop the spread of the widely believed myth of Communist world revolution. Had his view been the common rather than the exceptional one, the vicious cycle of mutually self-fulfilling prophecies of those who acted to advance and those who sought to prevent this world revolution might not have been set in motion so effectively that it affects East-West relations to the present day.

From the very beginning of the Bolshevik seizure of power in Russia, Karl Kautsky saw clearly and stated courageously that it was not and could not be a proletarian or a socialist, that is, Western anticapitalist, revolution. And, as the leading Marxist of his generation, he could authoritatively reject its claims to being Marxist as well. It is this message, delivered not as an impassioned plea to the emotions but as a calm and cool appeal to reason, that makes *The Dictatorship of the Proletariat* an important document in the history of Marxism and of the socialist movement and a milestone at that point of its path where Communism and democratic socialism parted ways.

Notes

1. For biographical and bibliographical data on Karl Kautsky see the Appendices, below, and my article in the *International Encyclopedia of the Social Sciences* (New York: Macmillan, 1968), 8:356–58.

2. For an amusing example, see Li Fu, Li Su-wen, and Wang Fu-ju, "On Kautskyism," *Hung-ch'i [Red Flag]* (Peking) nos. 8–9 (25 April 1962): 28–41, translated in Joint Publications Research Service, JPRS 13903 (29 May 1962) (Washington:

Department of Commerce): 76–120, which makes Kautsky out to be not only a Revisionist, but also, by implication, the ideological ancestor of Khrushchev.

3. Karl Kautsky, "Die Aussichten des Fünfjahresplanes," *Die Gesellschaft,* 8/1, no. 3 (March 1931): 261–62. This article appeared in translation as the preface to the English edition of Karl Kautsky, *Bolshevism at a Deadlock* (London: George Allen & Unwin, 1931), 7–23. It is, however, here translated from the German original.

4. Lenin, *The Proletarian Revolution and the Renegade Kautsky,* in *Collected Works,* 45 vols. (Moscow: Progress Publishers, 1960–70), 28:227–325. Kautsky, *Terrorism and Communism* (London: The National Labour Press, 1920; first German edition June 1919); Leon Trotsky, *Terrorism and Communism: A Reply to Karl Kautsky* (Ann Arbor: University of Michigan Press, 1961); Kautsky, *Von der Demokratie zur Staatssklaverei: Eine Auseinandersetzung mit Trotzki* (Berlin: Freiheit, 1921).

5. Trotsky, *Terrorism and Communism,* v–vii.

6. Kautsky, "Die Aussichten des Fünfjahresplanes," 262–63.

7. Karl Kautsky, *Demokratie oder Diktatur* (Berlin: Cassirer, 1918), 8.

8. For other comments by Kautsky on the dictatorship of the proletariat, see his *Von der Demokratie zur Staatssklaverei,* 38–43, 83–84; *The Labour Revolution* (New York: Dial Press, 1925), 59–89, where Kautsky takes issue with Lenin's *State and Revolution;* and *Social Democracy versus Communism* (New York: Rand School Press, 1946), 29–47.

9. The following are a few samples from Lenin, *The Proletarian Revolution and the Renegade Kautsky:* "awful theoretical muddle," "a schoolmaster who has become dry as dust," "in an incredibly tedious fashion chews the old cud," "twaddle," "this windbag," "monstrous distortion," "sophistry," "a lackey of the bourgeoisie," "monstrously absurd and untrue," "crass stupidity or very clumsy trickery" (all from 232–236). "It is impossible to enumerate all Kautsky's various absurdities, since every phrase he utters is a bottomless pit of apostasy" (240); "oh, civilized belly-crawling before the capitalists and bootlicking!" (245).

10. *The Dictatorship of the Proletariat* (Ann Arbor: University of Michigan Press, 1964; reprint, Westport, Conn.: Greenwood Press, 1981), 96.

11. *The Road to Power* (Chicago: Samuel A. Bloch, 1909). See my article on this book, above.

12. *The Dictatorship of the Proletariat,* 37. The 1893 article quoted here, as is noted in the German original but not in the English translation, is Kautsky "Ein sozialdemokratischer Katechismus," *Die Neue Zeit* 12/1 (1893): 361–70, 402–10. It was quoted at length by Kautsky in his *Road to Power* in 1909 (and not in 1900, as the translation states).

13. *The Dictatorship of the Proletariat,* 51.

14. Ibid., 6–7.

15. Kautsky's comments on agriculture and industry in the early Soviet state (in chapter 9) are, of course, entirely outdated, for these fields have undergone tremendous changes since then. His remarks on the socialization of agriculture, how-

ever, are still of some interest. He considered it impossible in backward Russia, because agriculture can only be socialized on the basis of large agricultural enterprises with a highly developed technology. Only then can such a new mode of production be so advantageous to the peasants that they would want to join the socialized enterprises. It did not even occur to Kautsky that force could be used to make the peasants join, as it was by Stalin a decade later. To Kautsky, socialization made no sense unless it improved the conditions of the workers involved. To Stalin, on the other hand, socialization served the goal of rapid industrialization, which, at least for a few decades, is not at all the same thing as the improvement of working and living conditions. Here again Kautsky saw the goals of the Bolsheviks through Western eyes. Twelve years later, at the beginning of the collectivization of agriculture in the Soviet Union, Kautsky still held that it was bound to fail because it was not accepted voluntarily by the peasants and because of Russia's technical backwardness. Kautsky, *Bolshevism at a Deadlock,* 27–58.

16. This does not mean that the former view is less "correct" than the latter one. One chooses one's categories of comparison depending on the subject to be investigated. It is merely suggested that the aspects of the Russian Revolution with which Kautsky was concerned can be more adequately analyzed by comparison with underdeveloped countries than with the West.

Appendix A

Biographical and Bibliographical Data

The story of Karl Kautsky's life is inseparable from that of his writings. Biographical and bibliographical data are therefore listed together here. The latter include all of Kautsky's writings cited in this book as well as other significant ones. Each work is listed under the year when it was first published in German, and the latest German edition and English translation are also noted there. For a virtually complete listing of Kautsky's publications, including translations, see Werner Blumenberg, *Karl Kautskys literarisches Werk* (The Hague: Mouton, 1960), which was helpful to me in compiling the present bibliography.

1854   16 October: Karl Kautsky born in Prague. His father was Johann Kautsky (1827–96), a theater painter; his mother was Minna Jaich Kautsky (1837–1912), an actress and then a novelist.

1863   Kautsky family moves from Prague to Vienna.

1864   11 August: Luise Ronsperger, Kautsky's future wife, born in Vienna.
    Kautsky enters the Gymnasium at the Benedictine monastery in Melk, which he attends until 1866.

1866   Kautsky enters the Akademische Gymnasium in Vienna.

1874   Kautsky enrolls at the University of Vienna, studies history, economics, natural science, influenced by Buckle, J. S. Mill, and especially Darwin.

223

1875   January: Kautsky joins the small and divided Austrian socialist party. He contributes articles to *Der Volksstaat* (*Vorwärts* beginning in 1876) (Leipzig), also in 1876–78, and to *Gleichheit* (Wiener Neustadt, Austria), also in 1876 and again 1887–89.

1876   Kautsky meets August Bebel and Wilhelm Liebknecht in Leipzig.

"Entwurf einer Entwicklungsgeschichte der Menschheit," published in *Die materialistische Geschichtsauffassung* (see 1927, below), 1:155–65.

1877   Kautsky contributes articles to *Der Sozialist* (Vienna), also many more in 1878 and 1879.

1878   Kautsky completes his first book, *Der Einfluss der Volksvermehrung auf den Fortschritt der Gesellschaft,* not published until 1880, on population growth and Malthusianism.

1879   Kautsky writes reports to *Der Sozialdemokrat* (Zurich; London in 1889) from Vienna.

1880   January: Invited by Karl Höchberg, a wealthy socialist scholar, Kautsky moves to Zurich, where he lives till May 1882. He contributes articles to publications supported by Höchberg, *Der Sozialdemokrat* (Zurich), also in 1880–82 and 1884–89, the *Jahrbuch fur Sozialwissenschaft und Sozialpolitik* (Zurich), also in 1881; *Staatswirthschaftliche Abhandlungen* (Leipzig), also in 1881.
    Kautsky also contributes articles to *Zeitschrift für Plastik* (Vienna), also in 1881–87.
    In close association with Eduard Bernstein, Höchberg's secretary, Kautsky studies Marxist literature, especially *Anti-Dühring* and *Capital.*

Der Einfluss der Volksvermehrung auf den Fortschritt der Gesellschaft (Vienna: Bloch & Hasbach).

1881   March–June: Kautsky visits Marx and Engels in London, becomes friendly with Engels. He continues study of prehistory and ethnology begun in Zurich and reads Bancroft, Bachofen, Morgan.

1882   May: Kautsky returns to Vienna. Beginning of friendship with Victor Adler.

Kautsky travels to the University of Jena, where Ernst Haeckel had accepted his study of the origin of marriage and the family as a doctoral dissertation, but the Dean would not let an anthropologist examine him, and so Kautsky never became a Ph.D.

Preparations, by Kautsky as editor and J. H. W. Dietz as publisher, for establishment of a monthly journal, *Die Neue Zeit,* in Stuttgart.

"Die Entstehung der Ehe und Familie." *Kosmos* (Stuttgart) 4:190–207, 256–72, 329–48.

1883 January: The first issue of *Die Neue Zeit* appears, just before Marx's death on 14 March; it is the first scholarly Marxist journal, which Kautsky will edit for thirty-five years as the outstanding international Marxist forum.

March: Kautsky marries Louise Strasser (1860–1950) and moves to Stuttgart. He visits Bernstein in Zurich, Engels in London.

"Die sozialen Triebe in der Tierwelt." *Die Neue Zeit* 1:20–27, 67–73; reprinted in *Die materialistische Geschichtsauffassung* (see 1927, below), 1:424–41.

"Ein materialistischer Historiker." *Die Neue Zeit* 1:537–47

"Die Entstehung der biblischen Urgeschichte." *Kosmos* (Stuttgart) 7:201–14.

1884 January: Kautsky moves back to Zurich.

Engages in polemic with C. A. Schramm against Rodbertus' economics.

"Die sozialen Triebe in der Menschenwelt." *Die Neue Zeit* 2:13–19, 49–59, 118–25; reprinted in *Die materialistische Geschichtsauffassung* (see 1927, below), 1:442–75.

"Das 'Kapital' von Rodbertus." *Die Neue Zeit* 2:337–50, 385–402.

1885 January: Kautsky moves to London, lives there till 1890, working with Engels, writing his three books published 1887–89, and beginning his study of early communist movements in the time of the Reformation, published in 1894.

1886 "Die Entstehung des Christenthums." *Die Neue Zeit* 3:481–99, 529–45.

"Die chinesischen Eisenbahnen und das euopäische Proletariat." *Die Neue Zeit* 4:515–25, 529–49.

1887   *Karl Marx' ökonomische Lehren.* Stuttgart: J. H. W. Dietz. 26th
       ed. Bonn: J. H. W. Dietz, 1980. *The Economic Doctrines of Karl
       Marx.* New York: Macmillan, 1936. Reprint: Westport, Conn.:
       Hyperion Press, 1979.
       "Die moderne Nationalität." *Die Neue Zeit* 5:392–405, 442–51.

1888   June: Kautsky returns to Vienna, where he remains till October 1889
       to go through the lengthy process of divorce from his first wife, Louise
       Strasser.
       Thomas More und seine Utopie. Stuttgart: J. H. W. Dietz. 7th ed.
       Bonn: J. H. W. Dietz, 1973. *Thomas More and His Utopia.*
       London: Lawrence & Wishart, 1979.

1889   *Die Klassengegensätze von 1789.* Stuttgart: J. H. W. Dietz. 2d ed.,
       *Die Klassengegensätze im Zeitalter der Französischen Revolu-
       tion,* 1908.
       "Die Bergarbeiter und der Bauernkrieg, vornehmlich in Thüringen."
       Die Neue Zeit 7:289–97, 337–50, 410–17, 443–53, 507–15.

1890   March: Kautsky leaves London for Vienna, where on 23 April he
       marries Luise Ronsperger.
       August: After fall of the Anti-Socialist Law, Kautsky moves to
       Stuttgart.
       September: *Die Neue Zeit* becomes a weekly.
1891   14 February: Birth of Kautsky's first son, Felix (who died in Califor-
       nia 3 February 1953).
       Kautsky's draft of the "theoretical" section of a new SPD program
       accepted at Erfurt Congress.

       "Der Entwurf des neuen Parteiprogramms." *Die Neue Zeit* 9/2:723–
       30, 749–58, 780–91, 814–27.

1892   13 January: Birth of Kautsky's second son, Karl, Jr. (who died in
       California 15 June 1978).
       Polemic with Georg von Vollmar against state socialism.

       Das Erfurter Programm. Stuttgart: J. H. W. Dietz. 19th ed. Bonn:
       J. H. W. Dietz, 1974. *The Class Struggle (Erfurt Program)* New
       York: Norton, 1971.
       "Grundsätzlicher Teil." In Karl Kautsky and Bruno Schönlank,
       Grundsätze und Forderungen der Sozialdemokratie. Berlin:
       Vorwärts. Reprinted in Karl Kautsky, *Texte zu den Programmen*

der deutschen Sozialdemokratie, ed. Albrecht Langner, 116–77. Cologne: Hegner, 1968.

"Vollmar und der Staatssozialismus." *Die Neue Zeit* 10/2:705–13.

"Der Parteitag und der Staatssozialismus." *Die Neue Zeit* 11/1:210–21.

1893   Kautsky attacks advocates of the replacement of parliamentarism by direct legislation. In his article criticizing a "Social-Democratic catechism," he favors the proletarian political revolution through the use of civil liberties, elections, and parliamentarism.

Der Parlamentarismus, die Volksgesetzgebung und die Sozialdemokratie. Stuttgart: J. H. W. Dietz. 3d ed. *Parlamentarismus und Demokratie,* 1920.

"Ein sozialdemokratischer Katechismnus." *Die Neue Zeit* 12/1:361–69, 402–10.

1894   1 November: Birth of Kautsky's third son, Benedikt (who died in Vienna 1 April 1960).

Kautsky opposes SPD favoring protection of peasantry and breakup of large agrarian enterprises.

"Der Kapitalismus fin de siècle." *Die Neue Zeit* 12/1:457–60, 517–26, 589–98.

1895   5 August: Engels dies.

Breslau SPD Congress favors Kautsky's position on agriculture. He continues to study agriculture till publication of his book, *Die Agrarfrage,* in 1899, the first systematic Marxist treatment of the subject, generally favoring cooperative large enterprises.

Die Vorläufer des Neueren Sozialismus. Stuttgart: J. H. W. Dietz. Vol. 1, 8th ed.; vol. 2, 9th ed., *Vorläufer des neueren Sozialismus.* Bonn: J. H. W. Dietz, 1976. Ed. by Hans-Jürgen Mende, Berlin: Dietz Verlag, 1991. Partially translated as *Communism in Central Europe in the Time of the Reformation.* New York: A. M. Kelley, 1966.

Friedrich Engels: Sein Leben. sein Wirken, seine Schriften. Berlin: Vorwärts. 2d rev. ed., 1908. *Frederick Engels: His Life, His Work, His Writings.* Chicago: Charles H. Kerr, 1899.

"Die Intelligenz und die Sozialdemokratie." *Die Neue Zeit* 13/2:10–16, 43–49, 74–80.

"Unser neuestes Agrarprogramm." *Die Neue Zeit* 13/2:557–65, 586–94, 610–24. "Our Latest Programme." In *Paths of Development in Capitalist Agriculture,* ed. Athar Hussain and Keith Tribe, 106–49. London: Macmillan, 1984.

"Der Breslauer Parteitag und die Agrarfrage." *Die Neue Zeit* 14/1:108–13.

"Die Breslauer Resolution und ihre Kritik." *Die Neue Zeit* 14/1:182–86.

1896   Kautsky's polemic with Belfort Bax on the Marxist conception of history.

"Finis Poloniae?" *Die Neue Zeit* 14/2:484–91, 513–25.

"Die materialistische Geschichtsauffasung und der psychologische Antrieb." *Die Neue Zeit* 14/2:652–59. *The Social-Democrat* (London) 6 (1902): 242–48.

"Was will und kann die materialistische Geschichtsauffassung leisten?" *Die Neue Zeit* 15/1:213–18, 228–38, 260–71. *The Social-Democrat* (London) 6 (1902): 296–99, 340–48, 375–82.

1897   Fall: The Kautsky family moves from Stuttgart to Berlin.

Kautsky favors SPD participation in elections to the Prussian legislature.

"Utopistischer und materialistischer Marxismus." *Die Neue Zeit* 15/1:716–27. *The Social-Democrat* (London) 7 (1903): 98–112.

"Umsturzgesetz und Landtagswahlen in Preussen." *Die Neue Zeit* 15/2:275–82.

"Die preussischen Landtagswahlen und die reaktionäre Masse." *Die Neue Zeit* 15/2:580–90.

1898   Beginning of conflict over Revisionism, involving Kautsky in the next few years in polemics over Marxist theory, agrarian policy, SPD–trade union relations, socialist participation in coalition governments, trade policy, the mass strike, ethics, and colonialism.

Kautsky writes his first article on imperialism, the first Marxist analysis of the subject.

"Der Kampf der Nationalitäten und das Staatsrecht in Oesterreich." *Die Neue Zeit* 16/1:516–24, 557–64.

"Aeltere und neuere Kolonialpolitik." *Die Neue Zeit* 16/1:769–81, 801–16.

1899   *Die Agrarfrage. Eine Übersicht über die Tendenzen der modernen Landwirtschaft und die Agrarpolitik der Sozialdemokratie.* Stuttgart: J. H. W. Dietz. Hanover: J. H. W. Dietz, 1966. *The Agrarian Question.* 2 vols. London: Zwan, 1988.

Bernstein und das sozialdemokratische Programm: Eine Anti-Kritik. Stuttgart: J. H. W. Dietz. 3d ed. Bonn: J. H. W. Dietz, 1979.

"Bernstein und die materialistische Geschichtsauffassung." *Die Neue Zeit* 17/2:4–16.

"Bernstein und die Dialektik." *Die Neue Zeit* 17/2:36–50.

"Bernstein über die Werttheorie und die Klassen." *Die Neue Zeit* 17/2:68–81.

"Zwei Kritiker meiner Agrarfrage." *Die Neue Zeit* 18/1:292–300, 338–46, 363–68, 428–36, 470–77.

"Die Schranken der kapitalistischen Landwirtschaft." *Archiv für soziale Gesetzgebung und Statistik* (Berlin) 13:255–90.

1900   "Die Neutralisierung der Gewerkschaften." *Die Neue Zeit* 18/2:388–94, 429–33, 457–66, 492–97.

"Die kommenden Kongresse." *Die Neue Zeit* 18/2:707–18.

"Die sozialistischen Kongresse und der sozialistische Minister." *Die Neue Zeit* 19/1:36–44.

1901   Kautsky turns *Die Neue Zeit* over to the SPD as its property. He opposes SPD advocacy of protective tariffs.

Handelspolitik und Sozialdemokratie. Berlin: Vorwärts. 2d ed. 1911.

"Tolstoi und Brentano." *Die Neue Zeit* 19/2:20–28.

"Akademiker und Proletarier." *Die Neue Zeit* 19/2:89–91.

"Problematischer gegen wissenschaftlichen Sozialismus." *Die Neue Zeit* 19/2:355–64.

"Bürgermeister und Minister." *Die Neue Zeit* 19/2:794–96.

"Der Parteitag in Lübeck." *Die Neue Zeit* 20/1:13–20.

"Die Revision des Programms der Sozialdemokratie in Oesterreich." *Die Neue Zeit* 20/1:68–82.

1902   Expecting a revolution in Russia with revolutionary consequences in Germany and Austria, Kautsky writes *Die soziale Revolution,* which Chancellor von Bülow calls the "Baedeker for the state of the future."

Die soziale Revolution. Berlin: Vorwärts. 2d enlarged ed., 1907. *The Social Revolution,* 3d ed., Chicago: Charles H. Kerr, 1916.

"Krisentheorien." *Die Neue Zeit* 20/2:37–47, 76–81, 110–18, 133–43.

1903   *Die Sozialdemokratie und die katholische Kirche.* Berlin: Vorwärts.
3d enlarged ed., Hamburg: Phönix, 1947.
"Klasseninteresse — Sonderinteresse — Gemeininteresse." *Die Neue Zeit* 21/2:240–45, 261–74.
"Zum Parteitag." *Die Neue Zeit* 21/2:729–39.

1904   Kautsky begins publication in three volumes (1904–10) of Marx's manuscript notes for a fourth volume of *Capital.*

Karl Marx, *Theorien über den Mehrwert,* ed. Karl Kautsky. 3 vols. Stuttgart: J. H. W. Dietz, 1904, 1905, 1910.
"Allerhand Revolutionäres." *Die Neue Zeit* 22/1:588–98, 620–27, 652–57, 685–95, 732–40. All but the first section reprinted in *Der politische Massenstreik* (see 1914, below), 68–103.
"Republik und Sozialdemokratie in Frankreich." *Die Neue Zeit* 23/1:260–70, 300–309, 332–41, 363–71, 397–414, 436–49, 467–81.

1905   Kautsky, in opposition to the trade unions and the *Vorwärts* editorial staff, advocates discussion and study of the mass strike as a complement to parliamentarism.

"Vorwort." *General-Register des Inhalts der Jahrgänge 1883 bis 1902 der Neuen Zeit,* iii–xiv. Stuttgart: Singer.
"Die zivilisierte Welt und der Zar." *Die Neue Zeit* 23/1:614–17.
"Die Bauern und die Revolution in Russland." *Die Neue Zeit* 23/1: 670–77.
"Die Lehren des Bergarbeiterstreiks." *Die Neue Zeit* 23/1: 772–82.
"Die Differenzen unter den russischen Sozialisten." *Die Neue Zeit* 23/2: 68–79.
"Die Spaltung der russischen Sozialdemokratie." *Leipziger Volkszeitung,* 15 June.

1906   Kautsky attacks the attempt to incorporate Kantian ethics into Marxism, and thus tries to fill a gap in Marxist thought.

Ethik und materialistische Geschichtsauffassung: Ein Versuch. Stuttgart: J. H. W. Dietz. Bonn: J. H. W. Dietz, 1973. *Ethics and the Materialist Conception of History,* 4th rev. ed., Chicago: Charles H. Kerr, 1918; photocopy, Ann Arbor: University Microfilms International, 1977.
"Der amerikanische Arbeiter." *Die Neue Zeit* 24/1:676–83, 717–27, 740–52, 773–87.

"Leben, Wissenschaft und Ethik." *Die Neue Zeit* 24/2: 516–29.
Partially translated in Karl Kautsky, *Selected Political Writings,*
ed. Patrick Goode, 46–52. London: Macmillan, 1983.
"Partei und Gewerkschaft." *Die Neue Zeit* 24/2:716–25, 749–54.
"Grundsätze oder Pläne?" *Die Neue Zeit* 24/2:781–88. Largely re-
printed in *Der politische Massenstreik* (see 1914, below), 137–
45.
"Triebkräfte und Aussichten der russischen Revolution." *Die Neue
Zeit* 25/1:284–90, 324–33.

1907   At the Congress of Second International, Kautsky successfully attacks
resolution envisaging a possible socialist colonial policy.

Sozialismus und Kolonialpolitik. Berlin: Vorwärts. *Socialism and
Colonial Policy.* Belfast: Athol Books, 1975.
"Der 25. Januar." *Die Neue Zeit* 25/1:588–96.

1908   Kautsky returns to his early interest in a Marxist analysis of early
Christianity.

Der Ursprung des Christentums: Eine historische Untersuchung.
Stuttgart: J. H. W. Dietz. 16th ed., Bonn: J. H. W. Dietz, 1977.
Foundations of Christianity. New York: Monthly Review Press,
1972.
Die historische Leistung von Karl Marx. Berlin: Vorwärts. 3d ed.,
Berlin: J. H. W. Dietz, 1933.
Nationalität und Internationalität. Stuttgart: Singer.
"Methoden der Kolonialverwaltung." *Die Neue Zeit* 26/1:614–21.
"Verelendung und Zusammenbruch." *Die Neue Zeit* 26/2:540–51,
607–12.
"Die Budgetbewilligung." *Die Neue Zeit* 26/2:809–26.
"Reform und Revolution." *Die Neue Zeit* 27/1:180–91, 220–32, 252–
59.

1909   Foreseeing a period of growing conflict and insecurity, Kautsky, in
Der Weg zur Macht, often seen as his most "revolutionary" work, demands the democratization of Prussia and the Reich and rejects compromise with bourgeois parties and the imperial regime.

*Der Weg zur Macht: Politische Betrachtungen über das Hinein-
wachsen in die Revolution.* Berlin: Vorwärts. Frankfurt: Euro-
paische Verlagsanstalt, 1972. *The Road to Power.* Atlantic
Highlands, N.J.: Humanities Press, 1994.

"Ein neues Buch über die französische Revolution." *Vorwärts*, 7 February.

"Sekte oder Klassenpartei?" *Die Neue Zeit* 27/2:4–14. *The Social-Democrat* (London) 13 (1909): 316–28.

"Positive Arbeit und Revolution." *Die Neue Zeit* 27/2:324–37.

"Leichtfertige Statistik." *Die Neue Zeit* 27/2:517–24.

"Nochmals die amerikanische Statistik." *Die Neue Zeit* 27/2:782–86, 821–32.

"Ludwig unter den Propheten." *Die Neue Zeit* 28/1:200–211.

1910   Kautsky returns to his early interest in population growth in nature and society.

Engages in polemics with advocates of the mass strike as a revolutionary weapon, including Rosa Luxemburg and, in 1910–11, Anton Pannekoek.

Vermehrung und Entwicklung in Natur und Gesellschaft. Stuttgart: J. H. W. Dietz. 3d ed., 1921.

"Was nun?" *Die Neue Zeit* 28/2:33–40, 68–80. Reprinted in *Der politische Massenstreik* (see 1914, below) 224–45 and in *Die Massenstreikdebatte*, ed. by Antonia Grunenberg, 96–121. Frankfurt: Europäische Verlagsanstalt, 1970. Partly translated in Karl Kautsky; *Selected Political Writings*, ed. Patrick Goode (see 1906, above), 54–73.

"Eine neue Strategie." *Die Neue Zeit* 28/2:332–41, 364–74, 412–21. Reprinted in *Die Massenstreikdebatte*, ed. Antonia Grunenberg, 153–90.

"Zwischen Baden und Luxemburg." *Die Neue Zeit* 28/2:652–67.

1911   "Finanzkapital und Krisen." *Die Neue Zeit* 29/1:764–72, 797–804, 838–46, 874–83. *The Social-Democrat* (London) 15 (1911): 326–30, 368–71, 423–27, 470–73, 517–23, 556–60.

"Der Kleinbetrieb in der Landwirtschaft." *Die Neue Zeit* 29/2:348–56, 408–17.

"Sklaverei und Kapitalismus." *Die Neue Zeit* 29/2:713–25.

"Die Aktion der Masse." *Die Neue Zeit* 30/1:43–49, 77–84, 106–17. Reprinted in *Der Politische Massenstreik* (see 1914, below), 255–81, and in *Die Massenstreikdebatte,* ed. Antonia Grunenberg (see 1910, above), 233–63.

1912   "Der improvisierte Bruch." *Die Neue Zeit* 30/2:461–67, 513–23.

"Die neue Taktik." *Die Neue Zeit* 30/2:654–64, 688–98, 723–33.

Reprinted in *Die Massenstreikdebatte,* ed. Antonia Grunenberg
(see 1910, above), 295–334.
"Der jüngste Radikalismus." *Die Neue Zeit* 31/1:436–46.

1913   "Nachgedanken zu den nachdenklichen Betrachtungen." *Die Neue Zeit* 31/2:558–68, 662–64.
"Die Einigung in England und Russland." *Die Neue Zeit* 32/1:465–73.

1914   Kautsky publishes an improved version of Vol. 1 of Marx's *Capital.* Vols. 2 and 3, edited by Kautsky in collaboration with his son Benedikt, were published, respectively, in 1926 and 1929.

Kautsky collects and reviews his and others' writings on the mass strike.

He attacks racial theories and anti-Semitism.

At the outbreak of World War I, Kautsky is isolated in the SPD between the majority supporting the imperial government's war policy and its Spartacist opponents; he advocates voting for the war credits only if the government committed itself to a purely defensive war without annexations. During the War, he attacks the supporters of the War and the government, especially Heinrich Cunow in 1915 and the Austrian Karl Renner, in *War Marxism (Kriegsmarxismus)* in 1918.

Karl Marx, *Das Kapital,* vol. 1, ed. Karl Kautsky. Stuttgart: J. H. W. Dietz.
Der politische Massenstreik. Berlin: Vorwärts.
Rasse und Judentum. Stuttgart: J. H. W. Dietz. 2d enlarged ed., 1921. *Are the Jews a Race?* New York: International Publishers, 1926. Reprint: Westport, Conn.: Greenwood Press, 1972.
"Der Imperialismus." *Die Neue Zeit* 32/2:908–22.

1915   19 June: Kautsky joins Bernstein and Haase in an appeal, "The Demand of the Hour," opposing both the Majority SPD and a party split.

Kautsky argues against both the Right and the Left that imperialist expansionism is not a necessary aspect of capitalism.

Nationalstaat, imperialistischer Staat und Staatenbund. Nuremberg: Fränkische Verlagsanstalt.
Die Internationalität und der Krieg. Berlin: Vorwärts.
"Zwei Schriften zum Umlernen." *Die Neue Zeit* 33/2:33–42, 71–81, 107–16, 138–46.
"Nochmals unsere Illusionen." *Die Neue Zeit* 33/2:230–41, 264–75.

"Imperialistische Tendenzen in der Sozialdemokratie." *Die Neue Zeit*
34/1:97–101.

"Das Gebot der Stunde: Aufruf Bernsteins, Kautskys und Haases."
Leipziger Volkszeitung 19 June, reprinted in Eugen Prager,
Geschichte der U.S.P.D., 72–74. Berlin: Freiheit, 1922.

1916   Still hoping to preserve party unity, Kautsky attacks the majority's
denial of freedom of expression to the minority. He associates himself
with Haase and Bernstein in the centrist Social-Democratic
"Arbeitsgemeinschaft" opposing the Majority SPD.

    Kautsky writes a number of studies in 1916–17 on questions of
nationalities, national self-determination, and war aims.

Überzeugung und Partei. Leipzig: Leipziger Buchdruckerei.
"Mitteleuropa." *Die Neue Zeit* 34/1:423–29, 453–68, 494–504, 522–
34, 561–69.
Die Vereinigten Staaten Mitteleuropas. Stuttgart: J. H. W. Dietz.

1917   April: Kautsky reluctantly joins the Independent Social-Democratic
Party (USPD) as it splits from the SPD. He is isolated between the
SPD and the majority in the USPD, but his manifesto for the new
party is accepted at its founding congress. Attacking both the Right
and the Left, he repeats that imperialism is not an economic necessity
of capitalism.

    In June, Kautsky argues that the revolution in Russia would and
should bring democracy and thus greater power to the proletariat, but
the social revolution for socialism could only come after capitalist
economic development.

    29 September: Kautsky dismissed as editor of *Die Neue Zeit* by the
SPD Executive Committee. Volume 35/2 is the last to appear under
his editorship.

*Serbien und Belgien in der Geschichte: Historische Studien zur
Frage der Nationalitäten und der Kriegsziele.* Stuttgart: J. H. W.
Dietz.
Elsass-Lothringen: Eine historische Studie. Stuttgart: J. H. W. Dietz.
3d ed. 1919.
Die Befreiung der Nationen. Stuttgart: J. H. W. Dietz. 4th ed, 1918.
"Der imperialistische Krieg." *Die Neue Zeit* 35/1:449–54, 475–87.
"Der Eispalast." *Die Neue Zeit* 35/1:609–13.
"Die Aussichten der russischen Revolution." *Die Neue Zeit* 35/2:9–
20.

"Imperialismus und reaktionäre Masse." *Die Neue Zeit* 35/2:102–15.

1918   Kautsky's study of the economic transition from war to peace, completed in March, is prevented by military censorship from publication until after the revolution.

By summer, Kautsky begins his attacks on the Bolsheviks, continued for the next twenty years, for attempting to introduce socialism in a backward country through terrorism and bureaucracy.

November–December: Kautsky, as a USPD representative, serves as undersecretary of state in the Foreign Office in the short-lived SPD-USPD revolutionary government.

November–January 1919: Kautsky serves (as chairman from December) in the Socialization Commission to study where and how socialization was appropriate.

> *Kriegsmarxismus: Eine theoretische Grundlegung der Politik des 4. August.* Vienna: Wiener Volksbuchhandlung. Also in *Marx-Studien* (Vienna) 4/1 (1918): 121–206.
> *Sozialdemokratische Bemerkungen zur Übergangswirtschaft.* Leipzig: Leipziger Buchdruckerei.
> *Die Diktatur des Proletariats.* Vienna: Wiener Volksbuchhandlung. Reprinted in *Demokratie oder Diktatur?*, 2 vols. ed. by Hans-Jürgen Mende, 1:7–87. Berlin: Dietz Verlag, 1990. Long excerpts in *Kautsky gegen Lenin,* ed. Peter Lübbe, 28–77. Bonn: J. H. W. Dietz, 1981. *The Dictatorship of the Proletariat.* Ann Arbor: University of Michigan Press, 1964. Reprint, Westport, Conn.: Greenwood Press, 1981. Excerpts in Karl Kautsky, *Selected Political Writings,* ed. Patrick Goode (see 1906, above), 98–125.
> *Demokratie oder Diktatur.* Berlin: Cassirer.
> *Habsburgs Glück und Ende.* Berlin: Cassirer.
> "Die Bolschewiki und wir." *Sozialistische Auslandspolitik* 4, no. 11 (13 March): 9.

1919   Kautsky continues through spring in the Foreign Office to collect the German documents on the war guilt of the imperial regime, published in the fall in four volumes.

January: Kautsky unsuccessfully mediates between the SPD government and Spartacist rebels in an attempt to avoid bloodshed and a victory for either side.

Kautsky declines offers of professorships at the universities of Berlin and Munich.

Terrorismus und Kommunismus: Ein Beitrag zur Naturgeschichte der Revolution. Berlin: Neues Vaterland. Reprinted in *Demokratie oder Diktatur?* ed. by Hans-Jürgen Mende (see 1918, above), 1:177–347. *Terrorism and Communism.* London: National Labour Press, 1920. Reprint, Westport, Conn.: Hyperion Press, 1973.

Die Wurzeln der Politik Wilsons. Berlin: Neues Vaterland.

Die Sozialisierung der Landwirtschaft. Berlin: Cassirer.

Die deutschen Dokumente zum Kriegsausbruch, ed. Max Montgelas and Walter Schücking, collected by K. Kautsky, 4 vols. Charlottenburg: Deutsche Verlagsgesellschaft für Politik und Geschichte. Rev. ed., 1927. *Outbreak of the World War: German Documents Collected by Karl Kautsky.* New York: Oxford University Press, 1924.

Wie der Weltkrieg entstand. Berlin: Cassirer. *The Guilt of William Hohenzollern.* London: Skeffington, 1920.

1920   End of September–early January 1921: Kautsky visits Georgia, then an independent republic with a social-democratic government.

In October, the USPD splits, the majority joining the KPD, the minority disintegrating or moving toward reunification with the SPD; Kautsky participates in the latter movement.

Vergangenheit und Zukunft der Internationale. Vienna: Wiener Volksbuchhandlung.

"Gustav Mayers Engels-Biographie." *Archiv für die Geschichte des Sozialismus und der Arbeiterbewegung* (Leipzig) 9:342–55.

1921   *Von der Demokratie zur Staatssklaverei: Eine Auseinandersetzung mit Trotzki.* Berlin: Freiheit. Reprinted in *Demokratie oder Diktatur?,* ed. Hans-Jürgen Mende (see 1918, above), 2:175–283.

Georgien, eine sozialdemokratische Bauernrepublik: Eindrücke und Beobachtungen. Vienna: Wiener Volksbuchhandlung. *Georgia, a Social-Democratic Peasant Republic: Impressions and Observations.* London: International Bookshops, 1921.

1922   June: Kautsky publishes his book proposing the bases of a new program for the reunited SPD.

Die proletarische Revolution und ihr Programm. Stuttgart: J. H. W. Dietz. 3d ed., 1932. *The Labour Revolution.* New York: Dial Press, 1925.

Mein Verhältnis zur Unabhängigen Sozialdemokratischen Partei: Ein Rückblick. Berlin: Breitscheid.

1923 Kautsky attacks Cunow's view of Marx's conception of the state.

Die Marxsche Staatsauffassung im Spiegelbild eines Marxisten. Jena: Thüringer Verlagsanstalt.

1924 Kautsky, following his three sons, moves from Berlin to Vienna where he lives till 1938.

"Karl Kautsky" [autobiographical sketch], in *Die Volkswirtschaftslehre der Gegenwart in Selbstdarstellungen,* ed. Felix Meiner, 1:117–53. Leipzig: Meiner. Reprinted as "Mein Lebenswerk," in *Ein Leben für den Sozialismus: Erinnerungen an Karl Kautsky,* ed. Benedikt Kautsky, 11–34. Hanover: J. H. W. Dietz, 1954.

1925 Amending the Erfurt Program he had drafted in 1891, Kautsky writes the "theoretical" section of the Heidelberg Program of the reunited SPD.
 Kautsky becomes involved in polemics over the nature of Communism and of the Soviet regime with the Menshevik Fyodor Dan and with Otto Bauer in 1925 and again in 1931 and with Friedrich Adler in 1933.

Die Internationale und Sowjetrussland. Berlin: J. H. W. Dietz.
"Grundsätzlicher Teil," in *Das Heidelberger Programm: Grundsätze und Forderungen der Sozialdemokratie,* ed. Paul Kampffmeyer, 5–26. Berlin: J. H. W. Dietz. Reprinted in Karl Kautsky, *Texte zu den Programmen der deutschen Sozialdemokratie,* ed. Albrecht Langner (see 1892, above), 275–328.
"Die Lehren des Oktoberexperiments." *Die Gesellschaft* 2/1, no. 4 (April): 374–80. Reprinted in *Kautsky gegen Lenin,* ed. Peter Lübbe (see 1918, above), 96–105.
"Die Internationale und Sowjetrussland." *Der Kampf* 18, no. 8–9 (August–September): 285–98.
"Das Proletariat in Russland." *Der Kampf* 18, no. 10 (October): 380–91. About half reprinted in *Kautsky gegen Lenin,* ed. Peter Lübbe, 106–18.

1927 Kautsky completes his magnum opus on the materialist conception of history, in which he thought he succeeded in realizing his early ambition of uniting the natural and social sciences in a consistent scheme.

> *Die materialistische Geschichtsauffassung.* 2 vols. Berlin: J. H. W. Dietz. Abridged edition, ed. John H. Kautsky, Bonn: J. H. W. Dietz, 1988. Abridged translation, *The Materialist Conception of History,* ed. John H. Kautsky, New Haven, Conn.: Yale University Press, 1988.

1928   *Wehrfrage und Sozialdemokratie.* Berlin: J. H. W. Dietz.

1929   "Natur und Gesellschaft." *Die Gesellschaft* 6/2, no. 12 (December): 481–505. Abridged translation, "Nature and Society," in *Karl Kautsky and the Social Science of Classical Marxism,* ed. John H. Kautsky, 73–79. Leiden: E. J. Brill, 1989.

1930   *Der Bolschewismus in der Sackgasse.* Berlin: J. H. W. Dietz. *Bolshevism at a Deadlock.* London: Allen & Unwin, 1931.

1931   "Sozialdemokratie und Bolschewismus." *Die Gesellschaft* 8/1, no. 1 (January): 54–71.
"Die Aussichten des Fünfjahresplanes." *Die Gesellschaft* 8/1, no. 3 (March): 255–64. Reprinted in *Kautsky gegen Lenin,* ed. Peter Lübbe (see 1918, above), 141–55. Translated as "Preface" to *Bolshevism at a Deadlock* (see 1930, above).
"Die Aussichten des Sozialismus in Sowjetrussland." *Die Gesellschaft* 8/2, no. 11 (November): 420–44.

1932   Kautsky publishes the first of four projected volumes on wars in their relation to democratic and then socialist movements. The manuscript of volume 2 was already set in type when the Nazis took power in Germany and confiscated the publishing house and the manuscript. Kautsky then wrote the projected fourth volume on socialist views of war as an independent book, which was completed in 1935 and published in 1937.

> *Krieg und Demokratie.* Berlin: J. H. W. Dietz. "Kommunismus und Sozialdemokratie." *Die Gesellschaft* 9/1, no. 3 (March): 260–78. Partially reprinted in *Kautsky gegen Lenin,* ed. Peter Lübbe (see 1918, above), 156–75. Partially translated in Karl Kautsky, *Social Democracy versus Communism,* ed. David Shub and Joseph Shaplen, 23–28, 48–74. New York: Rand School Press,

1946. Reprint: Westport, Conn.: Hyperion Press, 1979.
"Die Fabel von der Naturnotwendigkeit des Krieges." In *Der Internationale Kapitalismus und die Krise,* ed. Siegfried v. Kardorff et al., 132–50. Stuttgart: Ferdinand Enke, 1932.

1933   Kautsky tries to come to terms with the consequences of fascism for the socialist labor movement.

> *Neue Programme: Eine kritische Untersuchung.* Vienna: Prager.
> "Marx und Marxismus." *Die Gesellschaft* 10/1, no. 3 (March): 181–200. Almost completely translated in Karl Kautsky, "Marxism and Bolshevism — Democracy and Dictatorship." In *Socialism, Fascism, Communism,* ed. Joseph Shaplen and David Shub, 174–215. New York: American League for Democratic Socialism, 1934.
> "Demokratie und Diktatur." *Der Kampf* 26, no. 2 (February): 45–58. Almost completely translated in Karl Kautsky, "Marxism and Bolshevism" (see above).
> "Einige Ursachen und Wirkungen des deutschen National-sozialismus." *Der Kampf* 26, no. 6 (June): 235–45. Almost completely translated in Karl Kautsky, "Hitlerism and Social Democracy." In *Socialism, Fascism, Communism* (see above), 53–102.
> "Die blutige Revolution." *Der Kampf* 26, no. 8–9 (August–September): 346–61. Almost completely translated in Karl Kautsky, "Hitlerism and Social Democracy" (see above).
> "Die Ausrottung der Besten." *Arbeiter-Zeitung* (Vienna), 15 October; *Volksrecht* (Zurich), 30 October.

1934   Kautsky critically analyzes the February 1934 socialist uprising in Austria.

> *Grenzen der Gewalt: Aussichten und Wirkungen bewaffneter Erhebungen des Proletariats.* Anonymously published, Karlsbad: Graphia.

1935   Kautsky publishes the letters he had received from Engels.

> *Aus der Frühzeit des Marxismus: Engels' Briefwechsel mit Kautsky.* Prague: Orbis. 2d ed., adding Kautsky's letters to Engels', *Friedrich Engels' Briefwechsel mit Karl Kautsky,* ed. Benedikt Kautsky. Vienna: Danubia, 1955.

"Gedanken über die Einheitsfront." *Zeitschrift für Sozialismus* (Karlsbad) (April): 825-38. Reprinted in *Kautsky gegen Lenin*, ed. Peter Lübbe (see 1918, above), 181–200. "The United Front." *The New Leader* (New York), 4, 11, 18, and 25 January 1936.

1936   Kautsky begins work on his memoirs, but by the time of his death had completed only the very detailed description of his background and life until 1883. The work was published posthumously in 1960.

1937   *Sozialisten und Krieg: Ein Beitrag zur Ideengeschichte des Sozialismus von den Hussiten bis zum Völkerbund.* Prague: Orbis.
"Kommunismus und Demokratie." *Neuer Vorwärts* (Karlsbad), 5 December. Reprinted in *Kautsky gegen Lenin*, ed. Peter Lübbe (see 1918, above), 201–6.

1938   Kautsky is nominated by many European socialist parliamentarians and intellectuals for the Nobel Peace Prize — which was awarded to the Nansen International Office for Refugees in 1938.
12 March: As German troops enter Austria, Karl and Luise Kautsky escape across the Czech border to Bratislava, then travel to Prague and fly to Amsterdam. There he continues work on his memoirs.
In May, Kautsky's son Benedikt is taken to the concentration camp in Dachau and is then imprisoned in Buchenwald and Auschwitz until 1945. Karl, Jr., after imprisonment in Vienna, emigrates to Sweden and, in 1939, to the United States. Felix emigrates to England and, in 1939, to the United States.
17 October: Kautsky dies in Amsterdam, one day after his eighty-fourth birthday.

1944   August: Luise Kautsky, a few days after her eightieth birthday, is caught by the Gestapo in Amsterdam.
Early December: Luise Kautsky dies in Auschwitz.

1960   *Erinnerungen und Erörterungen,* ed. Benedikt Kautsky. The Hague: Mouton.

Appendix B

Edited Volumes Consisting Entirely or in Part of Writings by Karl Kautsky

Adler, Friedrich, ed. Victor Adler, *Briefwechsel mit August Bebel und Karl Kautsky*. Vienna: Wiener Volksbuchhandlung, 1954.

Goode, Patrick, ed. Karl Kautsky, *Selected Political Writings*. London: Macmillan, 1983.

Grunenberg, Antonia, ed. *Die Massenstreikdebatte*. Frankfurt: Europäische Verlagsanstalt, 1970.

Hussain, Athar, and Keith Tribe, eds. *Paths of Development in Capitalist Agriculture*. London: Macmillan, 1984.

Kautsky, Benedikt, ed. *Friedrich Engels' Briefwechsel mit Karl Kautsky*. Vienna: Danubia, 1955.

Kautsky, Karl, Jr., ed. *August Bebels Briefwechsel mit Karl Kautsky*. Assen: Van Gorcum, 1971.

Langner, Albrecht, ed. Karl Kautsky, *Texte zu den Programmen der deutschen Sozialdemokratie*. Cologne: Hegner, 1968.

Lübbe, Peter, ed. *Kautsky gegen Lenin*. Bonn: J. H. W. Dietz, 1981.

Mende, Hans-Jürgen, ed. *Demokratie oder Diktatur?* [title on dust-jacket only]. 2 vols. reprinting and using as titles of vol. 1: Karl Kautsky, *Die Diktatur des Proletariats;* I. Lenin, *Die proletarische Revolution und der Renegat Kautsky;* and Karl Kautsky *Terrorismus und Kommunismus;* and of vol. 2: Leo Trotzki, *Terrorismus und Kommunismus;* and Karl Kautsky *Von der Demokratie zur Staatssklaverei.* Berlin: Dietz Verlag, 1990.

Ratz, Ursula. "Briefe zum Erscheinen von Karl Kautskys 'Weg zur Macht.' " *International Review of Social History* 12, no. 3 (1967): 432–77.

Shaplen, Joseph, and David Shub, ed. *Socialism, Fascism, Communism.* New York: American League for Democratic Socialism, 1934.

Shub, David, and Joseph Shaplen, ed. Karl Kautsky, *Social Democracy versus*

Communism. New York: Rand School Press, 1946. Reprint: Westport, Conn.: Hyperion Press, 1979.

Weber, Henri, ed. Kautsky, Luxemburg, Pannekoek, *Socialisme: la voie occidentale.* Paris: Presses Universitaires de France, 1983.

Appendix C

Selected Writings on Karl Kautsky

The following list includes all writings devoted entirely or in large part to Kautsky that are cited in this book as well as some notable additional ones. Individual contributions to volumes on Kautsky cited in this book, especially nearly a dozen in *Marxismus und Demokratie,* edited by Jürgen Rojahn et al., are not listed separately. Werner Blumenberg, *Karl Kautskys literarisches Werk* (The Hague: Mouton, 1960) lists over six dozen shorter pieces on Kautsky, mostly in newspapers, that are not included here. I have marked a few, mostly relatively recent, especially good scholarly works with an asterisk.

Adler, Friedrich. "Karl Kautsky." *Der Sozialistische Kampf* (Paris) no. 12 (5 November 1938): 269–72.

Arenz, Horst, et al. (Projekt Klassenanalyse). *Kautsky: Marxistische Vergangenheit der SPD?* Berlin: Verlag für das Studium der Arbeiterbewegung.

Ascher, Abraham. "Axelrod and Kautsky." *Slavic Review* 26, no. 1 (March 1967): 94–112.

Bartel, Horst. "Karl Kautsky: Sein Anteil an der Entstehung und Propagierung des Erfurter Programms." In *Gestalten der Bismarckzeit,* ed. Gustav Seeber, 426–53. Berlin: Akademie-Verlag, 1978.

*Blumenberg, Werner. *Karl Kautskys literarisches Werk.* The Hague: Mouton, 1960.

Brill, Hermann. "Karl Kautsky: 16. Oktober 1854–17. Oktober 1938." *Zeitschrift für Politik* (new series) 1, no. 3 (October 1954): 211–40.

Bronner, Stephen Eric. "Karl Kautsky and the Twilight of Orthodoxy." *Political Theory* 10, no. 4 (November 1982): 580–605.

Bucharin, Nikolai. *Karl Kautsky und Sowjetrussland: Eine Antwort.* Vienna: Verlag für Literatur und Politik, 1925.

Claudín, Fernando. "Democracy and Dictatorship in Lenin and Kautsky." *New Left Review* no. 106 (November–December 1977): 59–76.

Fülberth, Georg. "Karl Kautskys Schrift 'Der Weg zur Macht' und seine Kontroverse mit dem Parteivorstand der SPD." Introduction to Karl Kautsky, *Der Weg zur Macht,* ed. Georg Fülberth, vii–xxiii. Frankfurt: Europäische Verlagsanstalt, 1972.

Geary, Dick. "Karl Kautsky and 'Scientific Marxism.'" *Radical Science Journal* (London) 11 (1981): 130–35.

———. "Karl Kautsky and German Marxism." In *Rediscoveries: Some Neglected European Thinkers,* ed. John A. Hall, 161–78. Oxford: Clarendon Press, 1986.

———. *Karl Kautsky.* Manchester: Manchester University Press, 1987.

———. "Max Weber, Karl Kautsky and German Social Democracy." In *Max Weber and his Contemporaries,* ed. Wolfgang J. Mommsen and Jürgen Osterhammel, 355–66. London: Allen & Unwin, 1987.

*Gilcher-Holtey, Ingrid. *Das Mandat des Intellektuellen: Karl Kautsky und die Sozialdemokratie.* Berlin: Siedler, 1986.

Gronow, Jukka. *On the Formation of Marxism: Karl Kautsky's Theory of Capitalism, the Marxism of the Second International and Karl Marx's Critique of Political Economy.* Helsinki: Finnish Society of Sciences and Letters, 1986.

Hilferding, Rudolf, ed. *Karl Kautsky zum 70. Geburtstage.* Special issue of *Die Gesellschaft.* Berlin: J. H. W. Dietz, 1924.

Holzheuer, Walter. *Karl Kautskys Werk als Weltanschauung.* Munich: C. H. Beck, 1972.

*Hünlich, Reinhold. *Karl Kautsky und der Marxismus der II. Internationale.* Marburg: Verlag Arbeiterbewegung und Gesellschaftswissenschaft, 1981.

Irrlitz, Gerd. "Bemerkungen über die Einheit politischer und theoretischer Wesenszüge des Zentrismus in der deutschen Sozialdemokratie." *Beiträge zur Geschichte der deutschen Arbeiterbewegung* 8, no. 1 (1966): 43–59.

Jacobs, Jack. "Marxism and Anti-Semitism: Kautsky's Perspective." *International Review of Social History* 30, no. 3 (1985): 400–430.

Karl Kautsky. der Denker und Kämpfer: Festgabe zu seinem siebzigsten Geburtstag. Vienna: Wiener Volksbuchhandlung, 1924.

Kautsky, Benedikt, ed. *Ein Leben für den Sozialismus: Erinnerungen an Karl Kautsky.* Hanover: J. H. W. Dietz, 1954.

Kautsky, John H. "Kautsky, Karl." In *International Encyclopedia of the Social Sciences* 8:356–58. New York: Macmillan, 1968.

———. "Introduction." In Karl Kautsky, *The Materialist Conception of History,* abridged edition, ed. John H. Kautsky, xxi–lxiv. New Haven, Conn.: Yale University Press, 1988.

———. "Karl Kautsky's Materialist Conception of History." *International*

Journal of Comparative Sociology 30, no. 1–2 (January–April 1989): 80–92.

*————, ed. *Karl Kautsky and the Social Science of Classical Marxism*. Leiden: E. J. Brill, 1989.

Korsch, Karl. "Die materialistische Geschichtsauffassung: Eine Auseinander-setzung mit Karl Kautsky." In Karl Korsch, *Die materialistische Geschicht-sauffassung*, ed. Erich Gerlach, 3–130. Frankfurt: Europäische Verlagsan-stalt, 1971.

Langkau-Alex, Ursula. "Karl Kautsky in den Niederlanden." In *öesterreichische Exilliteratur in den Niederlanden 1934–1940*, ed. Hans Würzner, 39–65. Amsterdam: Amsterdamer Publikationen zur Sprache und Literatur, 1986.

Laschitza, Annelies. "Karl Kautsky und der Zentrismus." *Beiträge zur Geschichte der deutschen Arbeiterbewegung* 10, no. 5 (1968): 798–832.

————. "Ich bin Redakteur und Parteimann, nicht blosser Privatgelehrter. Karl Kautsky." *Beiträge zur Geschichte der deutschen Arbeiterbewegung* 30, no. 5 (1988): 656–76.

Lenin, V. I. *Imperialism, the Highest Stage of Capitalism* (1916). In V. I. Lenin, *Collected Works*. 45 vols. Moscow: Progess Publishers, 1960–70. 22:185–304.

————. *The State and Revolution* (1917). In ibid. 25:385–497.

————. *The Proletarian Revolution and the Renegade Kautsky* (1918). In ibid. 28:227–325.

Li Fu, Li Su-wen, and Wang Fu-ju. "On Kautskyism." *Hung- ch'i [Red Flag]* (Peking) no. 8–9 (25 April 1962): 28–41. Translated in Joint Publications Research Service, JPRS 13903 (May 29, 1962): 76–120. Washington: De-partment of Commerce.

Matthias, Erich. "Kautsky und der Kautskyanismus: Die Funktion der Ideologie in der deutschen Sozialdemokratie vor dem ersten Weltkriege." In *Marxismusstudien*, 2d series, ed. Iring Fetscher, 151–97. Tübingen: J. C. B. Mohr, 1957.

Mende, Hans-Jürgen. *Karl Kautsky — vom Marxisten zum Opportunisten*. Ber-lin: Dietz Verlag, 1985.

Morgan, David W. "The Eclipse of Karl Kautsky, 1914–1924." *International Journal of Comparative Sociology* 30, no. 1–2 (January–April 1989): 57–67.

Osterroth, Franz. "Karl Kautsky." In *Biographisches Lexikon des Sozialismus*, ed. Franz Osterroth, 1:156–59. Hanover: J. H. W. Dietz, 19 60.

Panaccione, Andrea. *Kautsky e l'ideologia socialista*. Milan: Franco Angeli, 1987.

Papcke, Sven. "Karl Kautsky und der historische Fatalismus." In *Jahrbuch Arbeiterbewegung*, ed. Claudio Pozzoli, 3:231–46. Frankfurt: Fischer, 1975.

Plener, Ulla. "Karl Kautskys Opportunismus in Organisationsfragen (1900–1914)." *Beiträge zur Geschichte der deutschen Arbeiterbewegung* 3, no. 2 (1961): 349–70.

Projekt Klassenanalyse, *see* Arenz, Horst, et al.

Ratz, Ursula. "Karl Kautsky und die Abrüstungskontroverse in der deutschen Sozialdemokratie 1911–12." *International Review of Social History* 11, no. 2 (1966): 197–227.

———. "Perspektiven über Karl Kautsky." *Neue politische Literatur* 33, no. 1 (1988): 7–24.

Renner, Karl. *Karl Kautsky.* Berlin: J. H. W. Dietz, 1929.

*Rojahn, Jürgen, Till Schelz, and Hans-Josef Steinberg, eds. *Marxismus und Demokratie: Karl Kautskys Bedeutung in der sozialistischen Arbeiterbewegung.* Frankfurt: Campus Verlag, 1992.

Rónai, Zoltán. "Kautskys 'Materialistische Geschichtsauffassung.' " *Der Kampf* 21, no. 6 (June 1928): 233–45.

———. "Kautskys Klassen- und Staatslehre." *Der Kampf* 22, no. 10 (October 1929): 464–79.

Rubel, Maximilien. "Le magnum opus de Karl Kautsky: 'La conception matérialiste de l'histoire' (1927)." *La Révue Socialiste,* new series, no. 83 (January 1955): 4–14, and no. 85 (March 1955): 275–91.

*Salvadori, Massimo. *Karl Kautsky and the Socialist Revolution. 1880–1938.* London: NLB, 1979.

Schelz-Brandenburg, Till. *Eduard Bernstein und Karl Kautsky.* Cologne: Böhlau, 1992.

Schifrin, Alexander. "K. Kautsky und die marxistische Soziologie." *Die Gesellschaft* 6/2, no. 8 (August 1929): 149–69.

Schuster, Dieter. "Kautsky, Karl." In *Marxism, Communism and Western Society,* ed. C. D. Kernig, 5:1–7. New York: Herder & Herder, 1973.

Schwartz, Peter. "Imagining Socialism: Karl Kautsky and Thomas More." *International Journal of Comparative Sociology* 30, no. 1–2 (January–April 1989): 44–56.

*Steenson, Gary P. *Karl Kautsky. 1854–1938: Marxism in the Classical Years.* Pittsburgh: University of Pittsburgh Press, 1978; paperback ed., 1991.

*Steinberg, Hans-Josef. *Sozialismus und deutsche Sozialdemokratie.* 5th ed. Bonn: J. H. W. Dietz, 1979.

———. "Karl Kautsky und Eduard Bernstein." In *Deutsche Historiker,* ed. Hans-Ulrich Wehler, 4:53–64. Göttingen: Vanderhoek & Ruprecht, 1972.

———. "Kautsky, Karl." In *Lexikon linker Zeitfiguren,* 205–06. Frankfurt: Büchergilde Gutenberg, 1988.

Trotsky, Leon. *Terrorism and Communism. A Reply to Karl Kautsky* (1920). Ann Arbor: University of Michigan Press, 1961.

Waldenberg, Marek. *Mysl Polityczna Karola Kautsky'ego w okresie sporu z*

Rewizjonismem [Karl Kaytsky's political thought at the time of the Revisionist controversy]. Cracow: Panstwowe Wydawn. Naukowe oddz w Krakowie, 1970.

*————. *Wzlot i Upadek Karola Kautsky'ego* [Karl Kautsky's rise and fall]. 2 vols. Cracow: Wydawnictwo literackie, 1972.

Index

Titles of writings and names of their authors are indexed only as they appear in the text, not in notes or the appendices.